IMAGES
of Rail

YOSEMITE VALLEY RAILROAD

On the Cover: A Shay locomotive is being used to move log cars to the top of the big incline during the Yosemite Valley line's heyday. (Mariposa Heritage Press [MHP], Jim Law.)

IMAGES
of Rail

YOSEMITE VALLEY RAILROAD

Leroy Radanovich

ARCADIA
PUBLISHING

ISBN 978-0-7385-8111-9

Published by Arcadia Publishing
Charleston, South Carolina

Printed in the United States of America

Library of Congress Control Number: 2010923471

For all general information contact Arcadia Publishing at:
Telephone 843-853-2070
Fax 843-853-0044
E-mail sales@arcadiapublishing.com
For customer service and orders:
Toll-Free 1-888-313-2665

Visit us on the Internet at www.arcadiapublishing.com

This book is dedicated to Jim Law, Scott Pinkerton, Hank Johnston, Shirley Sargent, and Jack Burgess, who have all contributed to the knowledge and understanding of Mariposa County and Yosemite National Park.

Contents

ACKNOWLEDGMENTS

This volume is made up of material from Jim Law's *Memories of El Portal* published by Mariposa Heritage Press (MHP); Leroy Radanovich was both the editor and publisher. *Memories of El Portal* has gone out of print; however, it is still important to continue to have its history and photographs accessible. So I wish to acknowledge Arcadia Publishing for keeping a selection of the photographs and information available for the future. Almost all of the folks and activities that are contained in this volume no longer exist, and to have a national publisher show interest in continuing the history of my home for almost 77 years, Mariposa County, is very important. Other authors such as Hank Johnston and Jack Burgess have expertly covered other aspects of the life of this railroad.

With the information that has been provided by Jim Law and my partner, Scott Pinkerton, it is my intent to fill in the missing aspects of life in the Merced River Canyon and El Portal as they pertain to the Yosemite Valley Railroad.

About half of the photographs are from copyrighted books published by Mariposa Heritage Press and Arcadia Publishing. The remaining photographs are from my personal collection, which is originally from private sources from many years ago; the Yosemite Museum through Jim Law's publication; and the Mariposa Museum and History Center. My hope is that I fulfill Jim Law's desire that the lives of the men and women who lived during the early days on the Mother Lode, up the River Canyon, and in Yosemite are not forgotten.

Introduction

The canyon of the Merced River is the thread that connects the great San Joaquin Valley of California to the wonders of Yosemite Valley and beyond. The source of the river is the High Sierra of Yosemite National Park. It divides the county of Mariposa roughly in half as it passes on to the San Joaquin Valley. The yearly snowmelt fills the canyon with the rushing water captured behind Exchequer Dam to form Lake McClure, which provides the Merced Irrigation District with the ability to grow crops, dispense consumptive water, and provide many megawatts of electricity for the economy and pleasure of California.

During a critical period in the development of California, from 1906 until 1944, the Yosemite Valley Railroad snaked through the river canyon serving many purposes. At first, it was modern and convenient transportation for visitors to Yosemite National Park. No direct road from Merced could reach Yosemite Valley by an all-year low-level route. Seldom blocked by Sierra snow, the railroad could reach the park boundary at El Portal. It was there that a first-class hotel was constructed for comfort and accommodation. From El Portal, it was at first a four-and-a-half-hour carriage ride to Yosemite Valley, and after 1913, when the internal combustion engine was allowed in the park, the trip was shortened to a one-and-a-half-hour ride in a open-top bus.

In 1926, the "All Year Highway" 140 was opened from Merced through Mariposa to El Portal. The highway proved to be a difficult competitor for the already marginal railroad. However, the development of a number of industrial sites, including logging and mining, sustained the rail line until the resources being developed were depleted. A huge flood in 1937 damaged the right-of-way and tracks to such a degree that the railroad could not fully recover. Also, a number of events, including the beginning of World War II, ended the ability of the railroad, which seldom if ever showed a profit, to continue.

Through pictures and text, this book chronicles the history of the Yosemite Valley Railroad and its relationship to the Merced River Canyon, which includes the people who found employment with the railroad that played a large role in bringing industrial development and transportation to the Yosemite region. The story begins with the Gold Rush, which opened both the river canyon and Yosemite Valley and brought about the building of this unique railroad. I recommend two other books be referenced concerning the railroad itself: Hank Johnson's *Railroads of Yosemite Valley* by Stauffer Press and Jack Burgess's *Trains to Yosemite* by Signature Press. Each gives fundamental, detailed information on the rolling stock and construction. My purpose is to give a broader understanding of the people and activities within Merced and Mariposa Counties that were affected and influenced by the presence of such a railroad.

One

The Time Before

For thousands of years, the Merced River ran free and un-named. It provided salmon and trout, water for drinking, travel, death, and revival. For most of the year, it ran cold from the highest of the Sierra. Beginning with the melting snow and glacier ice, droplets formed little rivulets, small streams, creeks, and then a great river.

It ran roughly east and west because when the Sierra arose out of the earths crust, the course of the streams running north and south now dried and began a course toward the ocean many miles away. In those ancient rivers, the gravel settled into first the mud and then into old dry streambeds, which had been once subject to the volcanic discharge from the center of the earth. In that flow of molten rock, a rare shiny metal was casually deposited with the sand and rock at the bottom of those streams. Men and their animals came from the Pacific Coast to explore locations for missions like the ones that they established near the ocean. Soon after 1800, they came into the dry and hot central valley. While looking for water for themselves and their animals, they found a river that they called Mercy or Merced. They knew nothing of this river nor its source except it seemed to come from the snowy mountains, the Sierra Nevada. Change came in the form of other Europeans seeking that shiny metal.

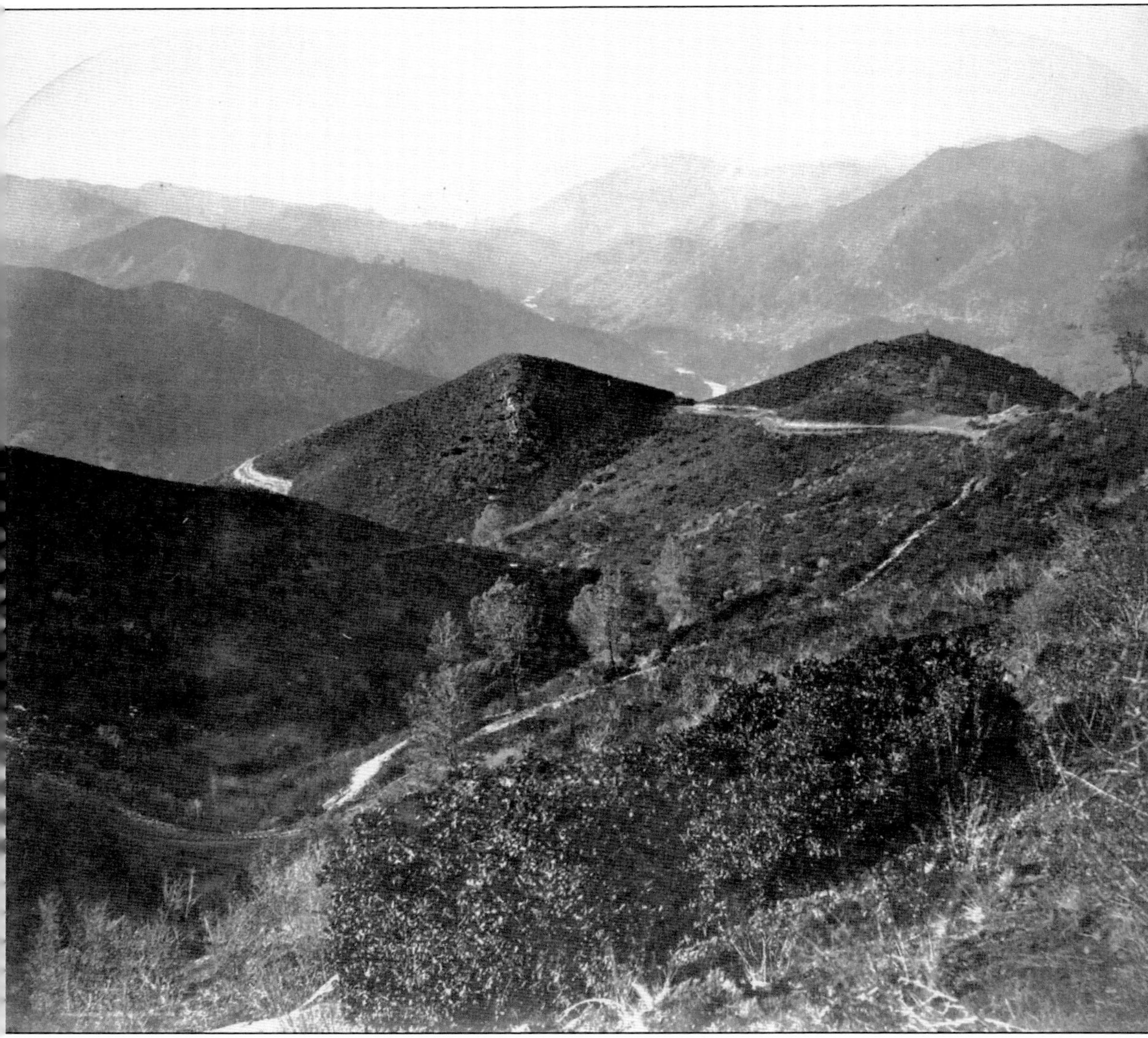

Crossing the canyon of the Merced, running roughly north and south, ran a great band of various kinds of minerals. The white man called it the Mother Lode because it contained varying amounts of the yellow metal called gold. Its presence caused many men to come to these mountains. (Photograph by Carlton E. Watkins, author's collection.)

For centuries, the Native Americans had learned to move through a relatively narrow territory seeking shelter, food, medicine, and companionship. The numbers of the new people was small, and the pioneers seemed intent on looking for the yellow metal. Unlike the Native Americans, although they had many skills, living off the land was a difficult choice. When the Native Americans saw one of these strangers hungry, they fed him. When they found him cold, they warmed him and sheltered him until the stranger began demanding more and taking not just what was offered, but also what was available to take, which upset the balance that had been achieved over centuries. (MHP.)

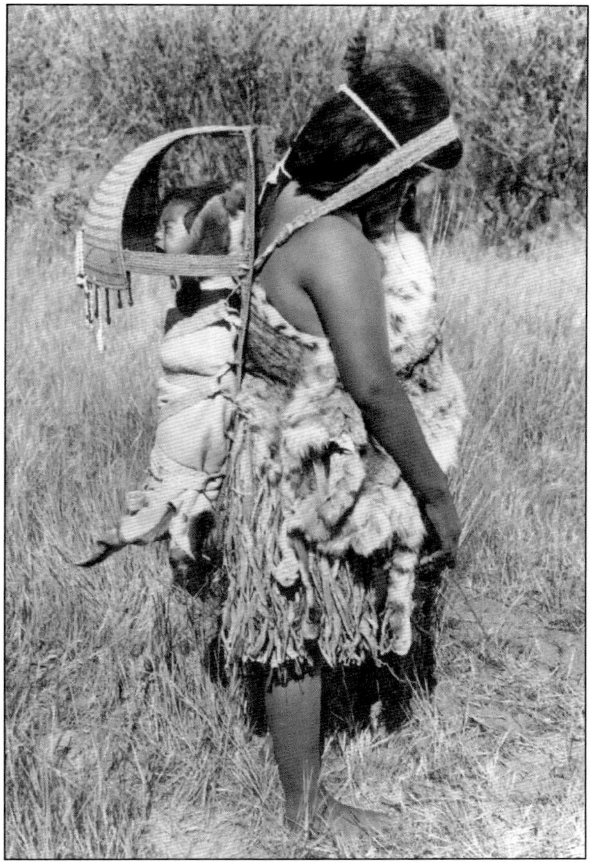

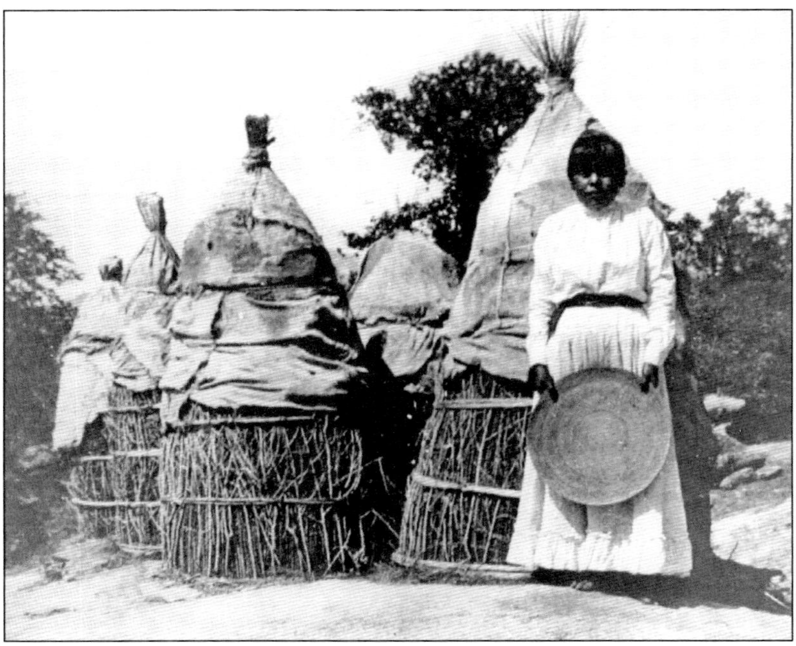

The Native Americans became afraid and worried and tried to repel these new people, but the strangers out numbered them and had too many weapons that could kill and injure. The game that had always sustained them disappeared. They were replaced by the horse and mule, which could be eaten when nothing else was available. (MHP.)

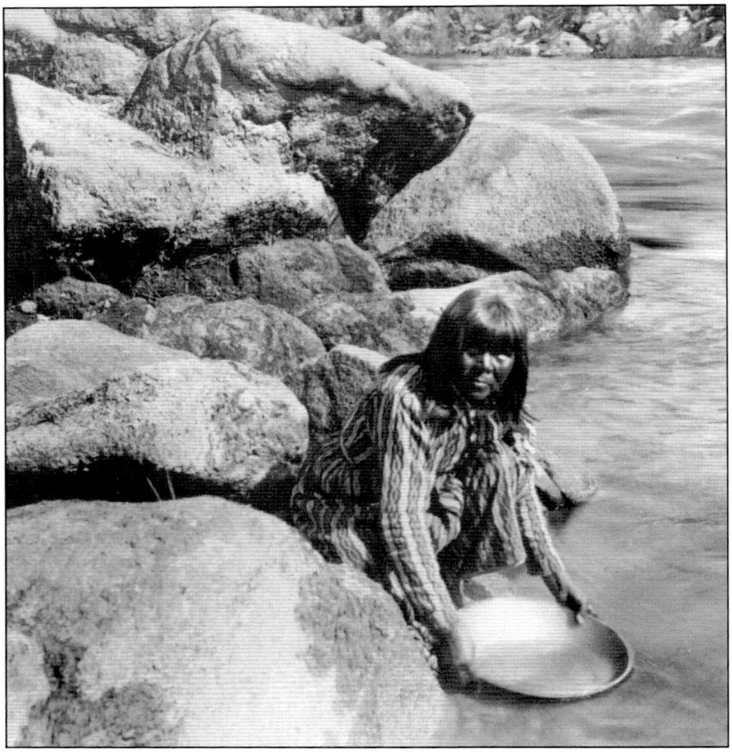

Replacing the wild game that was rapidly being depleted with the miners' animals caused the newcomers to become hostile towards the Native Americans and attack their previous benefactors. As the number of miners grew, the only course for the Natives was to be submissive. Feeling no respect from the newcomers, the natives attacked the mining camps, stores, and miners. The issues were the diminishing food supply and the spoiling of the water caused by mining. The natives also noted that the white men did not treat each other much better.(MHP.)

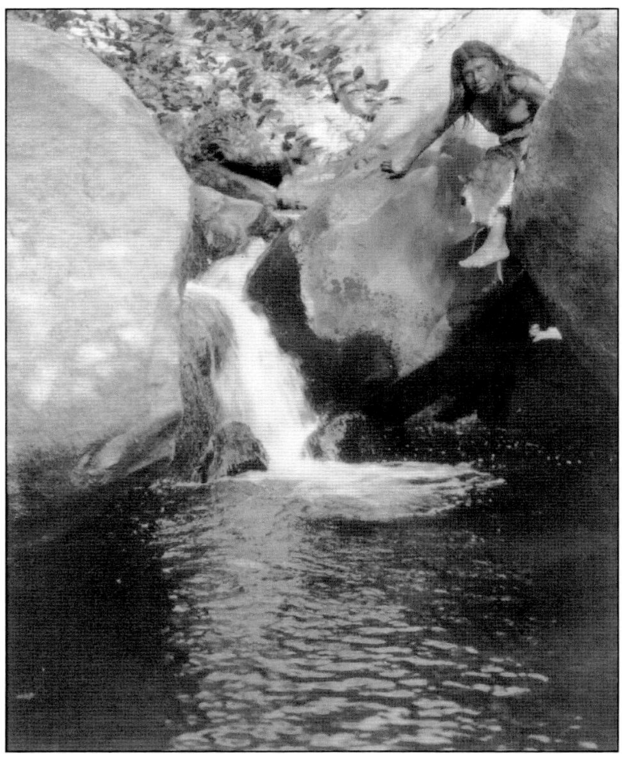

The Native Americans were forcefully herded into camps, which were not of their choosing, and were given strange clothing and inferior food. They were treated as if they were the stranger, not the native. Rapidly their homeland was being destroyed, and their water dammed and diverted, making it undrinkable. From time to time, their women were taken to be the wives of the newcomers. Some of the Native Americans knew of a marvelous valley high in the mountains, and they fought to protect this place from the newcomers. (MHP.)

A military leader and adventurer, John C. Fremont, understanding the presence of the gold, had acquired for himself a tract of land that did not have stable boundaries. He floated this tract into the land of the precious metal. Within a short time, a camp was built at Ridley's Ferry on the Merced River. (MHP.)

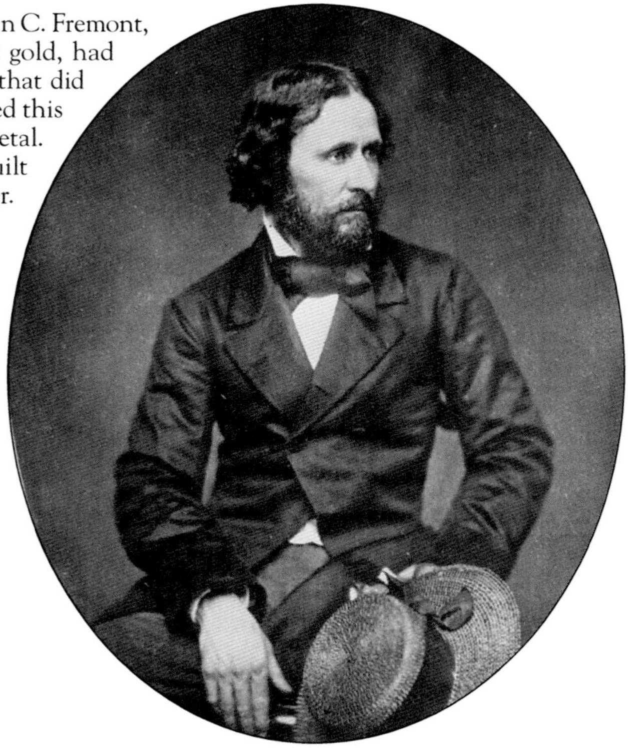

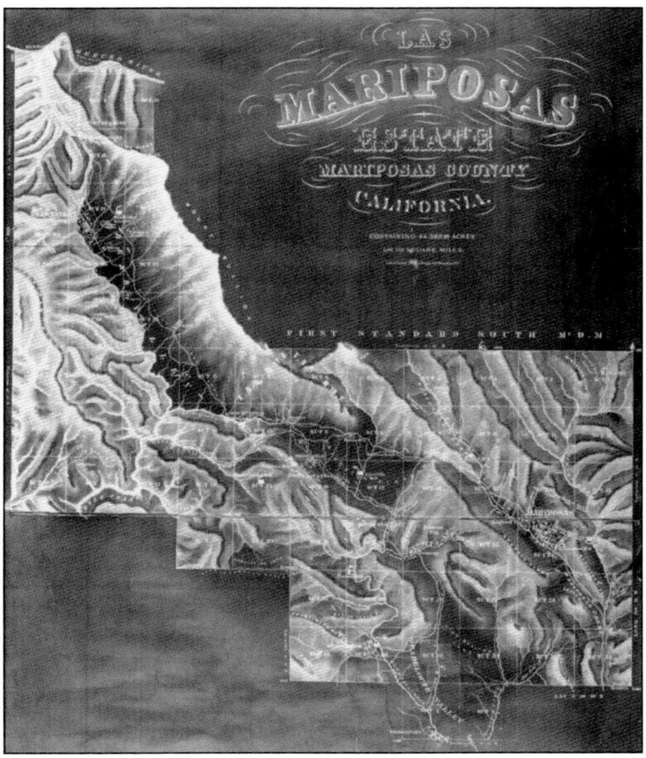

This grant covered 44,386 acres, which ran from the Merced River along the Mother Lode to beyond the town of Mariposa and covered the quality mining sites south of the river. (MHP.)

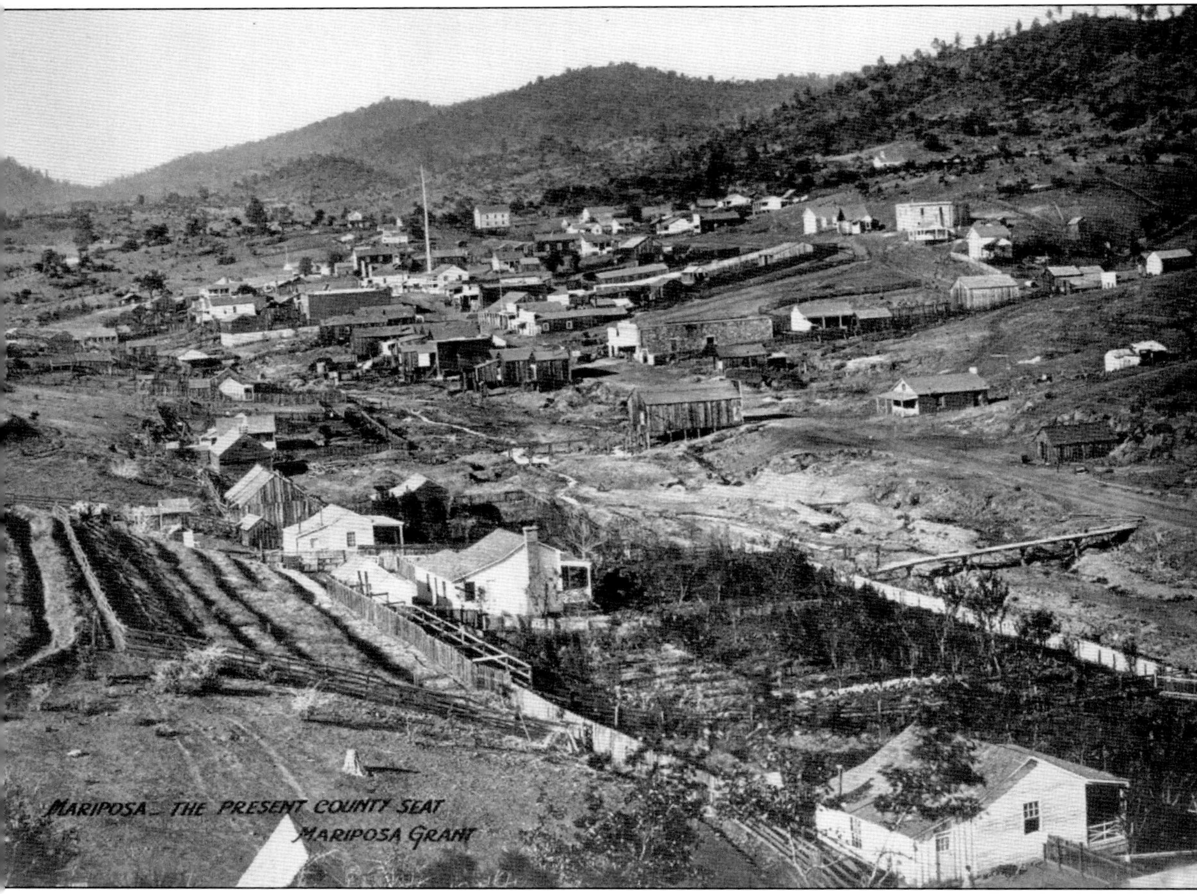

The earliest development along the Merced River was related to gold. By 1850, the town of Mariposa, soon to become the county seat of Mariposa County, was created by the banking investment firm of Palmer, Cooke, and Company of San Francisco under lease from John C. Fremont. (Photograph by Carlton E. Watkins, author's collection.)

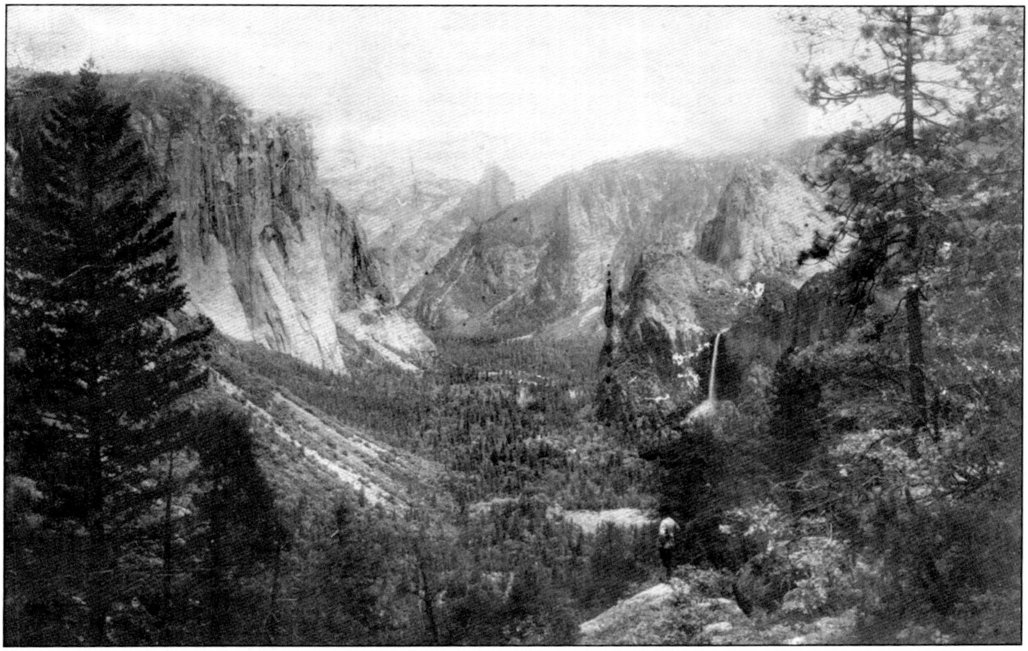

The competition for space and food caused the Native Americans to attack the miners and their stores. The miners organized to protect themselves and their possessions. Following the Native Americans into the mountains, they made a discovery that at first did not impress them. In 1851, the Mariposa Battalion entered Yosemite Valley seeking the Native Americans. By 1861, Yosemite Valley became recognized for its beauty and attractiveness for a more settled permanent population. (Photograph by Carlton E. Watkins, MHP)

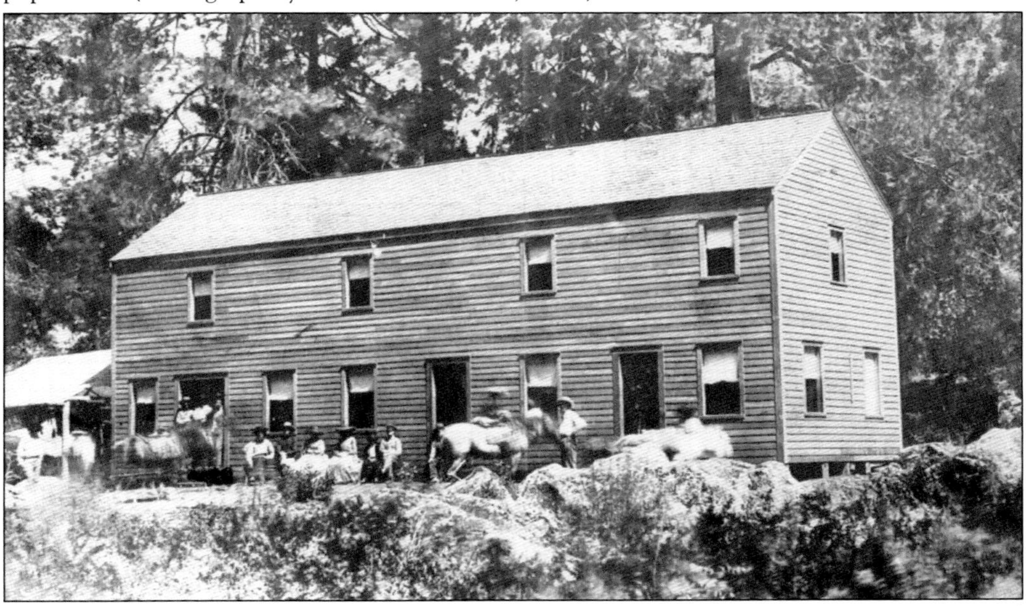

As the effort to gather gold became more difficult, other men began to turn their attention toward the valley above the gold mining areas on the Merced River. They saw Yosemite Valley as an opportunity to exploit the beauty and began limited development. (Chas. Weed, MHP.)

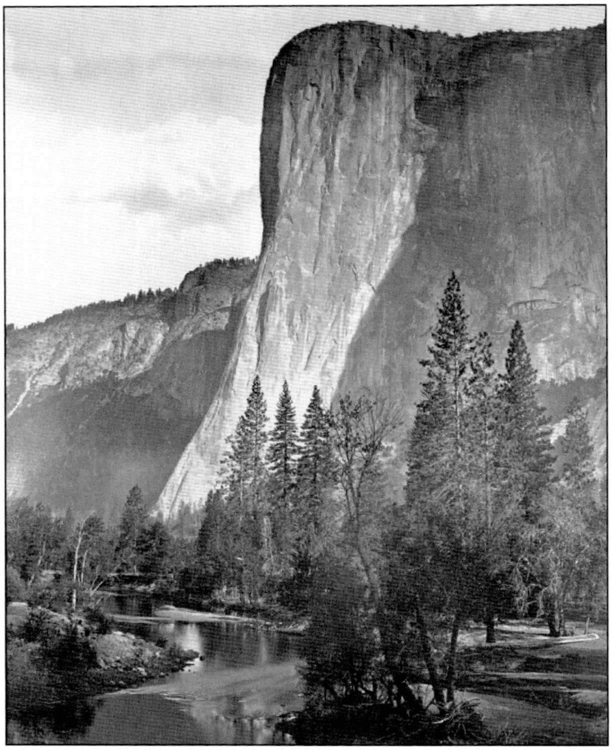

In 1860, the managers of the Fremont Grant brought a photographer, Carlton E. Watkins, to Mariposa to photograph the assets of the grant for purposes of seeking investment or sale. In the process, he photographed the area of the Merced River that was deeply involved in the industrial development of mining. In 1861, Watkins photographed extensively the area of the Sierra called Yosemite. (Photograph by Carlton E. Watkins, MHP.)

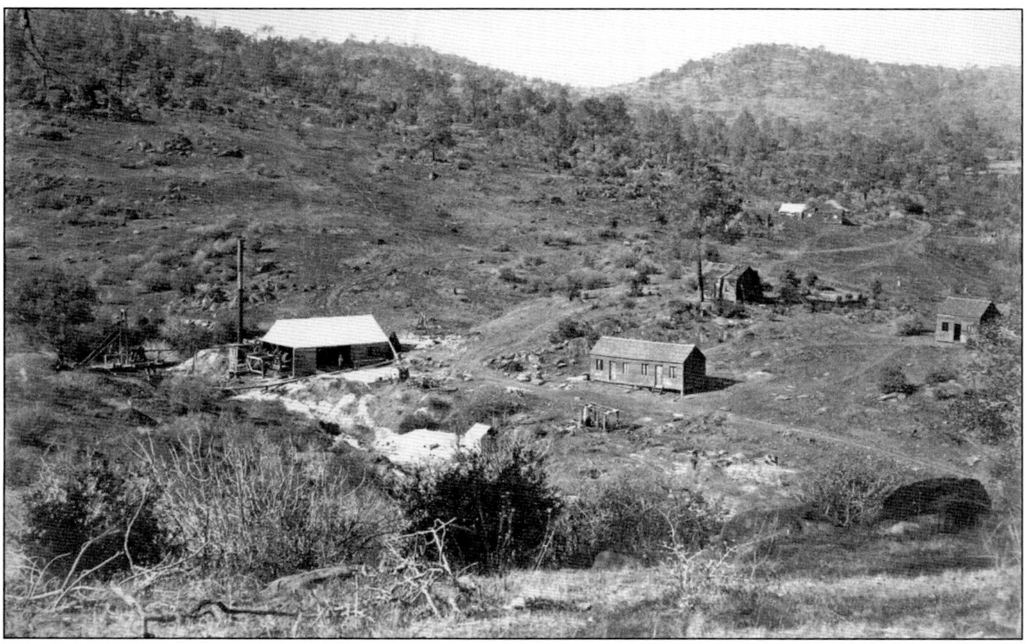

Above Ridley's Ferry, hard rock gold mines developed. The ore was milled at first in Bear Valley, south of the mining area, but a lack of available water caused John C. Fremont to relocate his processing to the Merced River. Thus, the mill named after his father-in-law, Senator Thomas Hart Benton of Missouri, was constructed. (Photograph by Carleton E. Watkins, author's collection.)

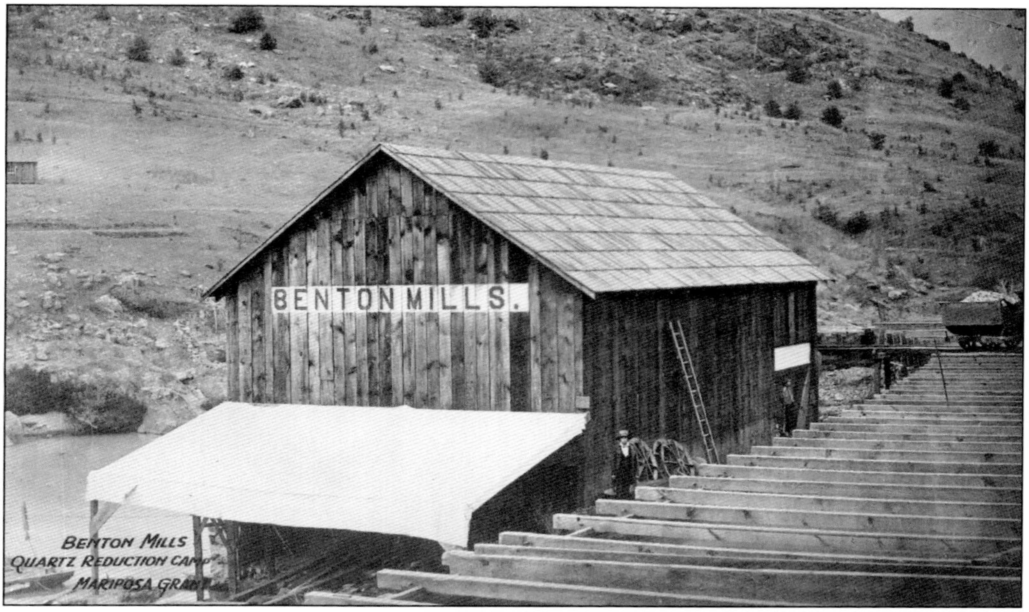

Originally named Ridley's Ferry, Benton Mills became the site of a large gold reduction mill, which served the mines of the John C. Fremont Grant on the mountains above the river. The river was dammed to provide the diversion of water to run the mill. In 1861, a great wall of water, which was caused by the breaking of a landslide upriver, washed the mill away. A larger mill was built higher on the riverbank. (Photograph by Carlton E. Watkins, author's collection.)

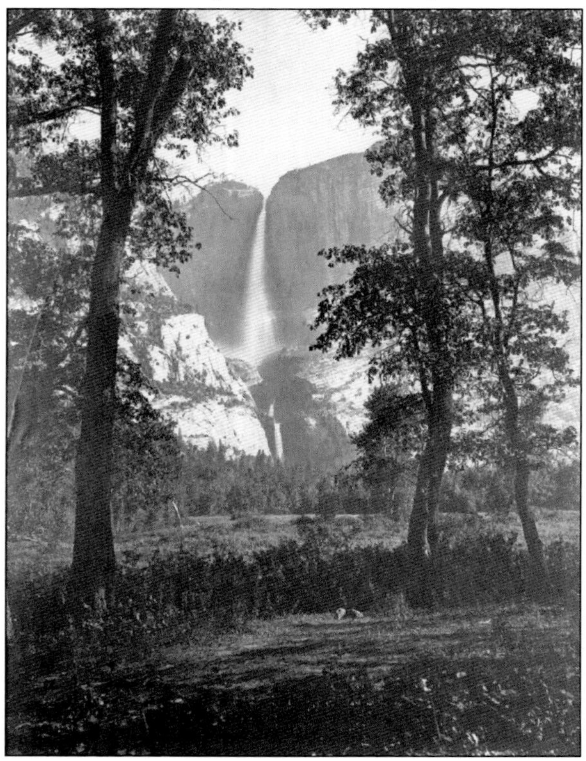

At first, the American discovery of Yosemite Valley in 1851 by the Mariposa Battalion did not attract much attention because the people that discovered it were miners following Native Americans. By 1861, as the result of Watkins's photography and publicity generated by James Mason Hutchings's *California Magazine*, Yosemite Valley became recognized for its beauty and attractiveness. (Photograph by Carlton E. Watkins, author's collection.)

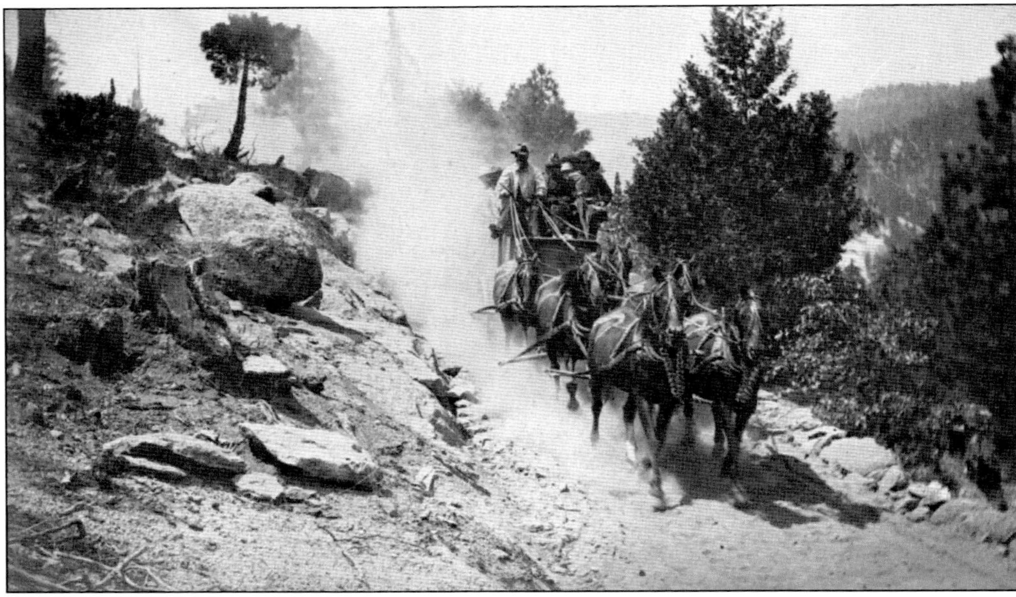

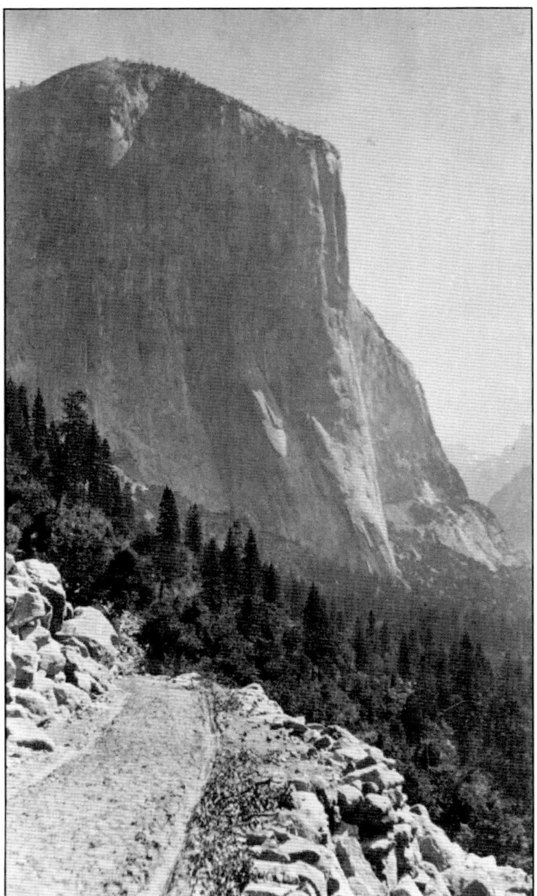

Promoters attempted to attract the growing population of California to visit the area. Hotels and other facilities for the guest were created. The trails made it difficult to visit the Sierra at first. The roads for the coaches and horses were laid out over steep and rugged terrain, so the Merced River Canyon seemed to be the answer for easy transport of visitors to Yosemite Valley. (Photograph by George Fiske, author's collection.)

Many speculative attempts were made to locate a wagon road and then a rail line up the river to the park. Different routes from the north and south of the valley were examined and built by 1876, but none met the level of quality and ease of the river canyon. Travel to the valley by these roads could only be done during the summer because of the heavy snow during the winter months. (Yosemite Museum.)

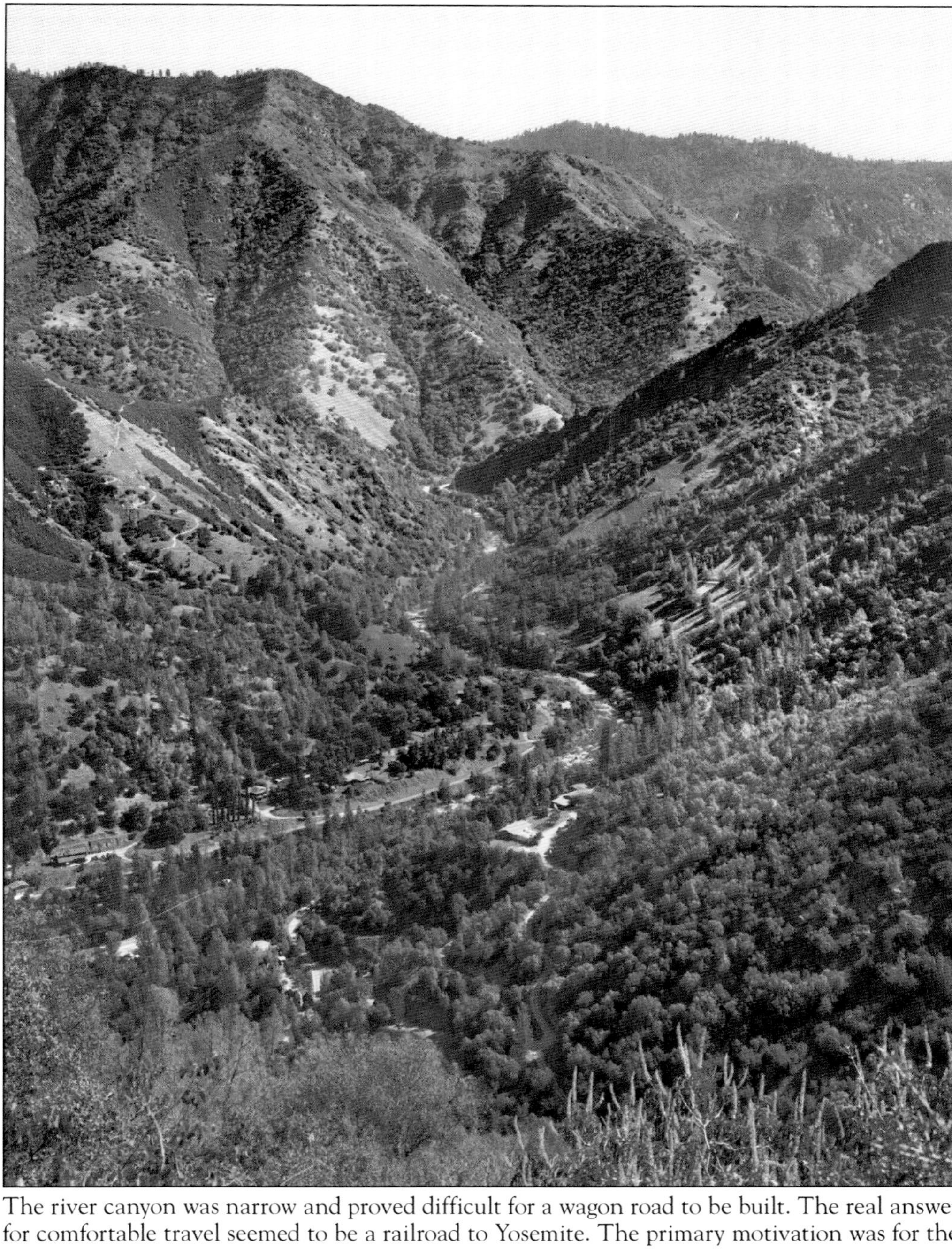

The river canyon was narrow and proved difficult for a wagon road to be built. The real answer for comfortable travel seemed to be a railroad to Yosemite. The primary motivation was for the railroad to be first tourist transportation to Yosemite National Park. (Author's collection.)

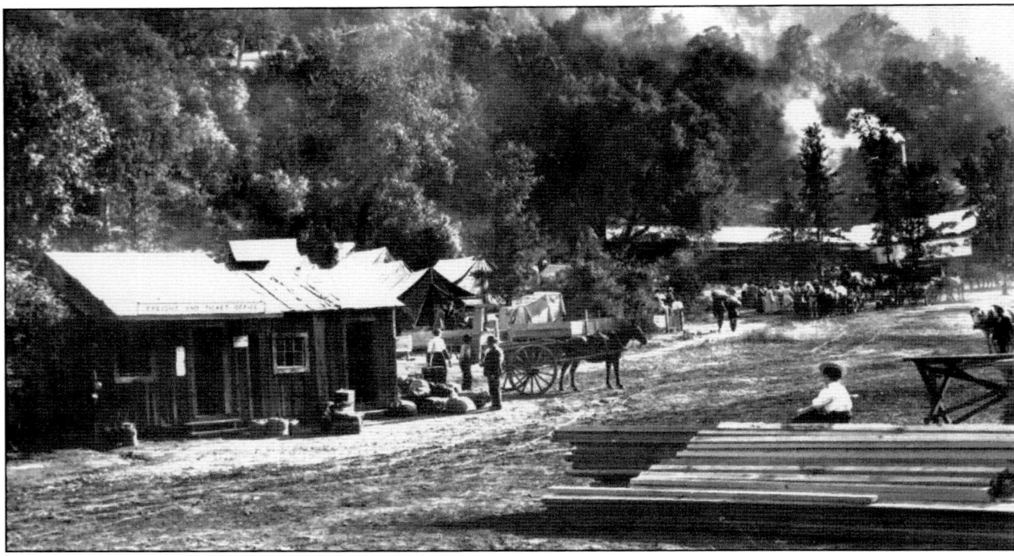

The desire to expand visitation to the park required as much year-round travel as possible. Planning and financing for a low-level route took a number of years. A serious effort was made to build a railroad, and by 1906, it reached the park boundary. (MHP.)

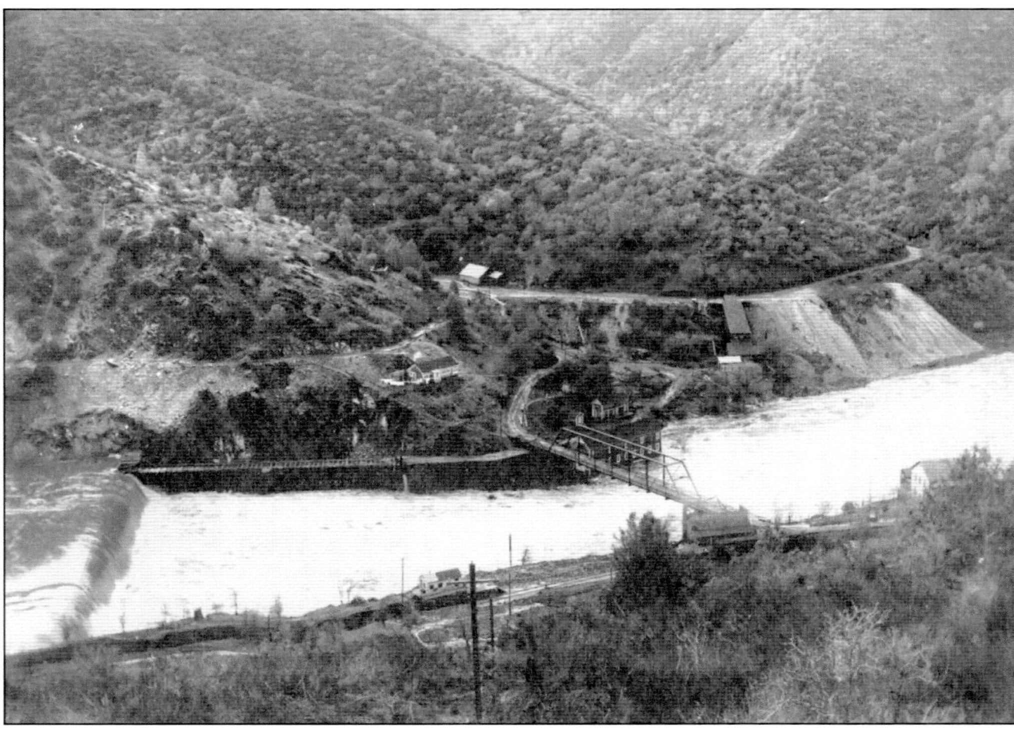

The arrival of Abner Bagby in 1898 began the development of the town of Bagby on the north side of the river at Benton Mills. The town was named after him as part of the location of a post office. Soon the Yosemite Valley Railroad reached Bagby, and it became a major stop along the line. (Photograph by Carlton E. Watkins.)

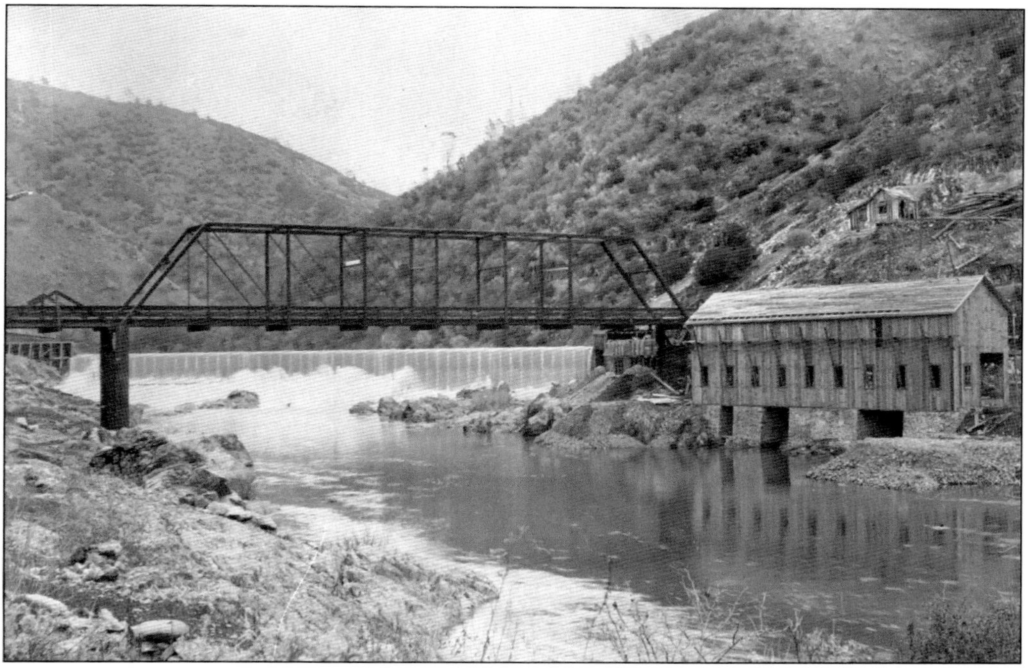

Around 1898, the mining company, now called the Mariposa Commercial and Mining Company, built a power station on the foundations of the old Fremont Mill at Benton Mills, now called Bagby. (MHP.)

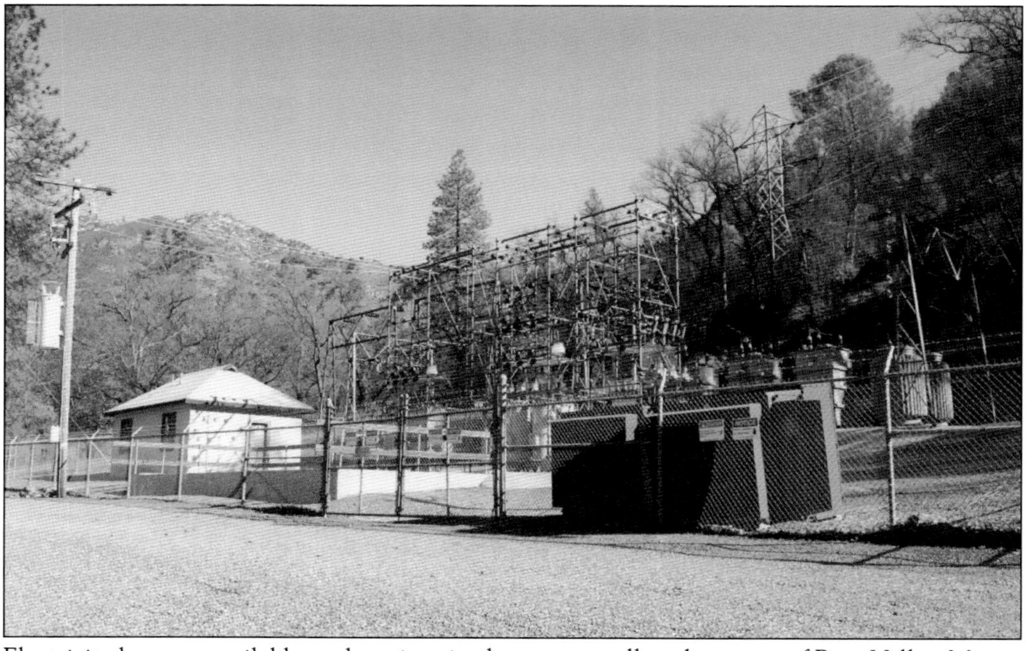

Electricity became available to the mines in the area as well as the towns of Bear Valley, Mount Bullion, and Mariposa. By 1923, electric transmission was brought up the river canyon as far as the logging at the incline, which is formerly known as Indian Flat, and a substation was built. (Author's collection.)

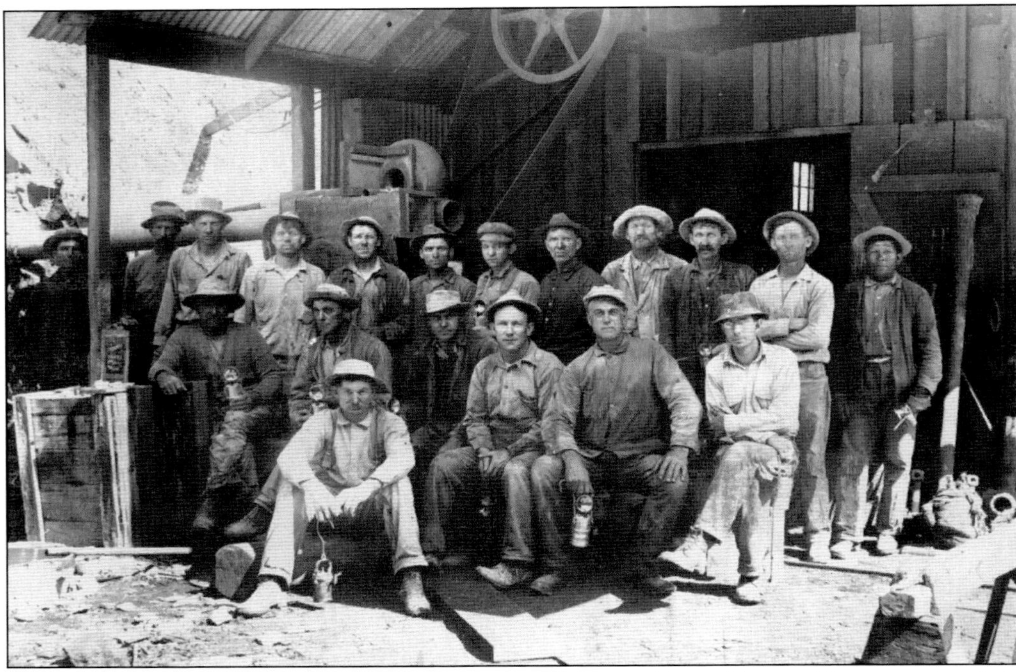

A mining project, which was first called the Original Mine and later Clearing House, predated the railroad. The presence of the railroad, as well as having electrical power, increased the industrial development of the river canyon. (MHP.)

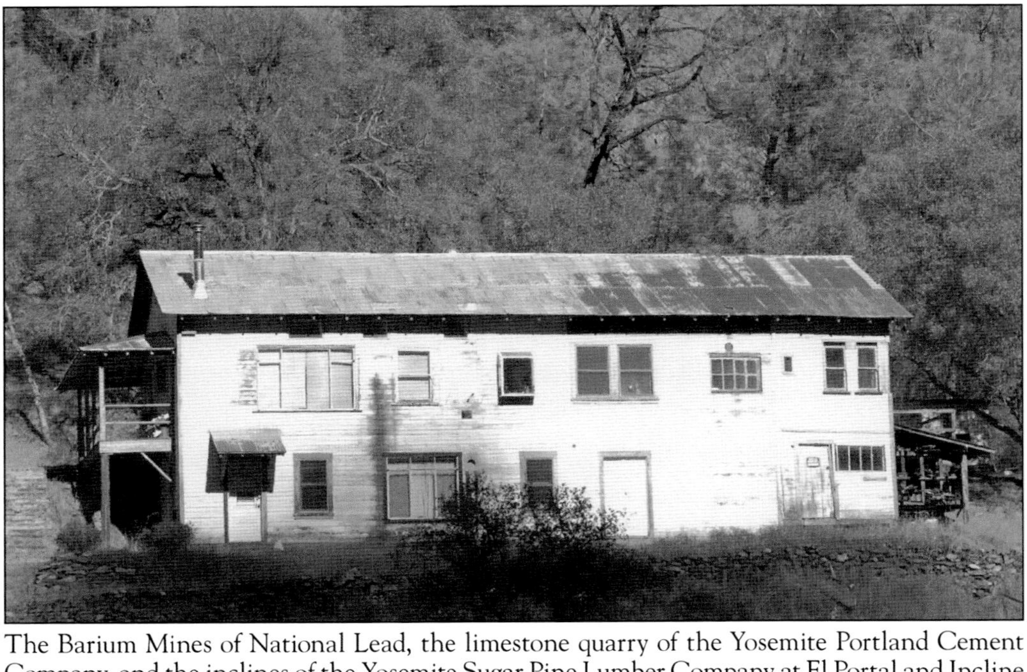

The Barium Mines of National Lead, the limestone quarry of the Yosemite Portland Cement Company, and the inclines of the Yosemite Sugar Pine Lumber Company at El Portal and Incline all used the services of the railroad. (Author's collection.)

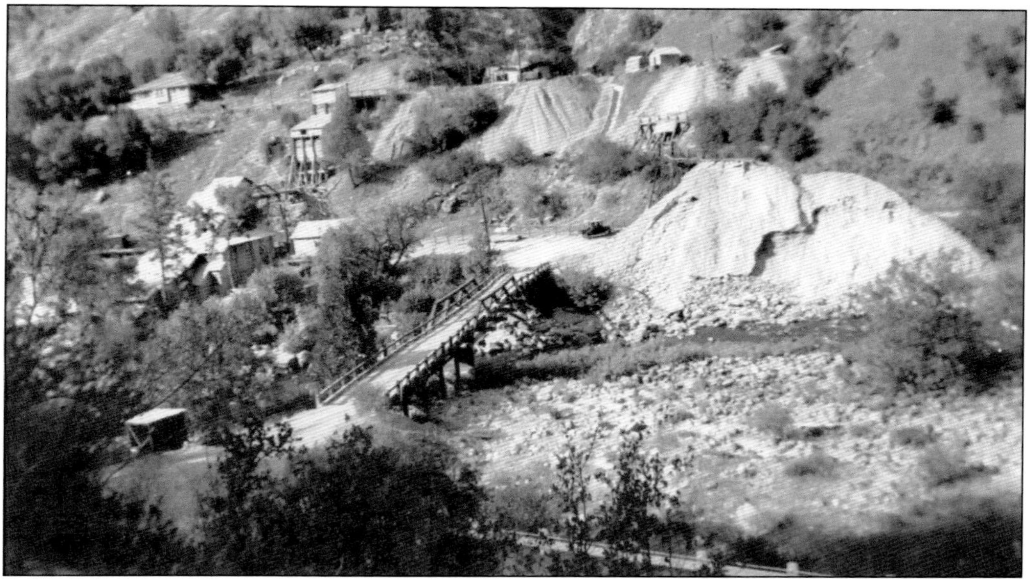

Augmented by the railroad, the development of the area lead to almost 40 years of industrial growth based on its natural resources. (MHP.)

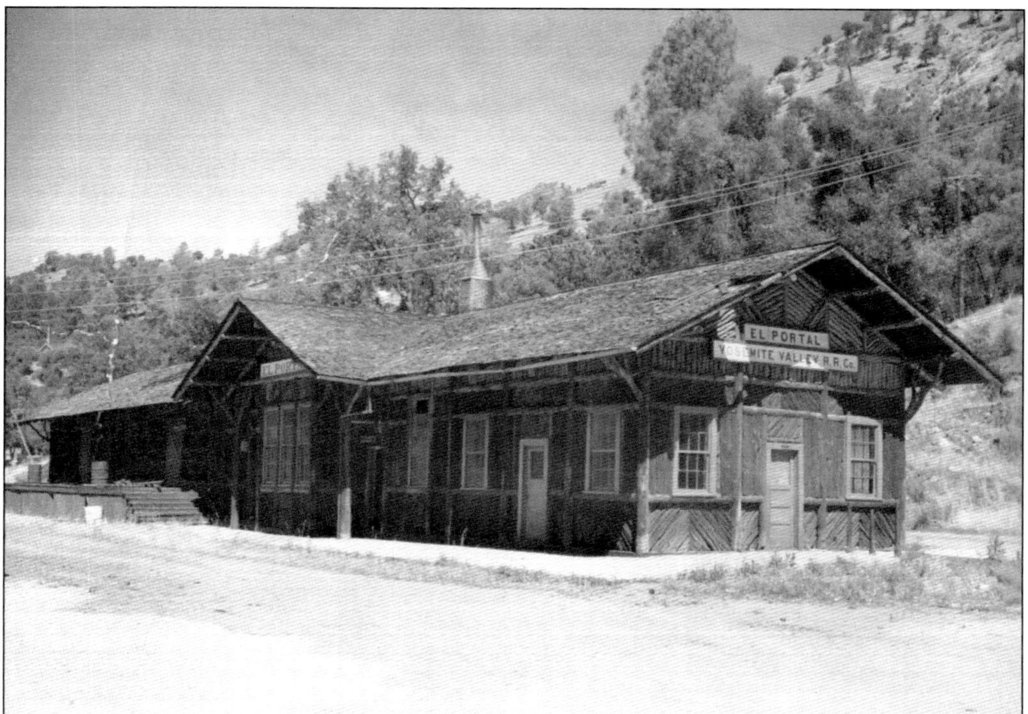

The first run on the entire line from Merced to El Portal occurred in May 1907. At El Portal, a more modern and attractive terminal replaced the temporary station. (MHP.)

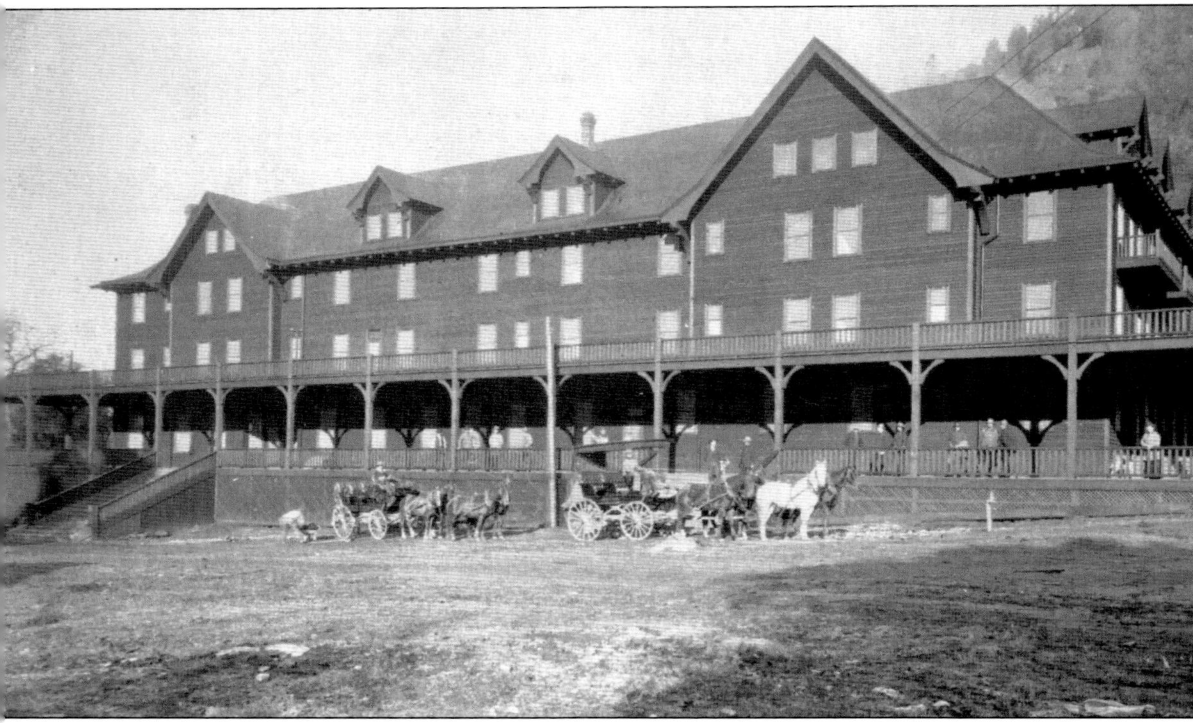

The Del Portal Hotel was started by the railroad, and it was the most elegant hotel in the Yosemite area for a short time. As Yosemite Valley had no first-class accommodations, this hotel was a welcome establishment for travelers at the end of the slow 67-mile trip from Merced. (MHP.)

Two

Establishment of the Yosemite Valley Railroad

With the establishment of Yosemite National Park in 1890, the development of a railroad to haul visitors and supplies began to take form. Yosemite Valley and the Mariposa Grove of Big Trees were already state parks that were granted by U.S. president Abraham Lincoln in 1863. Hotels in Yosemite Valley started soon after its discovery; however, the trip to get to the hotels was arduous. The primary route, long and steep, was the Mariposa Trail that went from Wawona via Paregoy Meadows. The Coulterville Free Trail, built by George Coulter, passed through Greeley Hill, Hazel Green, and the Merced Grove of Big Trees, and entered the state park at Gentry Station near Cascade Creek. Both routes required long difficult rides, so three roads were proposed and constructed to help make the trip easier. By 1876, the Big Oak Flat Road from Chinese Camp, the Coulterville Road from Coulterville, and the Mariposa Road from Mariposa and Wawona were opened. While passengers rode in relative comfort in a coach, it was still a long and dusty trip to Yosemite Valley. Each route reached the valley by a steep final section that was not only difficult, but also dangerous.

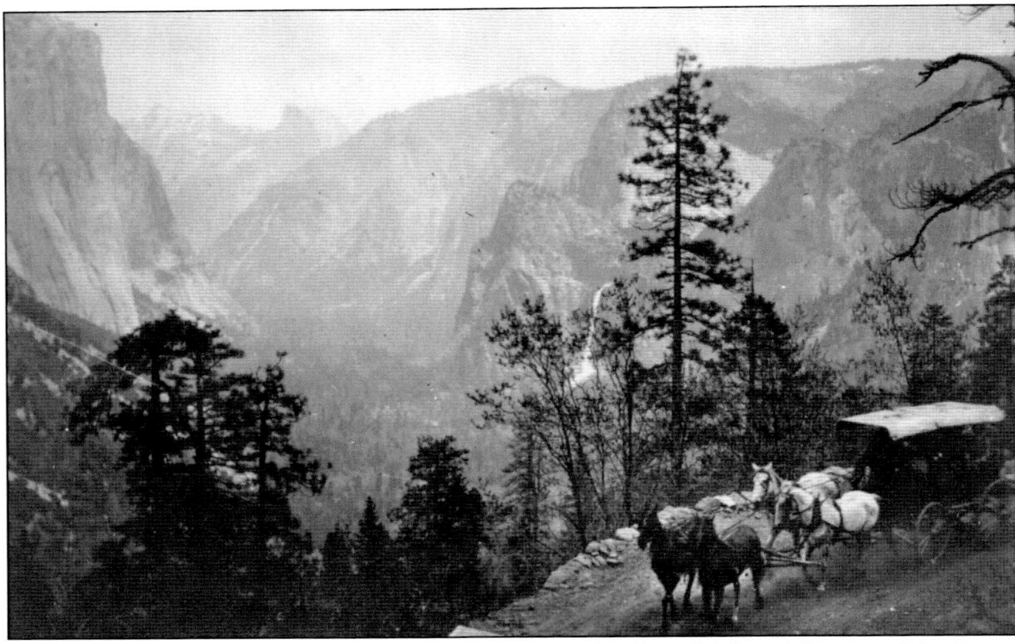

The final pitch on the Mariposa Road was subject to rock falls and delays. (Photograph by George Fiske, MHP.)

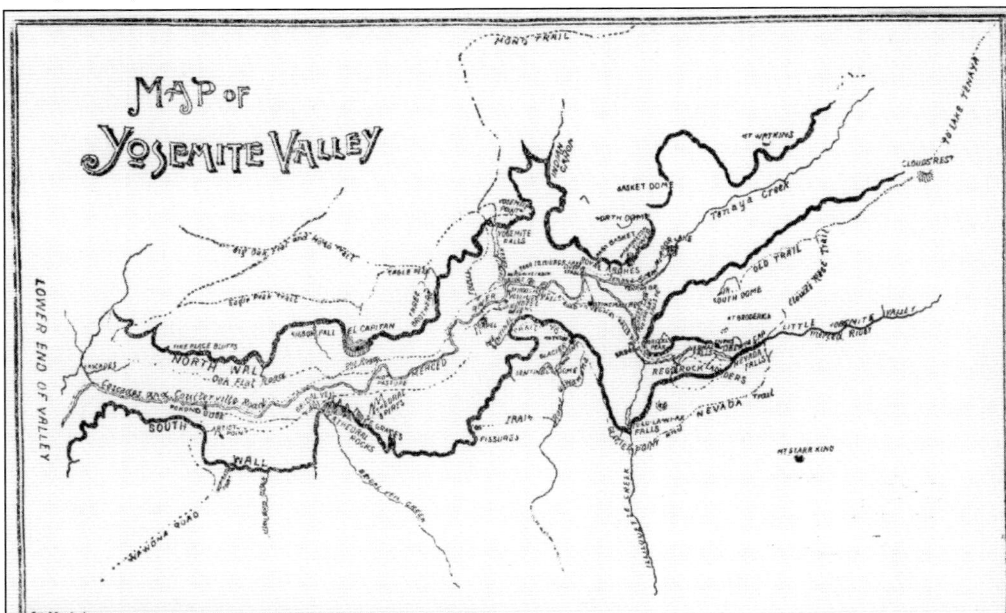

In 1863, Yosemite Valley and the Mariposa Grove of Big Trees became California State Parks by cession of the federal government. The administration of these areas lasted until 1906. The balance of the area around Yosemite Valley was eventually designated a national park in 1890. The boundaries were established, which encompassed large areas of timber and water that had been claimed privately. Newer perimeter agreements were adopted to recognize these private claims. (MHP.)

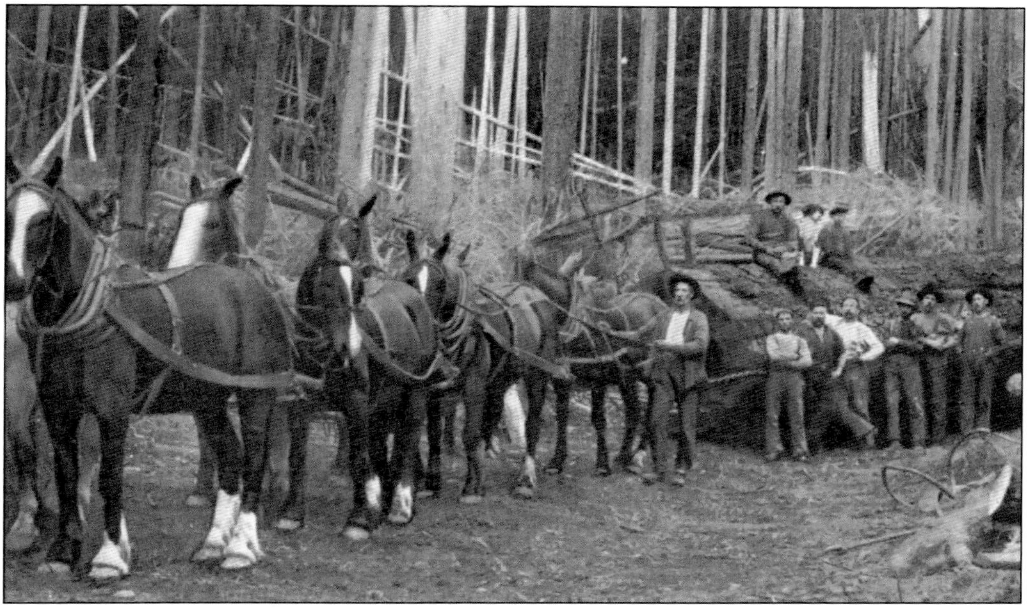

This opened the door for development of a railroad to the park boundary and roads within the park itself. It also made private timber claims available for harvesting. Timber claims had been filed prior to the establishment of Yosemite National Park but were not developed. After returning Yosemite Valley to the park, the desire for attracting public use was strengthened by the Secretary of Interior. This meant the need for transportation and lodging facilities. (MHP.)

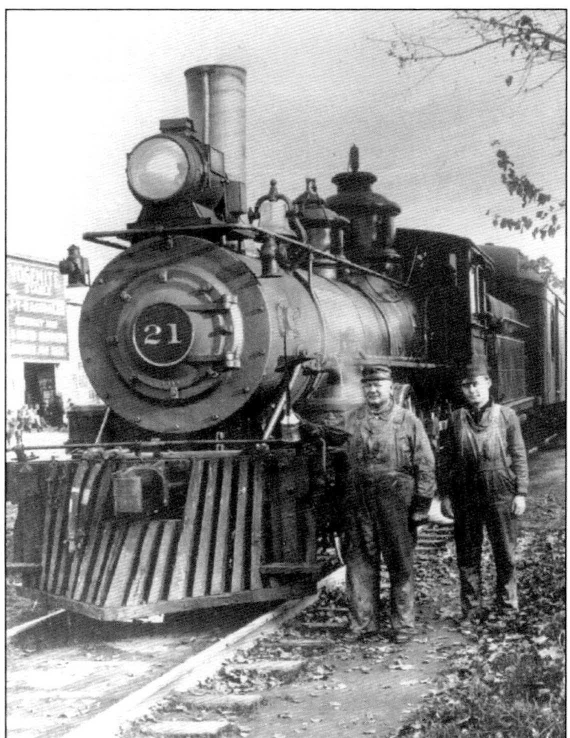

The strong desire to build first-class accommodations in Yosemite Valley was the dream of many. The answer was a railroad from the San Joaquin Valley. A number of attempts and surveys were made, and in 1902, a group in San Francisco started the Yosemite Valley Railroad. (MHP.)

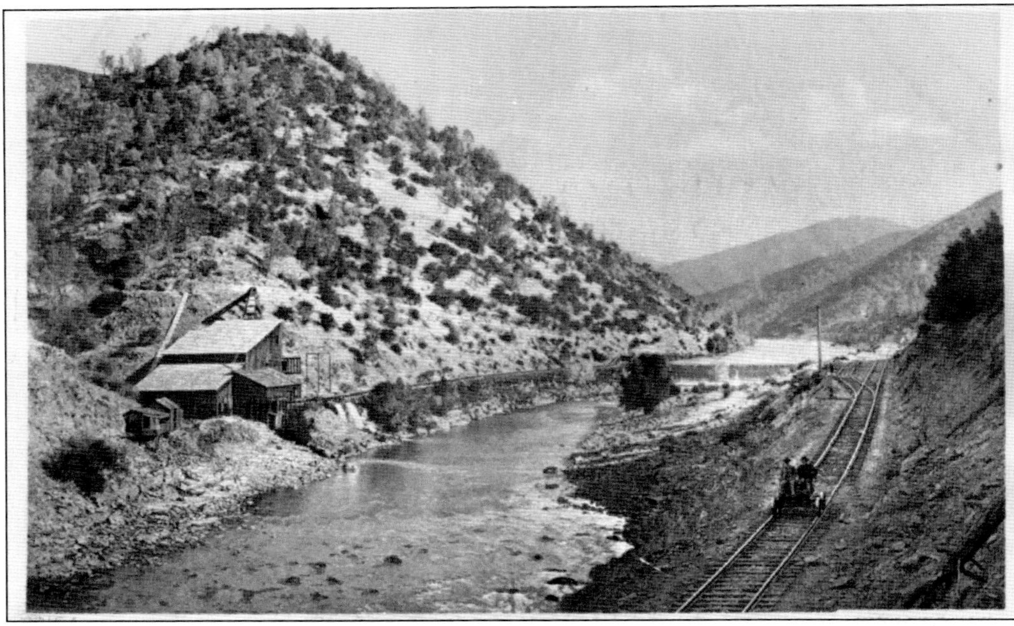

The Merced River Canyon was the most feasible location for a railroad route. By September 1905, grading began from Merced. Construction was done by mule scrapers, wheelbarrows, and as many as 1,800 men with shovels. About 2.9 million pounds of black powder blasted a rail bed through sandstone and granite. (MHP.)

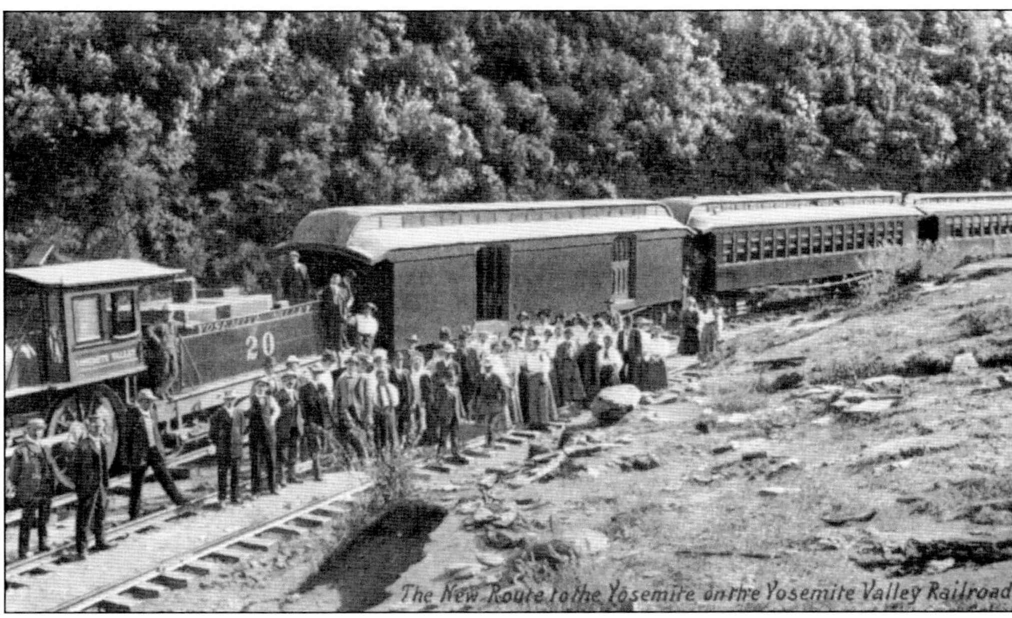

A railhead at the park boundary was established and was christened by the railroad as El Portal. With the exception of tents near the railhead, there were few services at first. (MHP.)

The railroad built a wagon road to the Cascades with the permission of the park service. There it joined the Coulterville Road. The new road was donated to the park service. This road became the basis for the arch rock entrance. (MHP.)

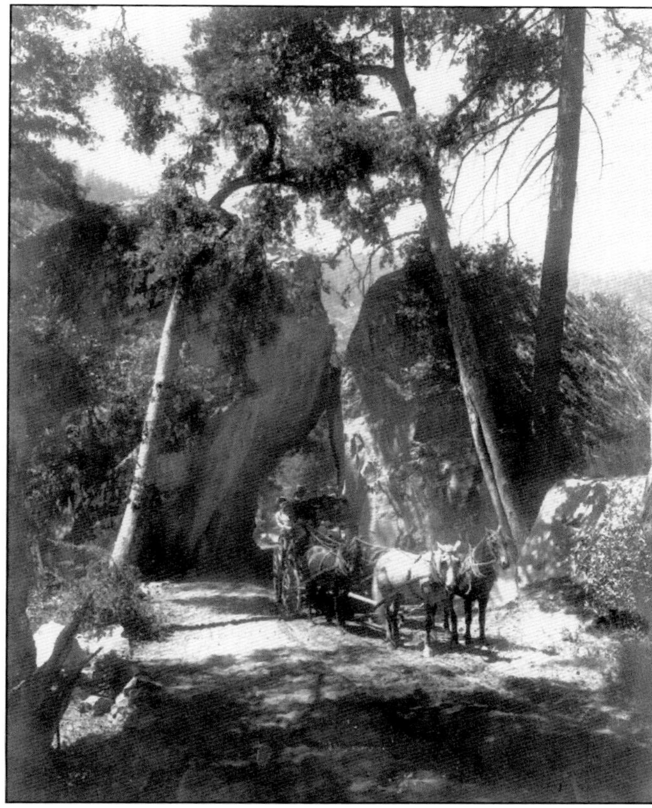

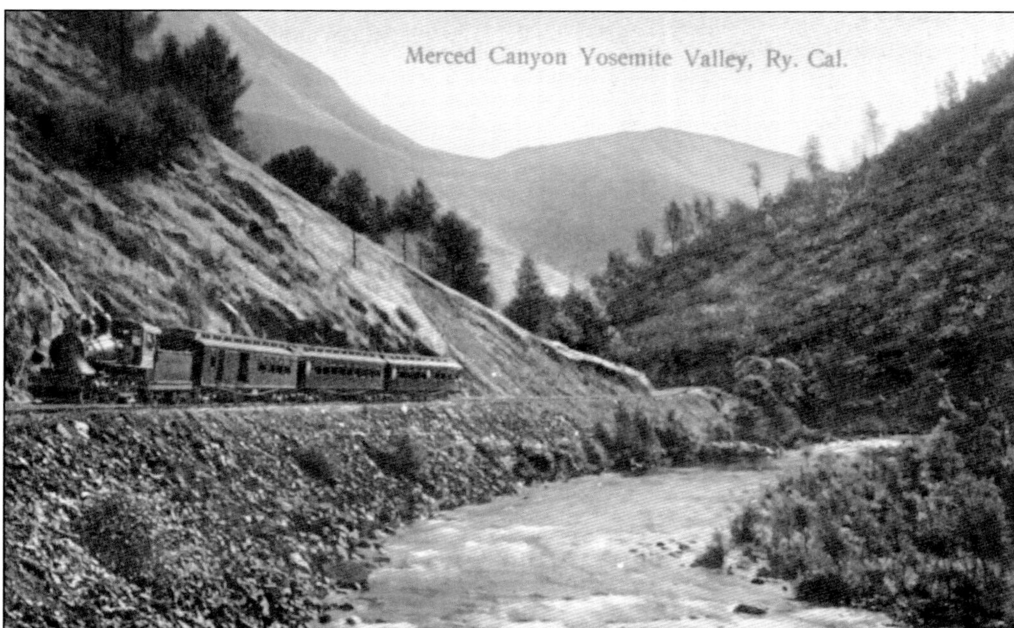

This image shows the Yosemite Valley Railroad as it passes alongside the Merced River. (Author's collection.)

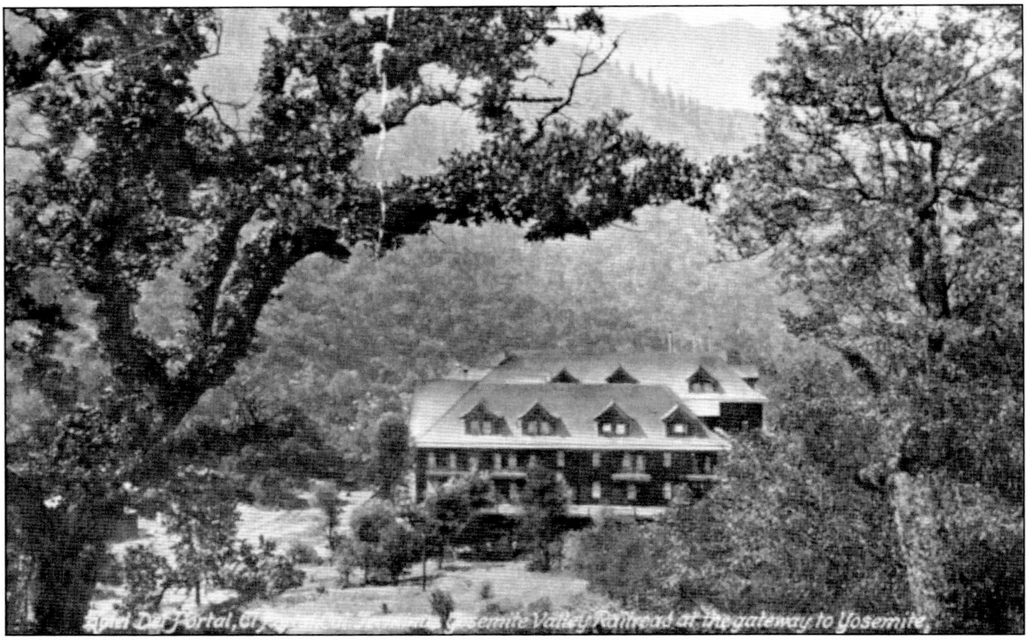

The Del Portal Hotel set the standard for elegance in the Yosemite region. (Courtesy of MHP.)

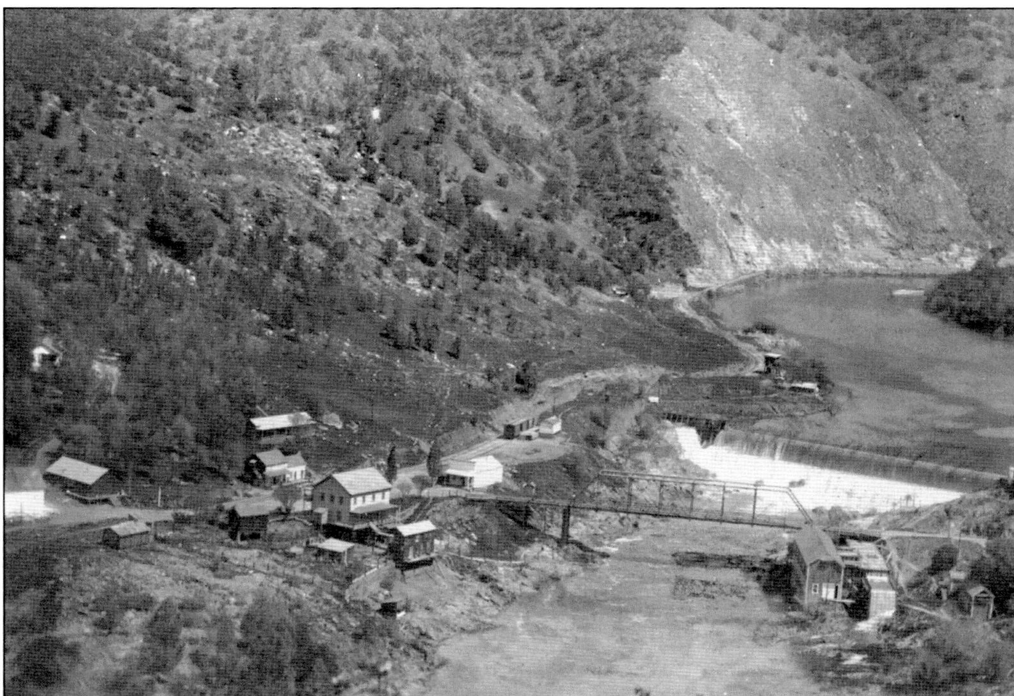
Postal and Wells Fargo Stations were established along the route. Bagby became an important stop. From this point, passengers and freight traveling to Mariposa could be transferred to supply the mines south of the Merced River. (MHP.)

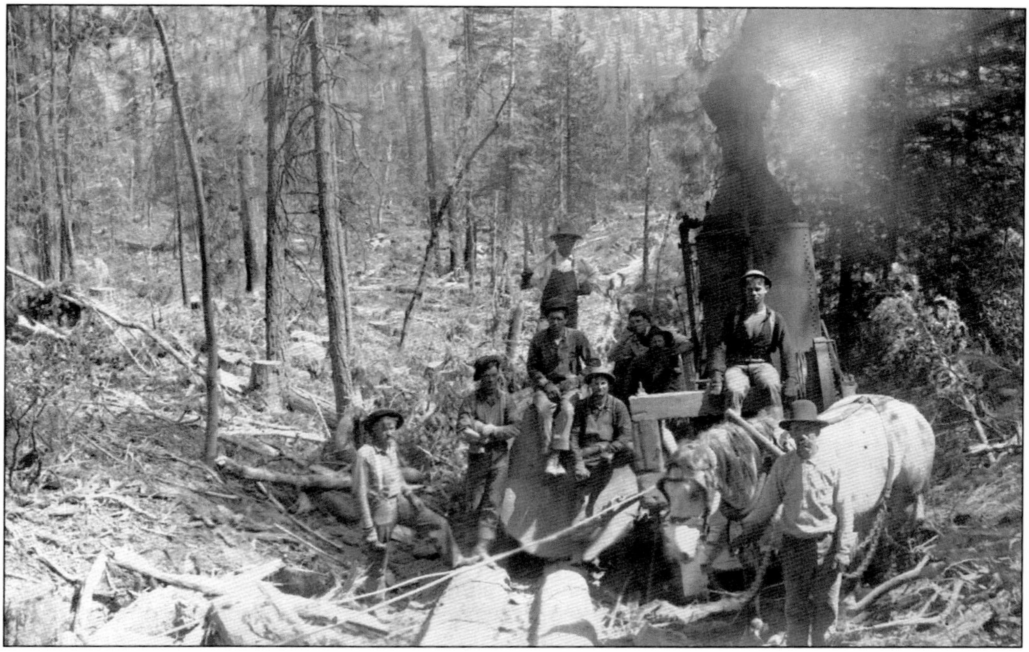

Aside from the travelers to Yosemite National Park, the presence of many acres of privately claimed undeveloped forests on both sides of the river helped encourage the building of the rail line. The possibility of mineral development, while noticed, did not prove to be of much interest, possibly because of the erratic nature of mining and its markets. (MHP.)

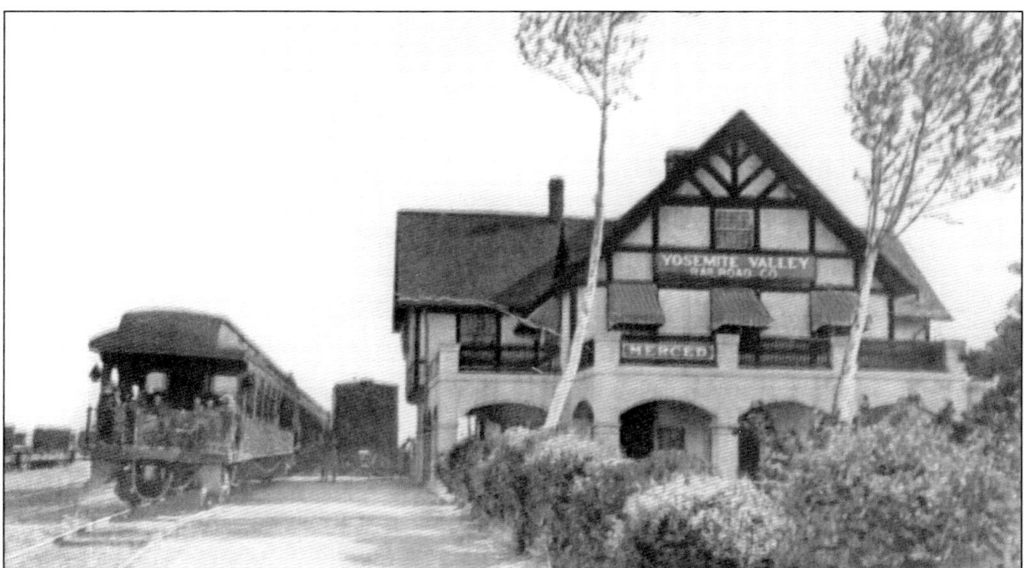

The railroad general offices were relocated to Merced after the 1906 earthquake in San Francisco. Tracks were laid that connected the Yosemite Valley Railroad to the Southern Pacific. (MHP.)

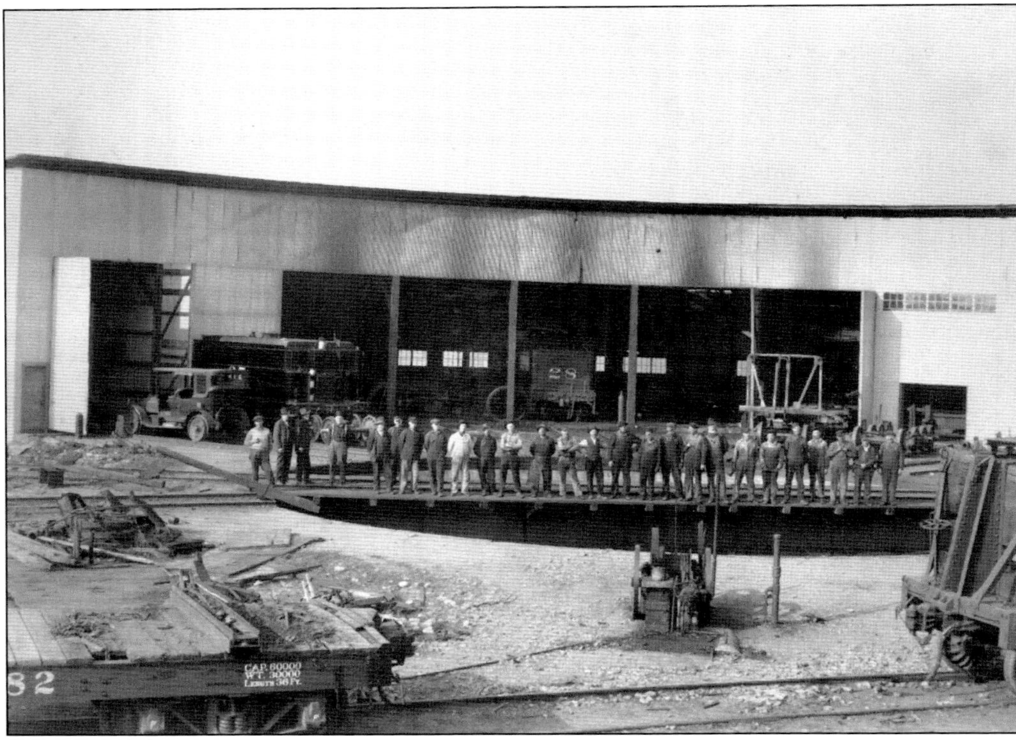

Shops and a roundhouse was established at the Merced terminus, as well as connections to the Southern Pacific line. Pullman service was started, and one could travel from Oakland to El Portal in relative comfort. At first there were some complaints about sparks from the wood burning engine, but soon other fuels were used. (MHP.)

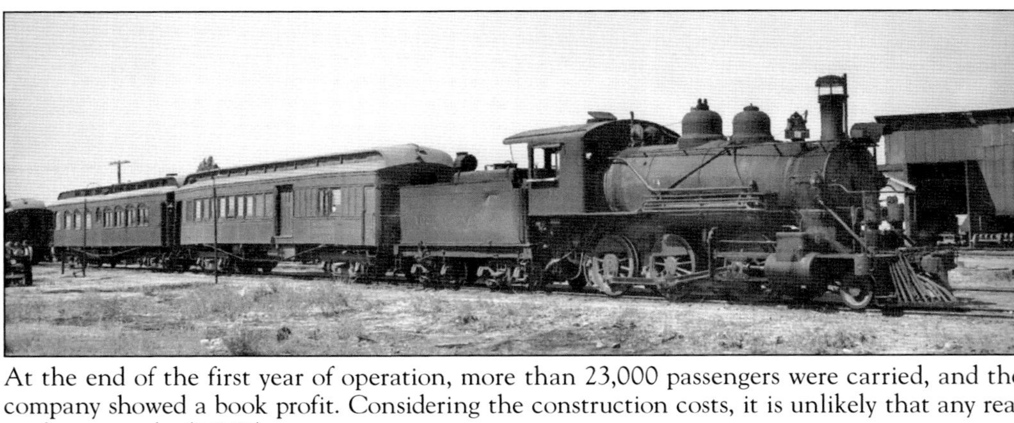

At the end of the first year of operation, more than 23,000 passengers were carried, and the company showed a book profit. Considering the construction costs, it is unlikely that any real profit was made. (MHP.)

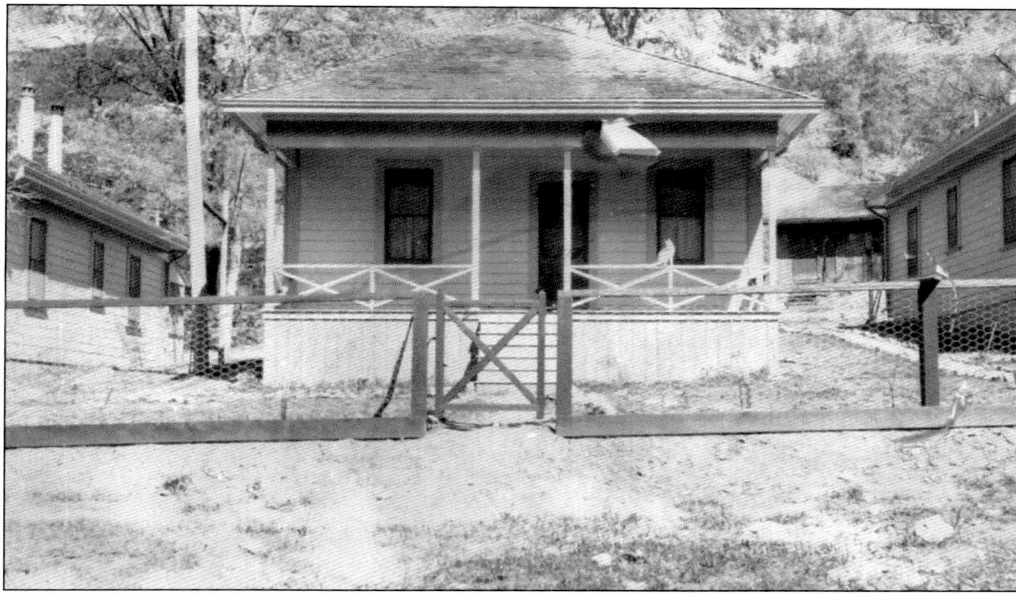

At the park boundary, El Portal developed as the residential area for the employees of the railroad. The railroad built residences for key employees. (MHP.)

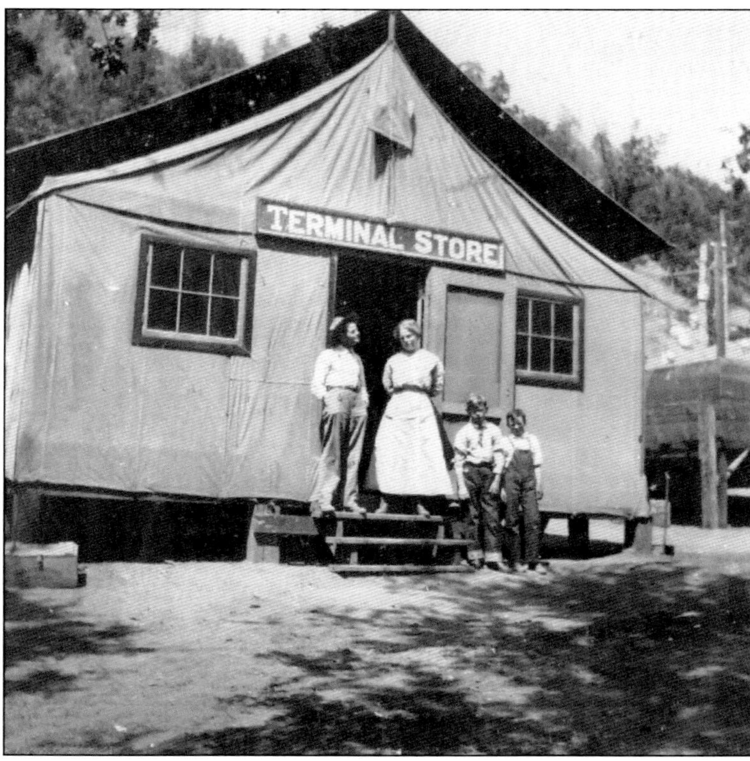

The railroad owned everything, including the Terminal Store. (MHP.)

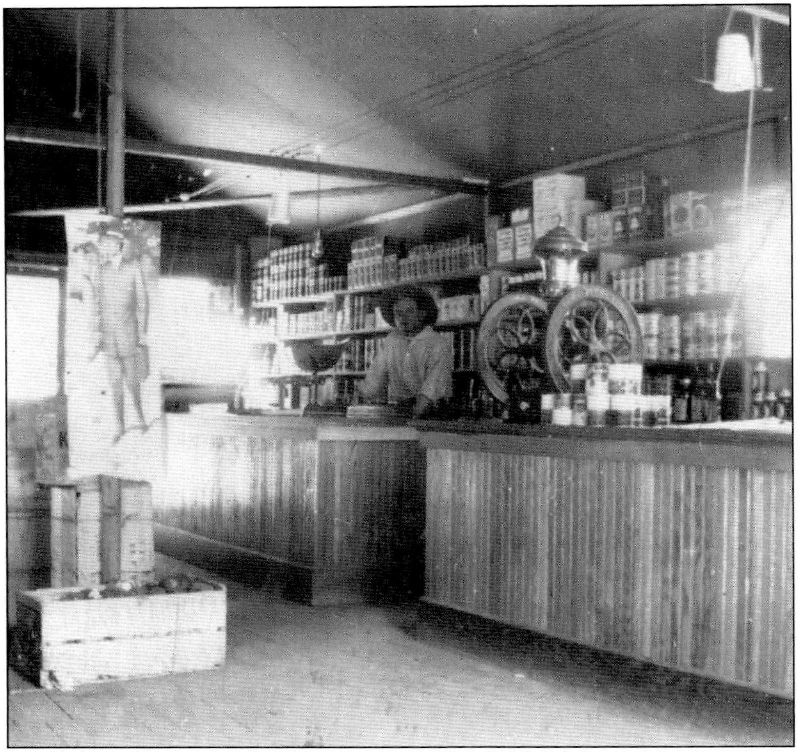

Billy Nelson, who was later one of the first rangers in Yosemite, tended to the Terminal Store. Nelson always wore twin ivory-handled pistols, even when he was a ranger. He was a genuine character and passed away in Mariposa during the 1950s (MHP.)

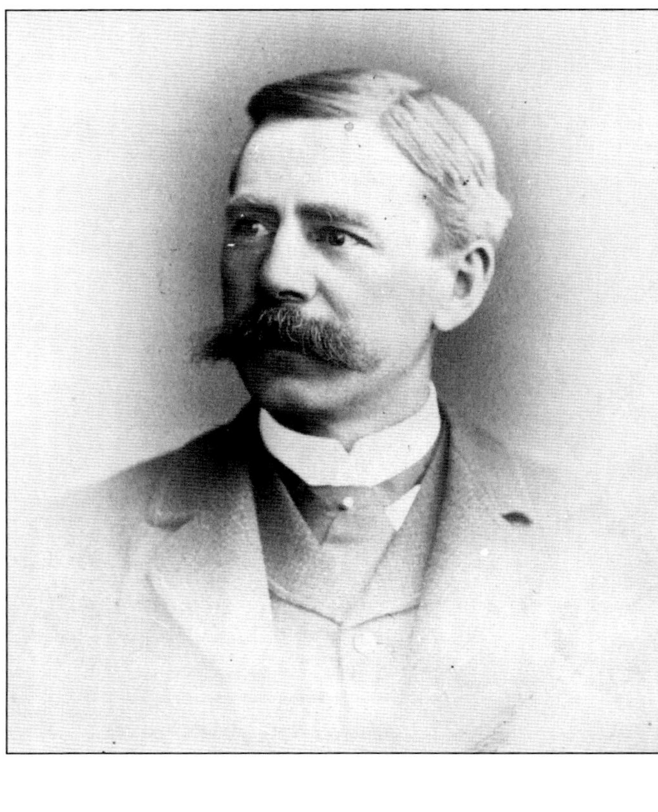

The site of El Portal was on land that was owned by Augustus H. "Cap" Ward. Ward sold the site to the Yosemite Valley Railroad. The area was quite primitive, with no roads. Native Americans were the main inhabitants, and the closest wagon road was at Cascades. (MHP.)

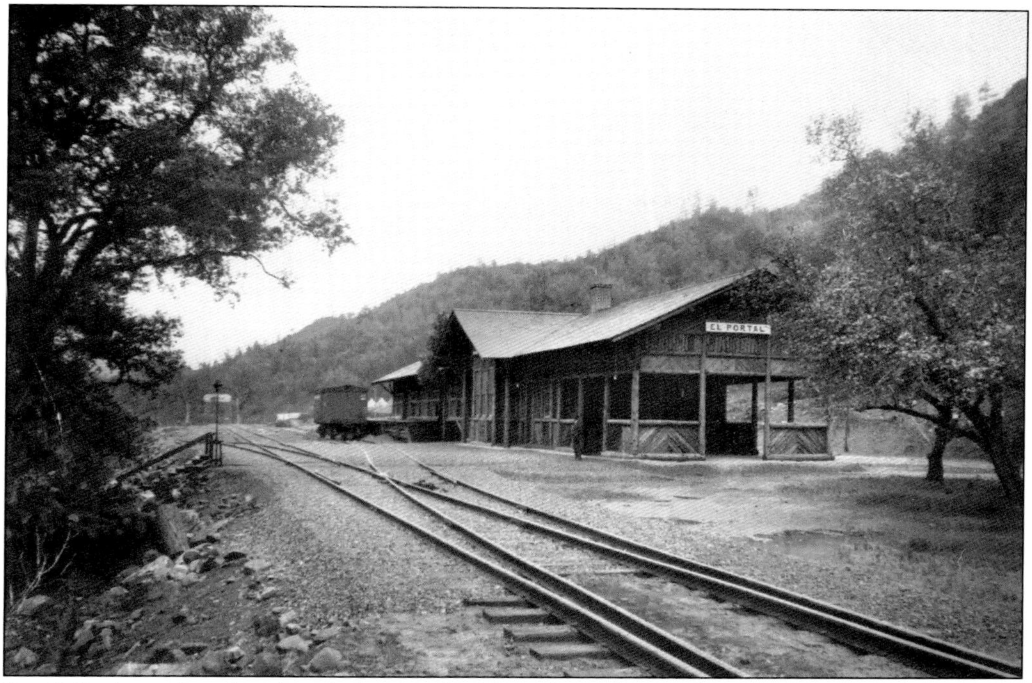

By 1909, the railroad replaced the ramshackle ticket office with a proper station house with baggage and freight sections. (MHP.)

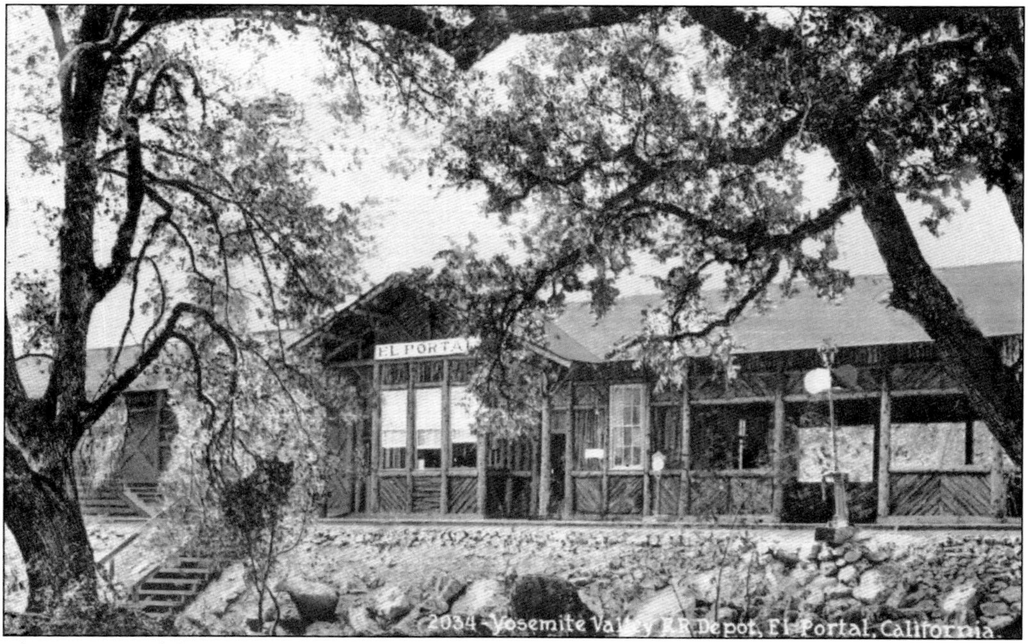

The exterior of the station was covered with split cedar with the bark intact. It looked quite nice, but its dryness made it quite flammable. (MHP.)

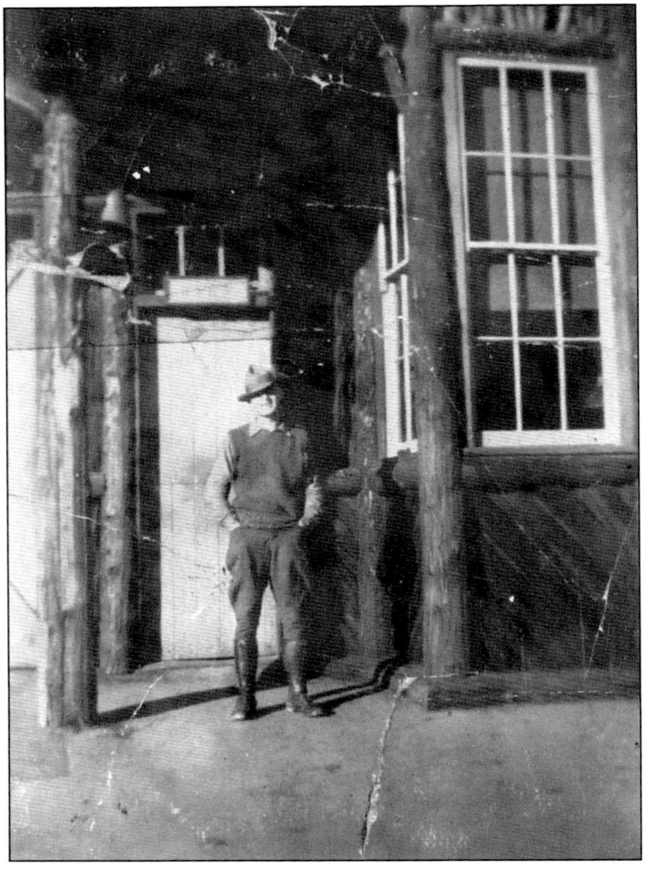

Agent George Farber is pictured at the El Portal station in 1920. Although just 11 years old, the cedar siding shows its lack of permanence. Farber also served as a Wells Fargo agent in Yosemite. (MHP.)

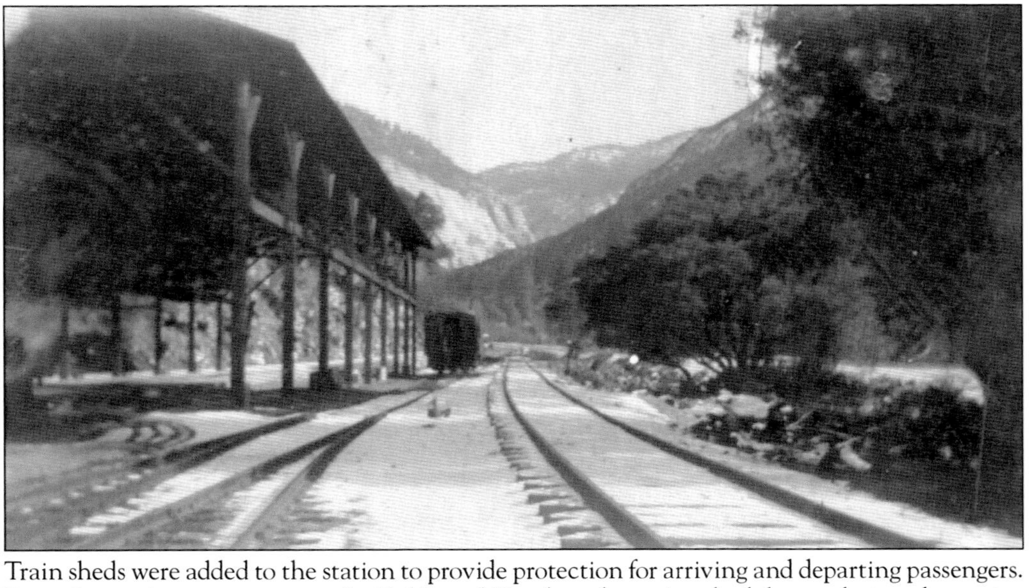

Train sheds were added to the station to provide protection for arriving and departing passengers. From the station, most went to the Del Portal Hotel, as the train schedule was designed to arrive in the late afternoon and leave after breakfast. (MHP.)

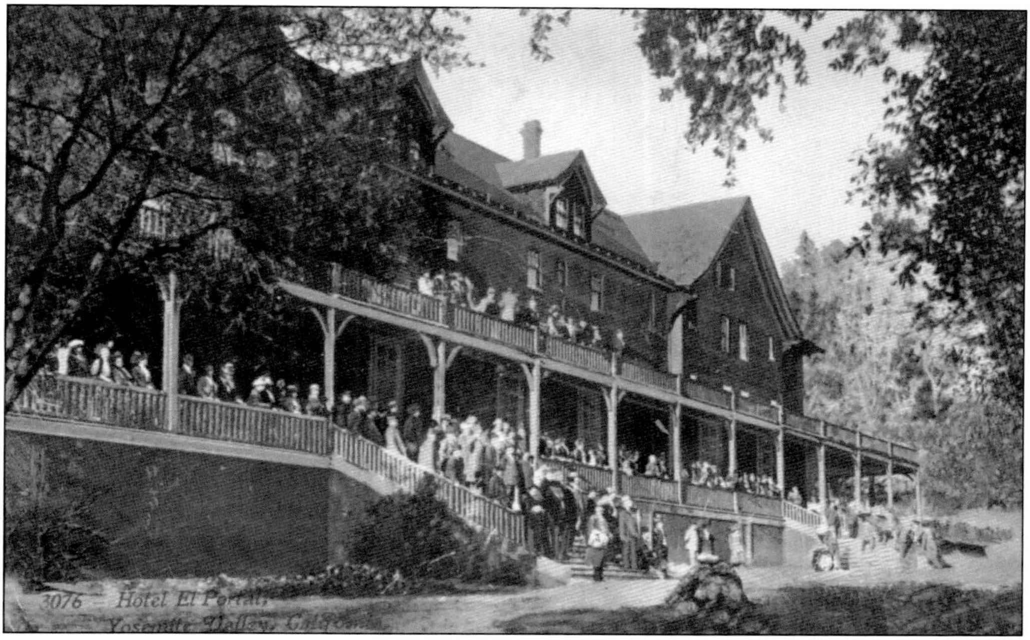

The Del Portal Hotel, built in 1908, replaced a number of tents that had been the first quarters for the passengers. (MHP.)

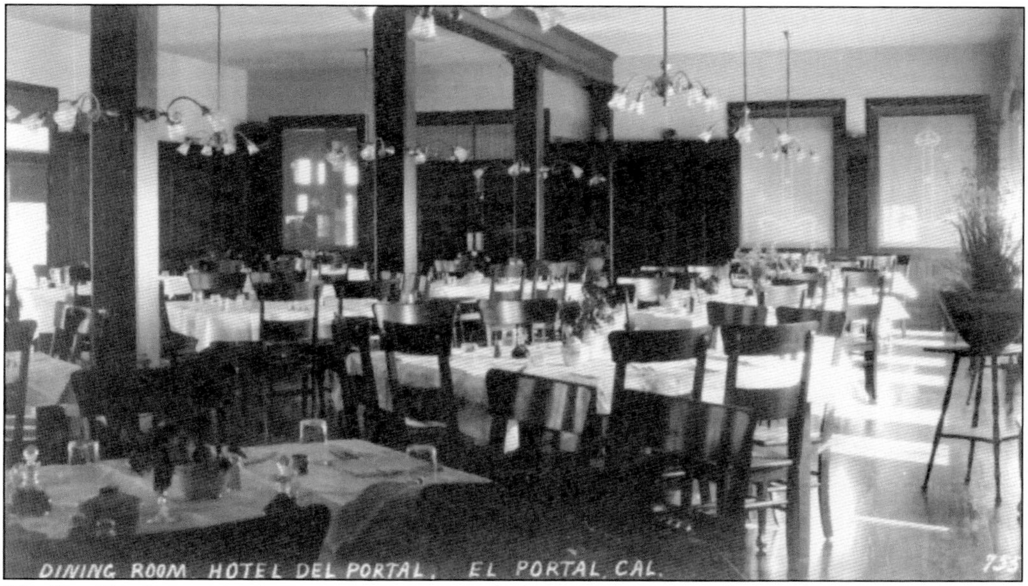

The hotel had many modern conveniences, including running water (hot and cold) and electricity from a power plant on Crane Creek. It also had many luxuries such as ferns in the polished dinning room and a menu offering a fine selection of food, ranging from trout to game. (MHP.)

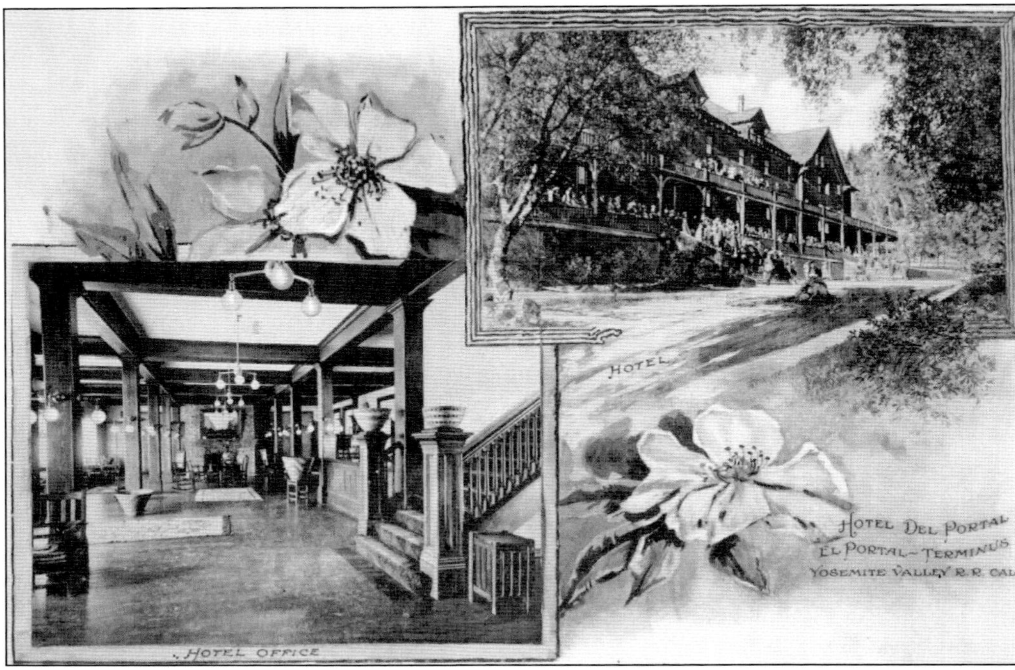

The advertising card by the Pillsbury Picture Company shows a first-class facility decorated with dogwood blossoms and ferns. (MHP.)

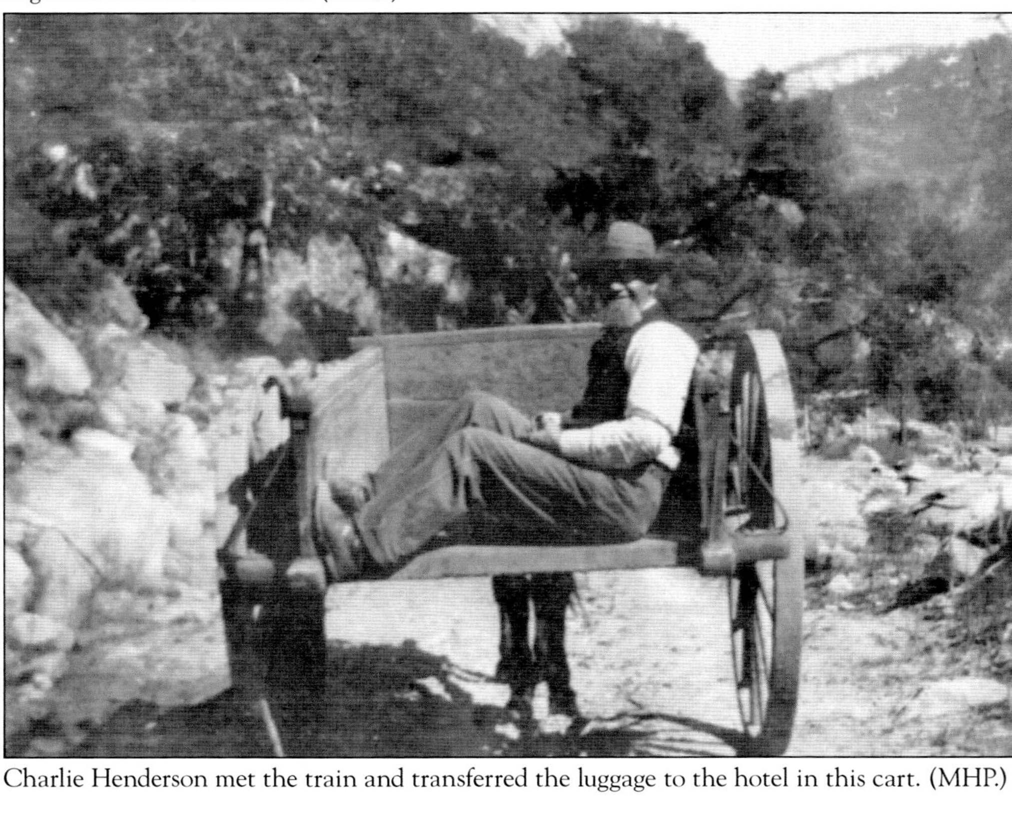

Charlie Henderson met the train and transferred the luggage to the hotel in this cart. (MHP.)

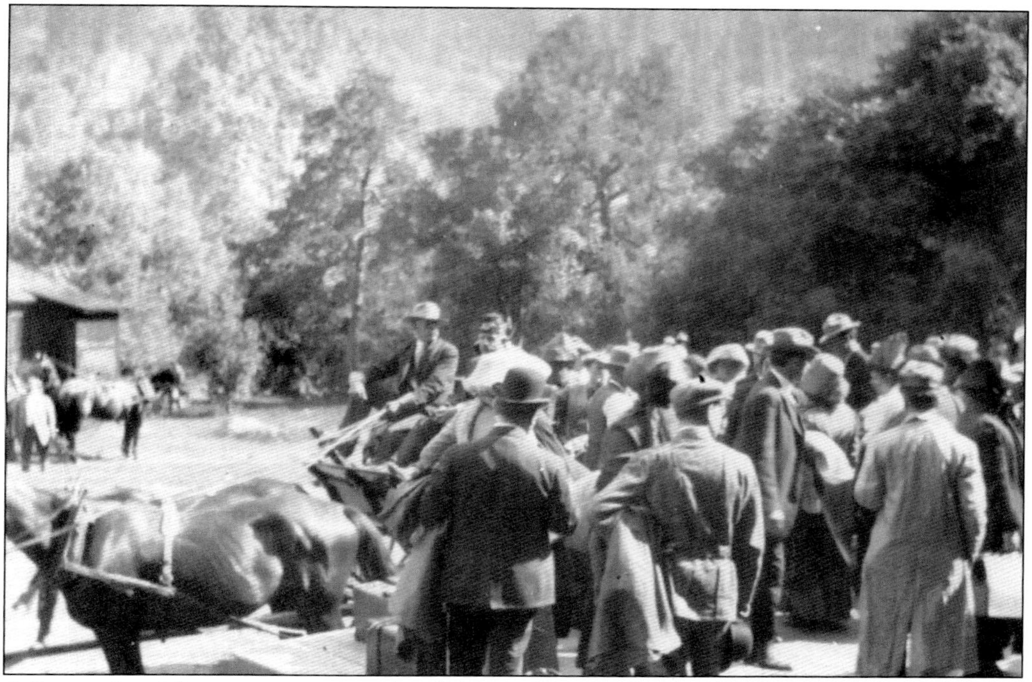

Following breakfast, passengers were loaded into the carriages that lined up in front of the hotel. Then they were engaged in a slow, dusty trip to Yosemite Valley. (MHP.)

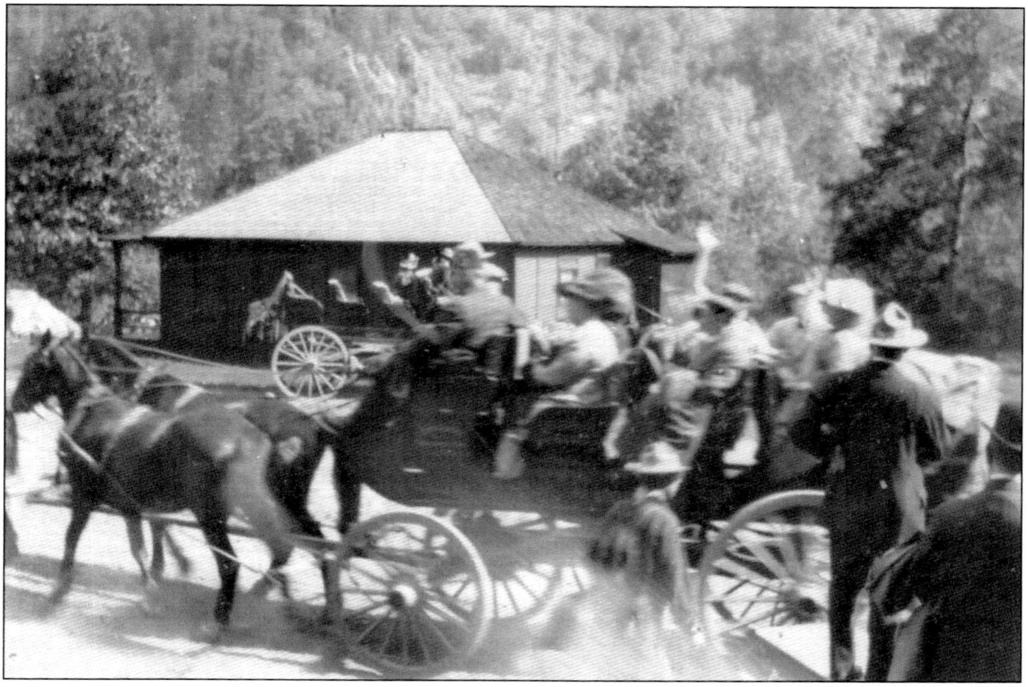

To get to the park, visitors endured a trip that often lasted four hours. Horses were changed at least twice during the trip, once at Arch Rock and again at Cascades, at the Coulterville Road. (MHP.)

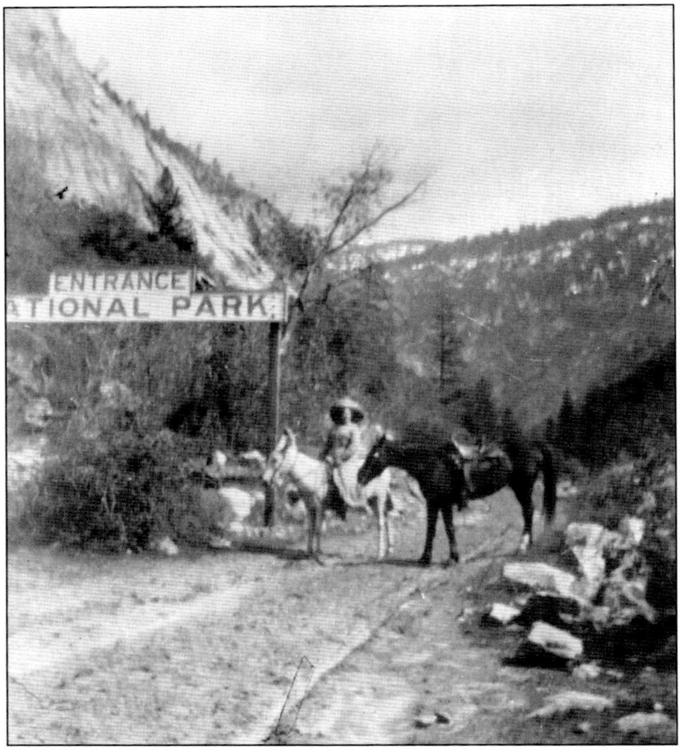

The first landmark, the entrance to Yosemite National Park, was a short distance from Yosemite Valley. The Yosemite Transportation Company ran the stages. The road was built by the railroad and was donated to the park. (MHP.)

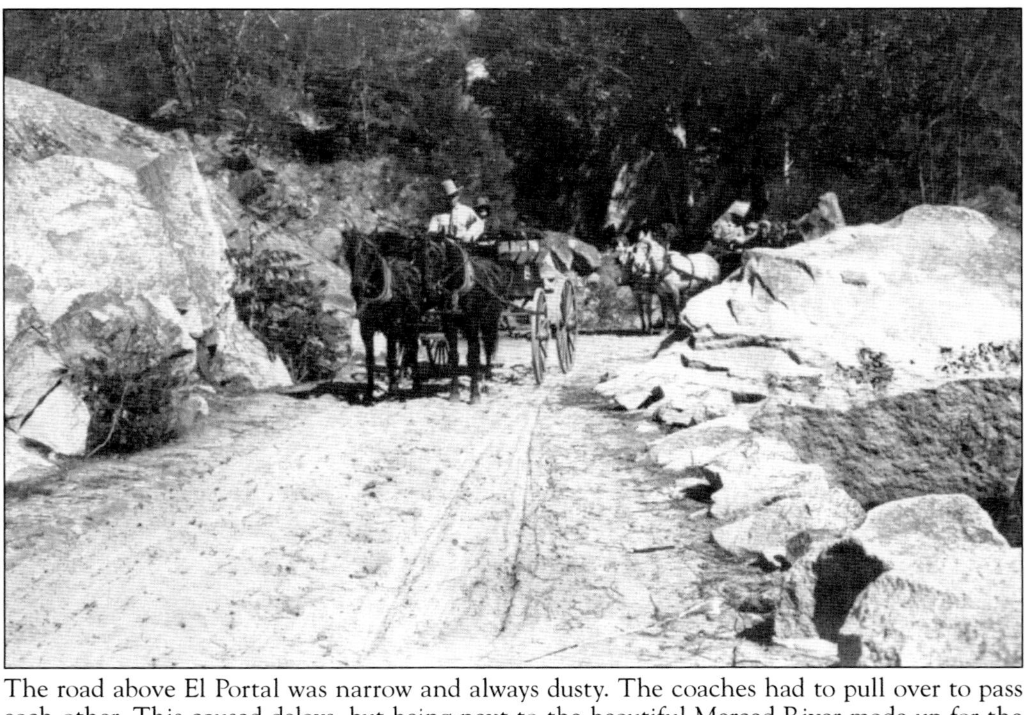

The road above El Portal was narrow and always dusty. The coaches had to pull over to pass each other. This caused delays, but being next to the beautiful Merced River made up for the lost time. (MHP.)

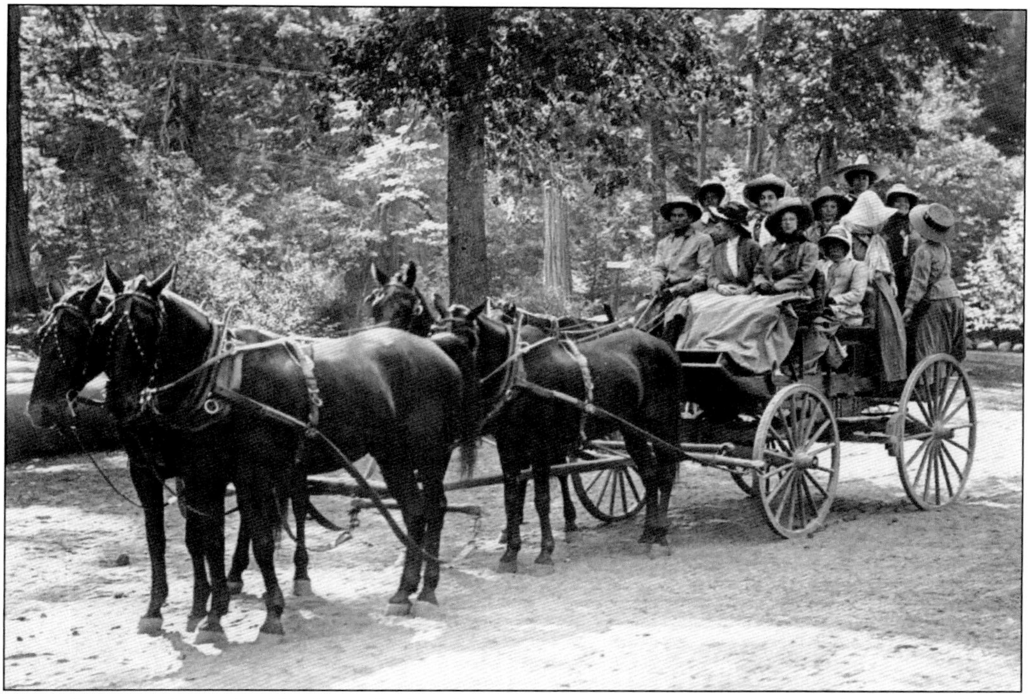

Cascades was where the Coulterville Road intersected. There was a blacksmith shop and horse corrals. Cascade Falls was the first of the major waterfalls in Yosemite. (MHP.)

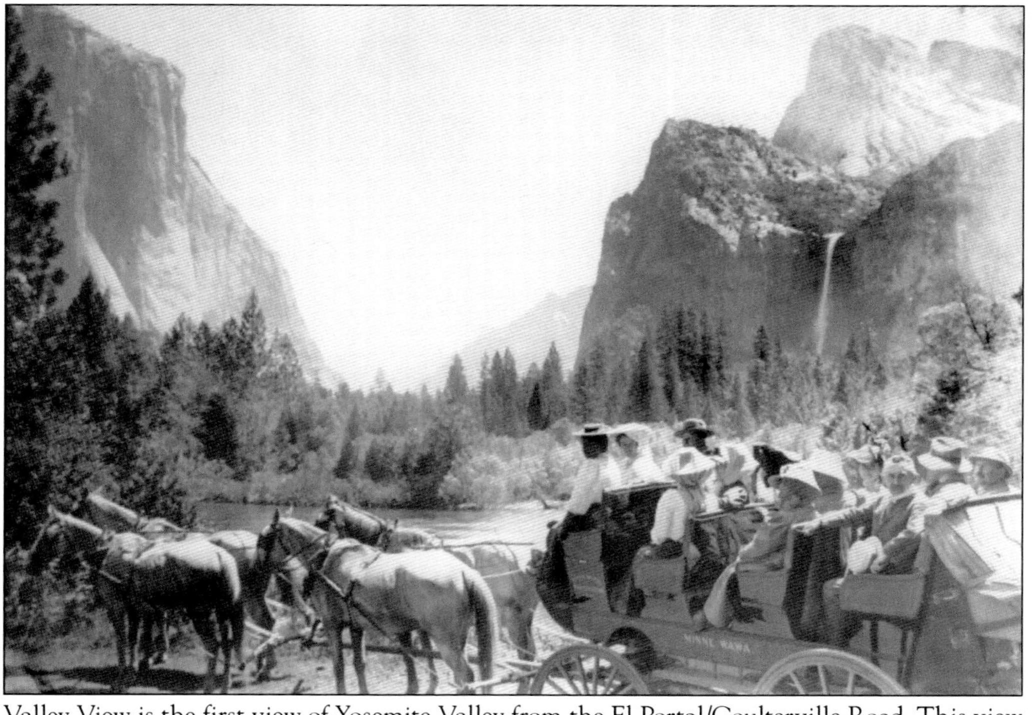

Valley View is the first view of Yosemite Valley from the El Portal/Coulterville Road. This view along the Merced River is still a favorite among visitors. (MHP.)

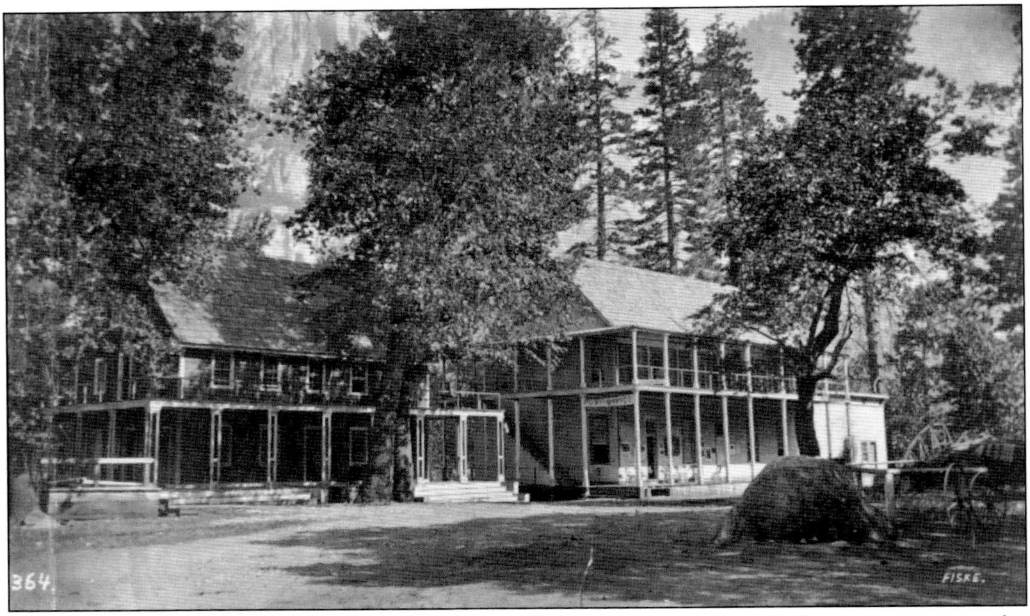

The Sentinel Hotel in Yosemite Valley was one of the destinations for the passengers on the Yosemite Valley Railroad. (Photograph by Fiske, MHP.)

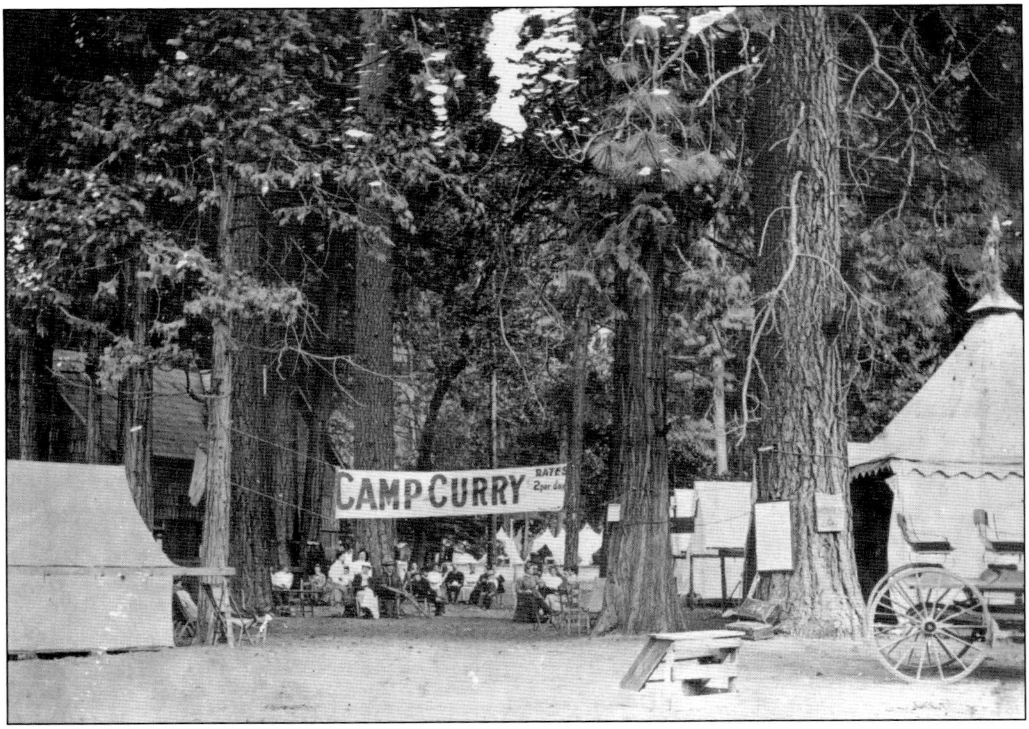

Started in 1899 as Camp Sequoia, Camp Curry became the favorite of many of the rail passengers. Accommodations where inexpensive, and a full program of nightly entertainment was offered. During the summer season, many of the employees were college students from Stanford University. (MHP.)

David Curry and his wife, Jenny, founded Camp Curry. A platform in front of the camp was the place for greeting and wishing farewell to the guests. Curry, a bombastic hotel keeper, would send off the stages with a shouted farewell. (MHP.)

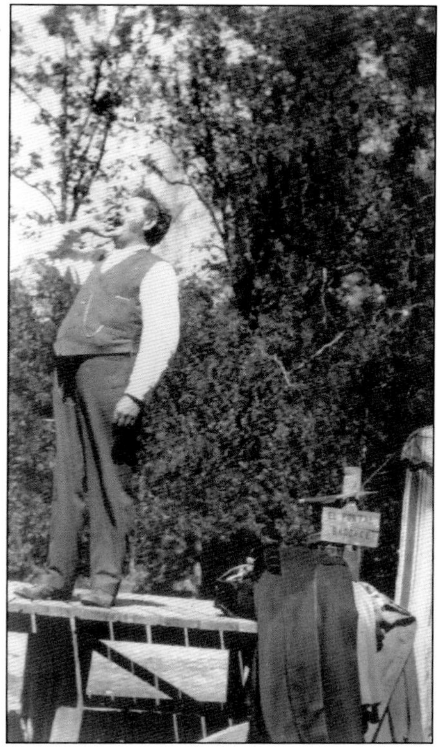

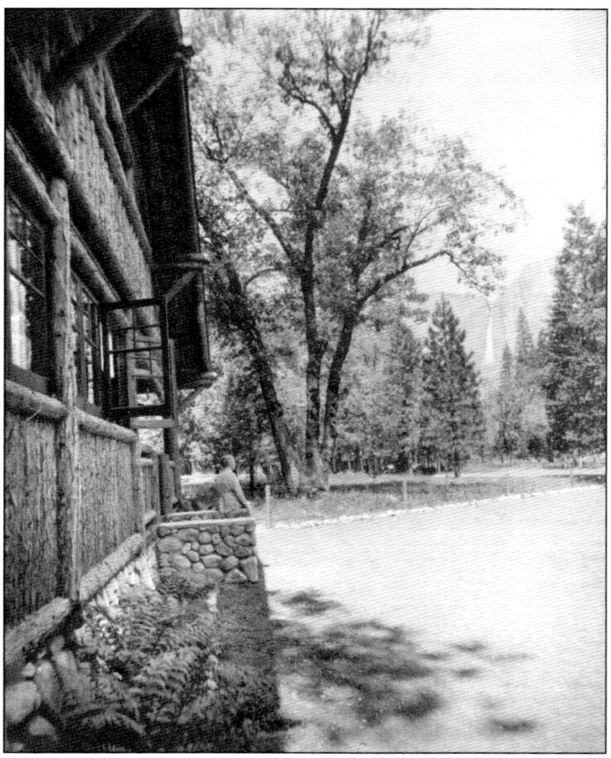

Jenny Curry sits in front of her cabin, with Yosemite Falls in the background. The Curry family continued the tradition as innkeepers until 1966, with the departure of John Foster Curry. (MHP.)

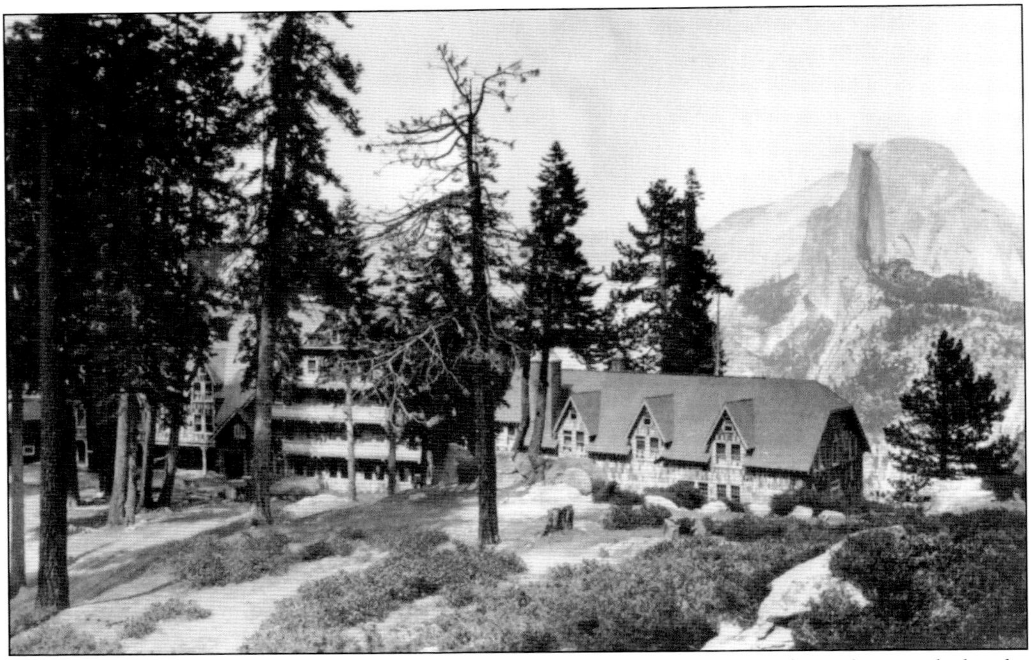

The Glacier Point Hotel, built by the Desmond Company in 1918, was also a favorite lodge for railroad passengers. The views of both Yosemite Valley and the High Country attracted many seasonal guests. The hotel burned in 1969. (MHP.)

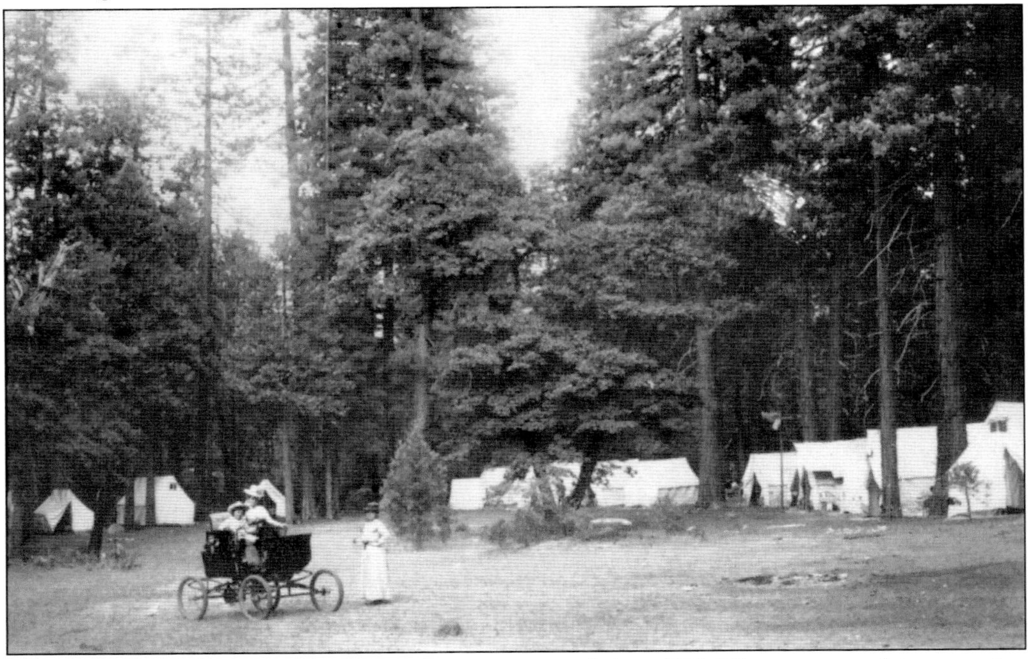

In Camp Curry, Oliver Lippencot drives a steam automobile in 1901. The presence of the steaming and puffing vehicle frightened the horses and mules. Automobiles would not be allowed into the park until 1913. The arrival of the internal combustion engine changed the operation of the railroad. (MHP.)

Three

The Yosemite Valley Railroad Diversifies

Even though Yosemite National Park allowed the internal combustion engine into the park by 1913, it took awhile for the railroad and the transportation contractor, Yosemite Transportation System, to convert from horse-drawn stages to buses. The bus cut two to three hours off the trip from El Portal to Yosemite Valley. The railroad was not doing well with tourist travel alone, because of the seasonable nature of travel. The company knew of the possibility of timber harvest and transport as a potential revenue generator when it was formed. In 1911, the Yosemite Lumber Company began by purchasing 10,000 acres of timber allotments between Yosemite Valley and Wawona. These allotments had been created before Yosemite National Park was formed. The problem had always been how to get the timber to the mill. The Yosemite Valley Railroad solved the problem. A lumber mill was constructed at Merced Falls, which was 53.5 miles by rail from the forest. The mill would employ 350 workers and caused the creation of a town with its own hospital, stores, theater, and hotel. In order to access the timber, an incline railroad was constructed at El Portal that rose 7,800 feet above the river canyon. The Yosemite Valley Railroad participated in many of the costs of the operation, including the bunk cars necessary for hauling the timber down the incline and on to Merced Falls.

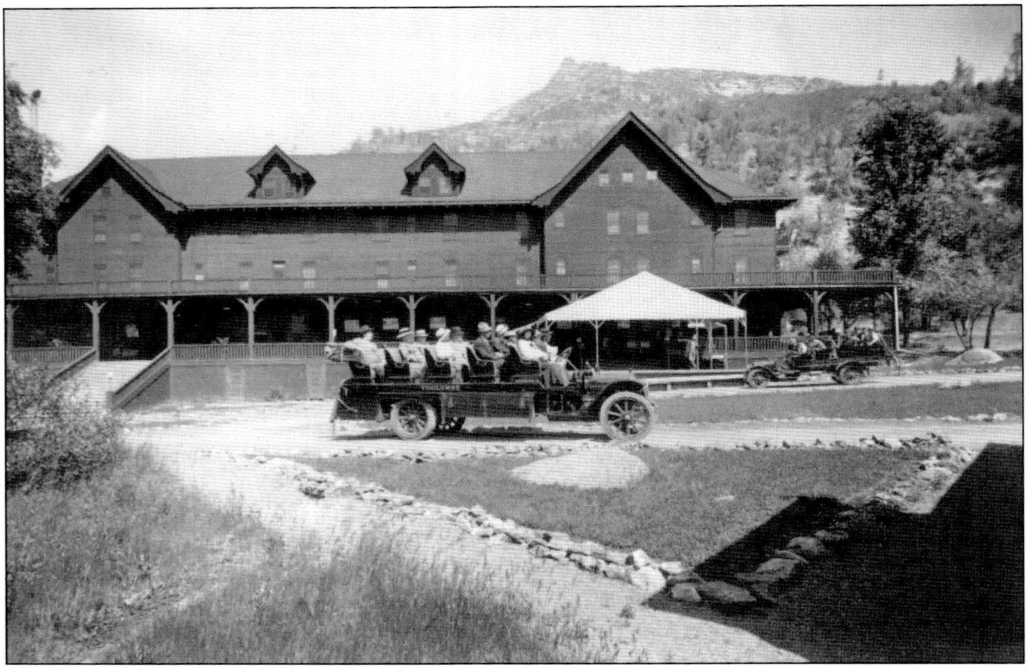

Automobile stages replace horses and wagons for the transportation of guests from the Del Portal Hotel to the valley floor. (MHP.)

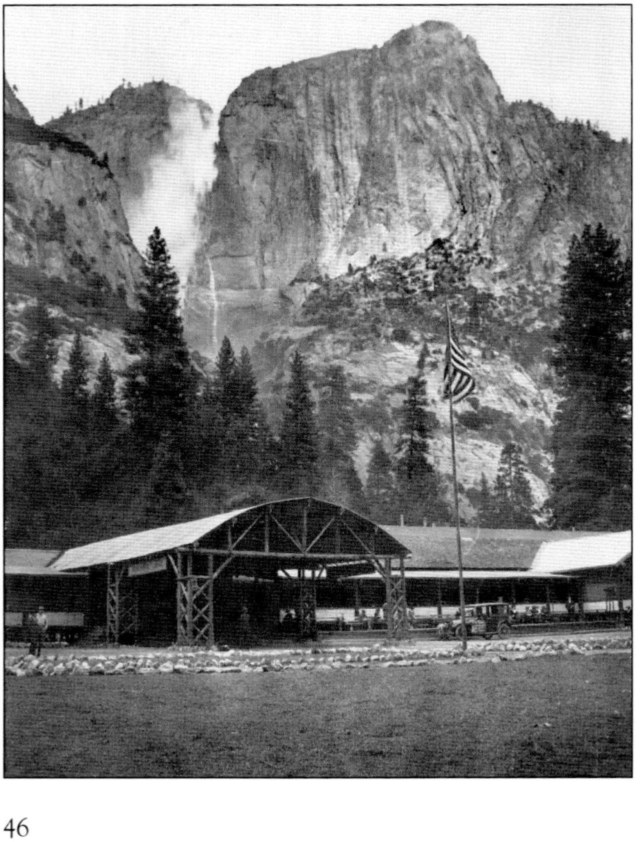

Constructed by the Dorman Company, Yosemite Lodge consisted of a number of U.S. Army barracks joined together with a cafeteria, which were added to the south end. The porte-cochere protected the arriving buses from the elements. (MHP.)

Open-top automobile stages did not spare the riders from the dust, but the ride was shorter. Riders enjoyed the beautiful sight of Yosemite Falls while parked in front of Yosemite Lodge. (MHP.)

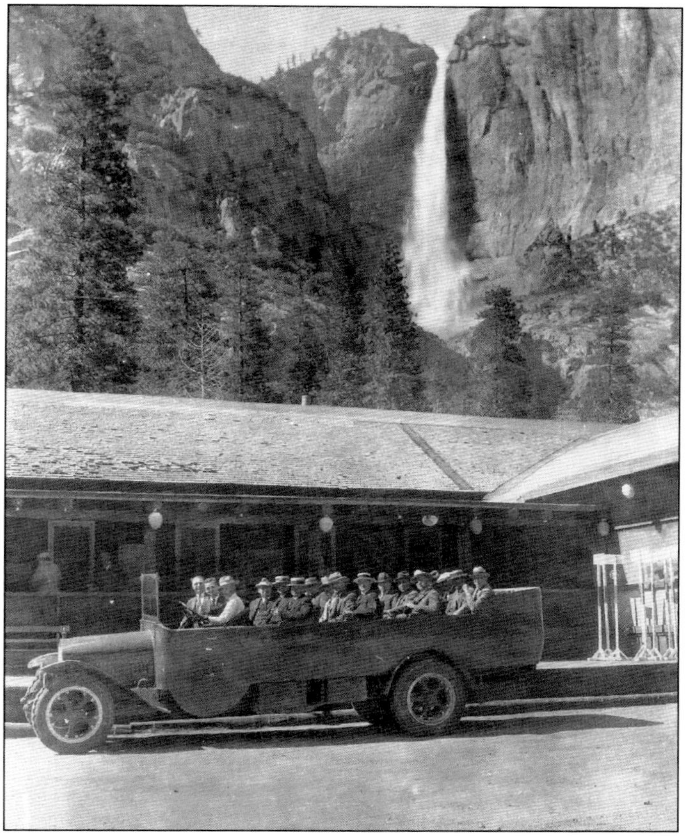

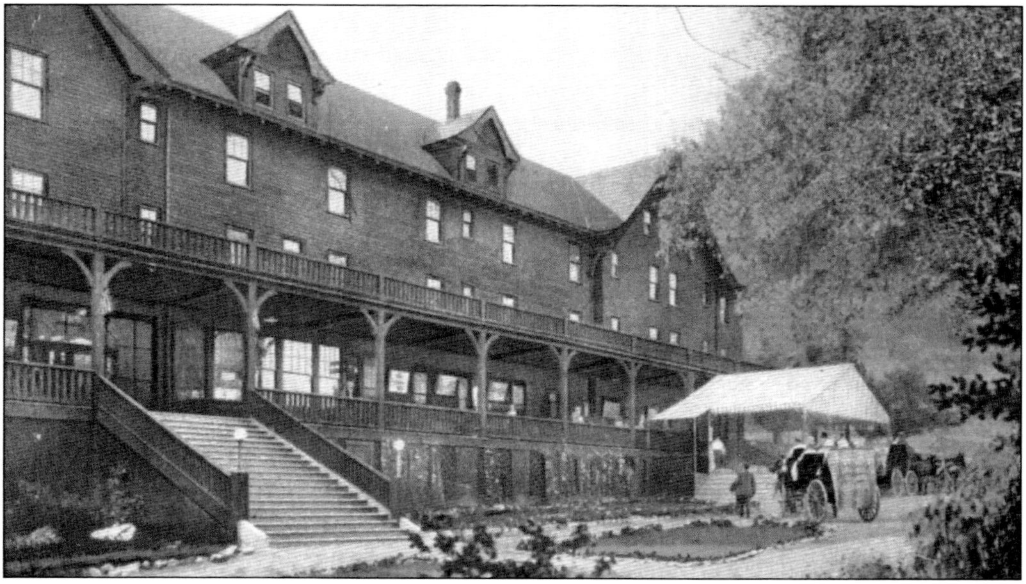

With the institution of motor-driven stages, business at the Del Portal Hotel began to dwindle. With the buses, passengers were loaded directly from the train onto the buses that took them to Yosemite Valley. World War I also had an effect on tourist travel. (MHP.)

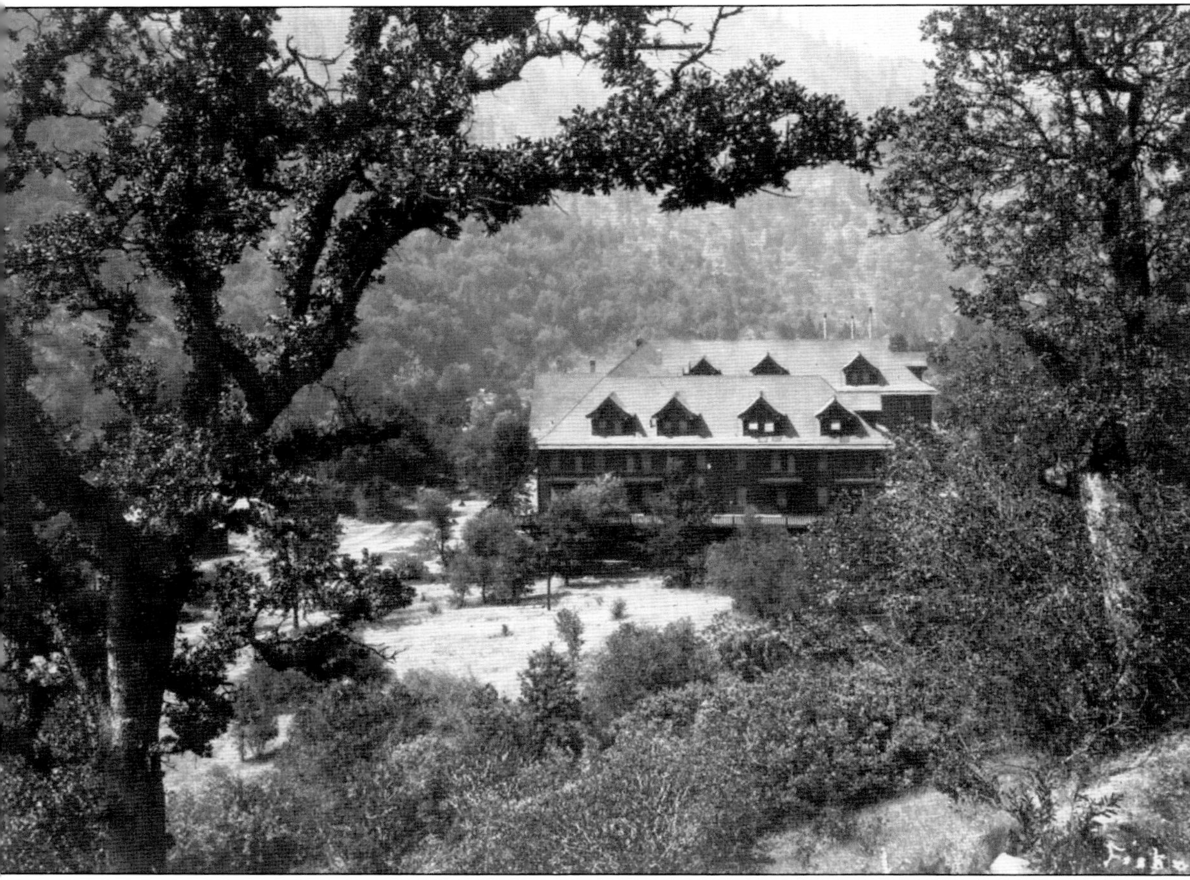

On October 27, 1917, this beautiful hotel went up in flames. It is said that a defective flue in the kitchen caused the fire. All guests and employees escaped unharmed. (MHP.)

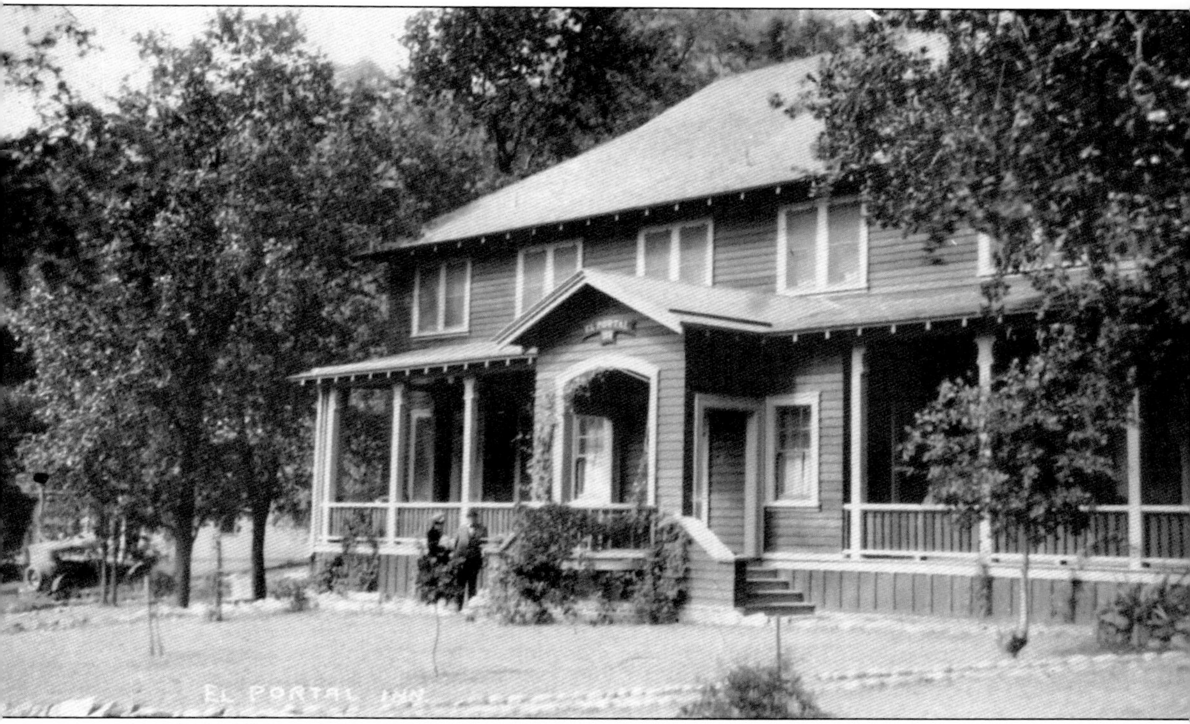

A new hotel, the El Portal, was constructed. It was much smaller and less elegant. The same kitchen equipment from the Del Portal was installed. During the 1930s, this hotel, which was little used except by train crews, also burned. The defective kitchen equipment was to blame. (MHP.)

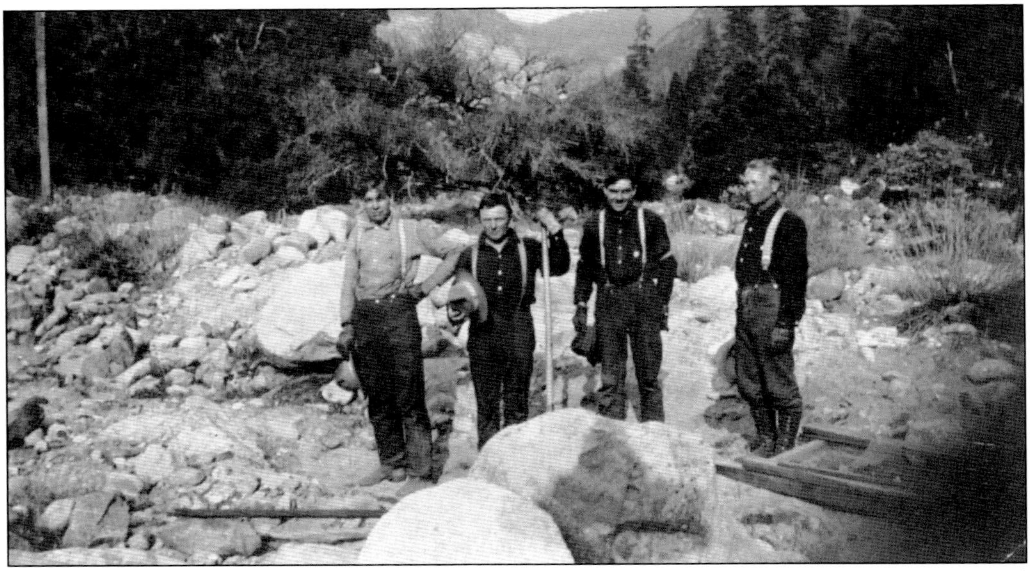

Construction of the Yosemite Lumber Company trestle across the Merced River in El Portal connected the south side incline to the main line. Local men built the trestle. Pictured from left to right are Bert Branson, Joe Lind, Milton Branson, and Ray Scott. (MHP.)

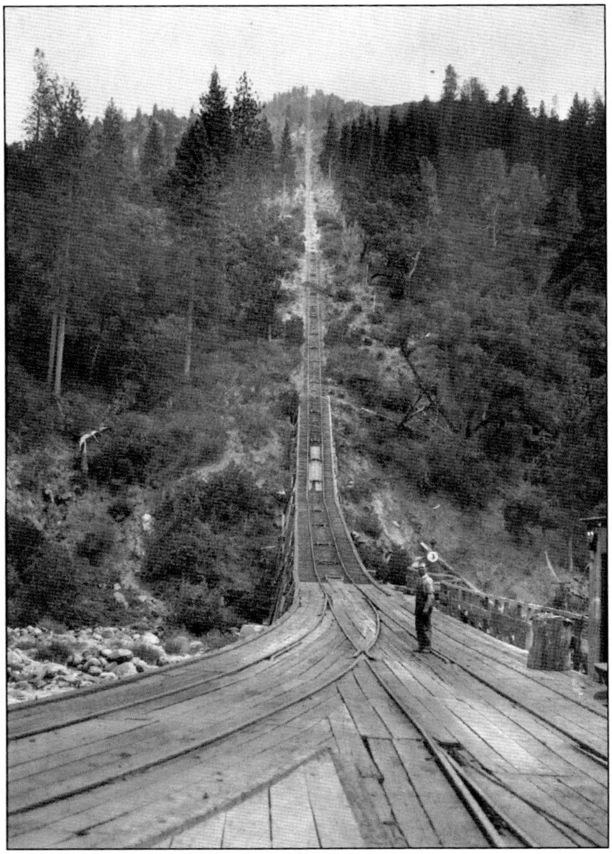

The first foreman, Frank McFadden stands on the finished trestle at the bottom of the incline in 1912. (MHP.)

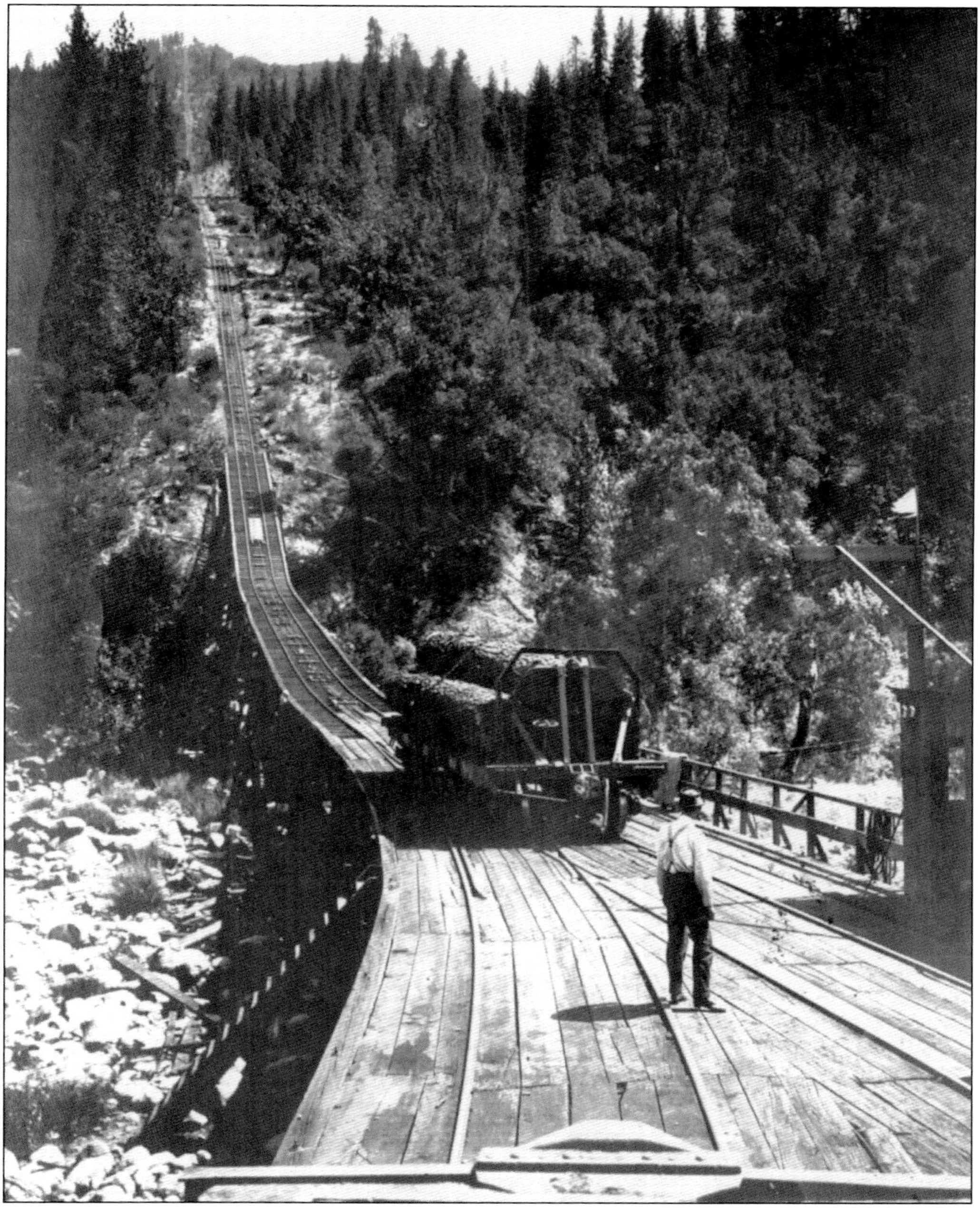

This section of the South Side Incline is at a pitch of 78 degrees. The steam donkey engine was pulling itself to the top when it lost its brakes near the top of the 1,000-foot pitch. The engineer, W. W. McNicoll, was killed when the machine came crashing down. (MHP.)

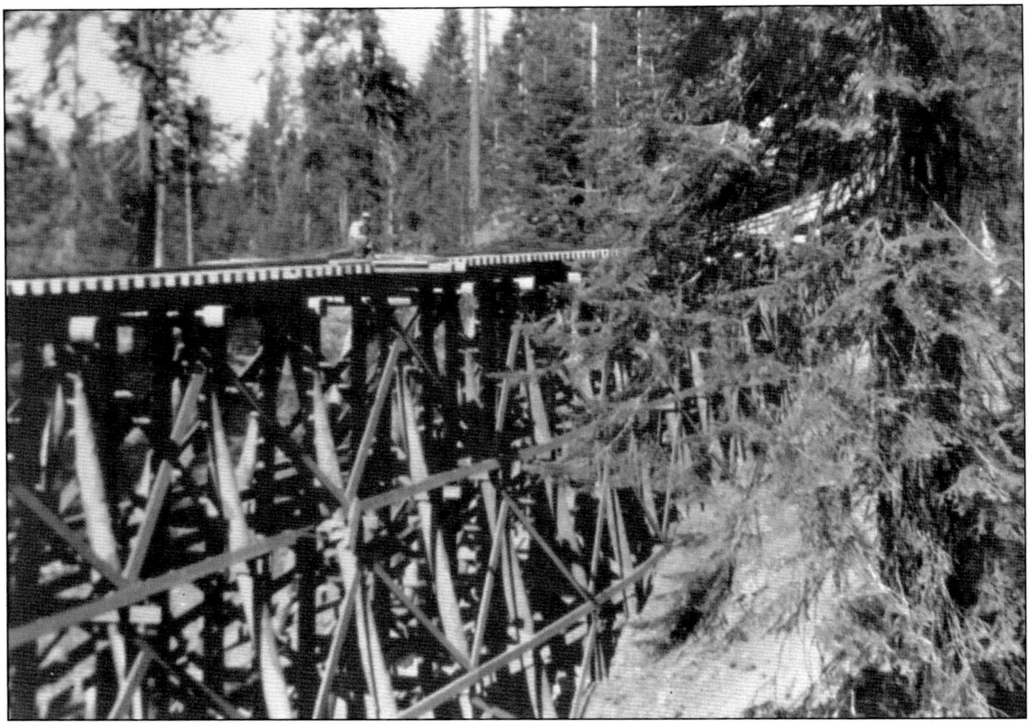

Shown are the bottom supports of the El Portal incline trestle, which were located at the top and right before reaching Camp No. 1. (MHP.)

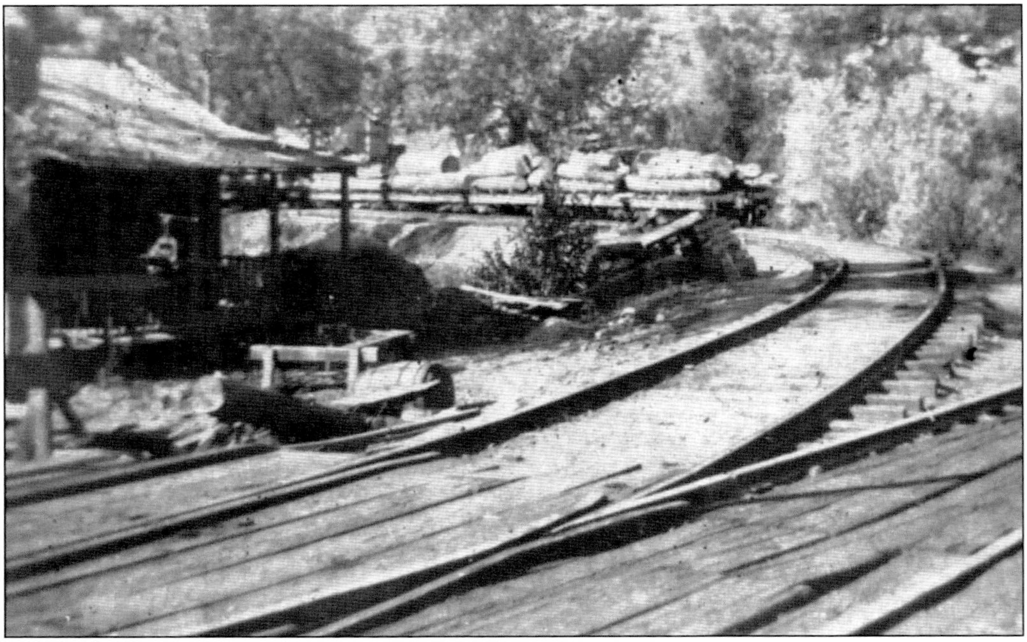

The Yosemite Lumber Company's foreman's house was located at the lower end of the El Portal incline in 1916. Pictured here are bunk cars of logs waited to be shipped to the mill at Merced Falls. (MHP.)

Jim Law, chronicler of the history of the logging industry in El Portal, stands top left with a crew in 1917 ready to install new 1.5-inch cable on the incline. (MHP.)

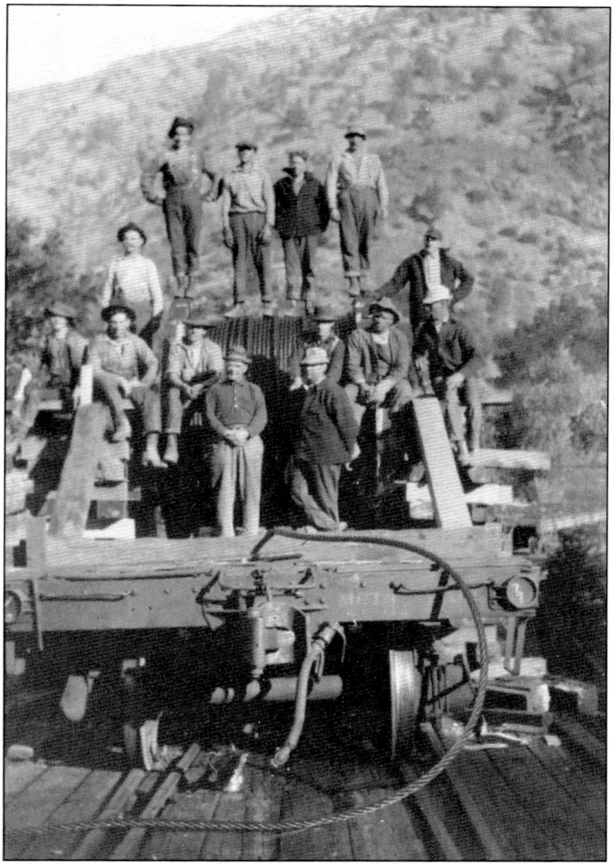

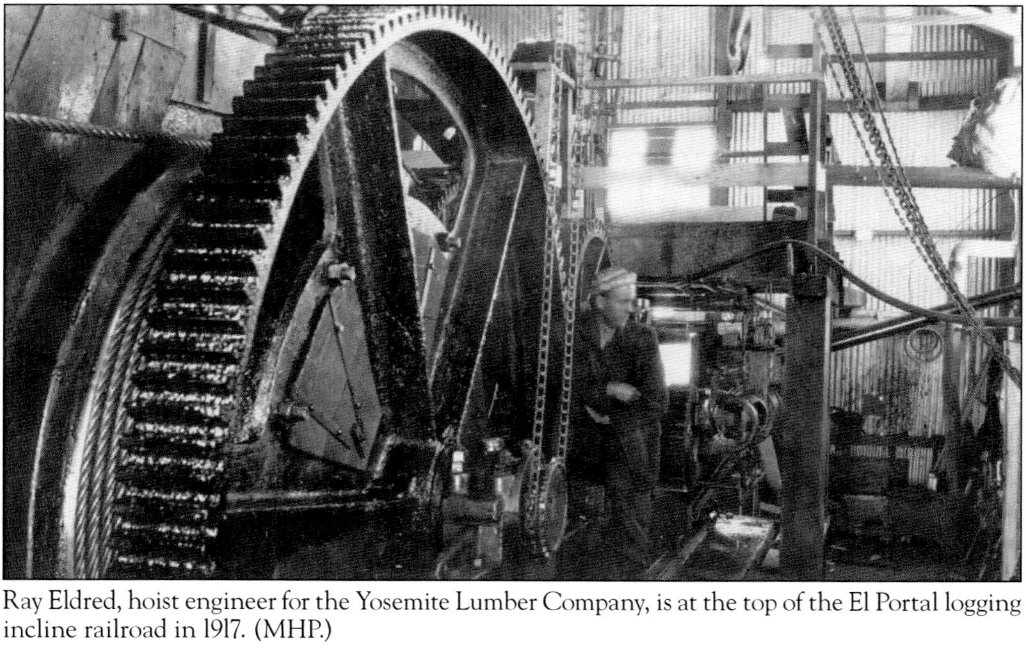

Ray Eldred, hoist engineer for the Yosemite Lumber Company, is at the top of the El Portal logging incline railroad in 1917. (MHP.)

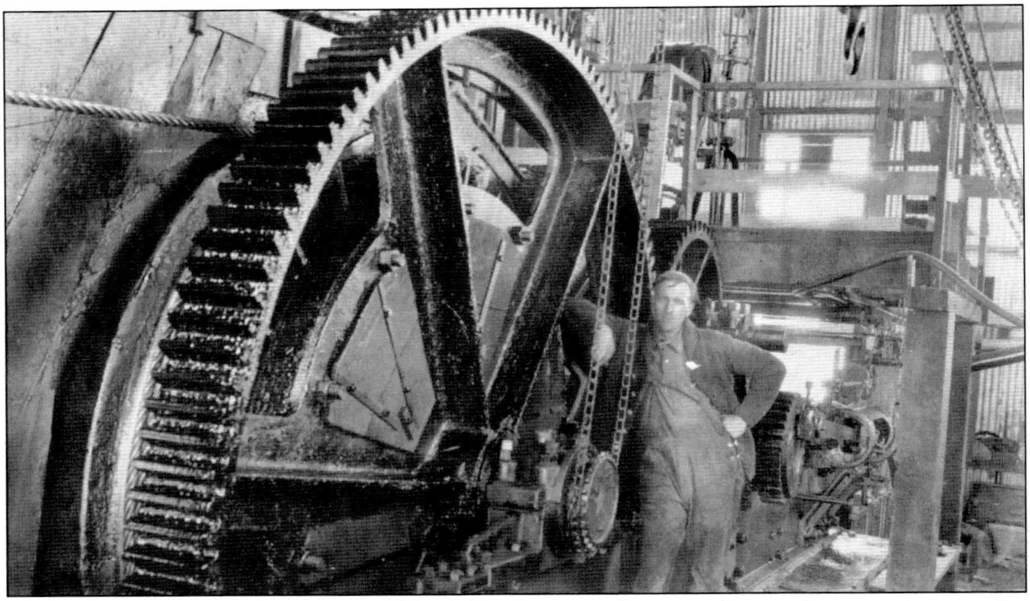

In 1917, Errol Eldred, who was Ray Eldred's brother, was the second steam hoist engineer at the top of Yosemite Lumber Company's logging incline railroad. (MHP.)

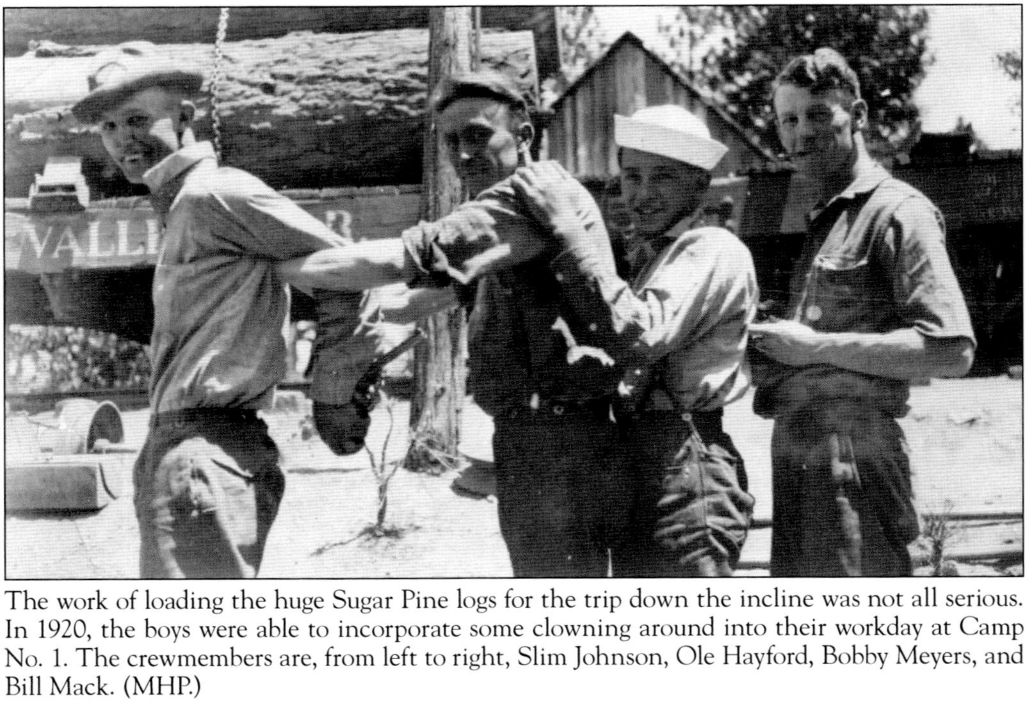

The work of loading the huge Sugar Pine logs for the trip down the incline was not all serious. In 1920, the boys were able to incorporate some clowning around into their workday at Camp No. 1. The crewmembers are, from left to right, Slim Johnson, Ole Hayford, Bobby Meyers, and Bill Mack. (MHP.)

Pictured in 1920 at the top of the incline are, from left to right, Kenneth "Ole" Hayford, foreman; Bill Renner, brakeman; and Bobby Meyers, bellhop. Each job was a serious part of the operation, and they depended on the skills of the workmen to survive. (MHP.)

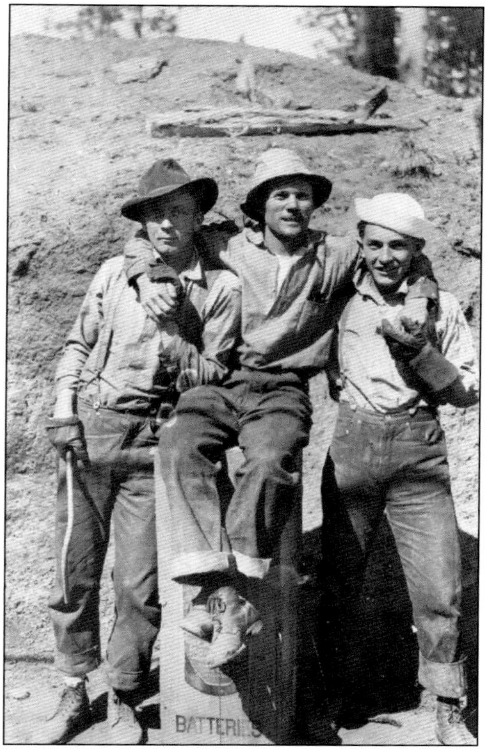

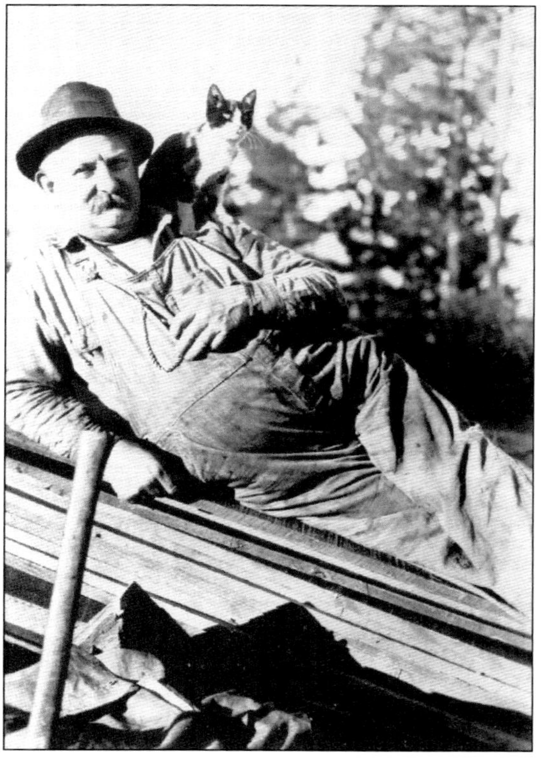

In 1919, Ed Fenner was the fireman on the steam hoist at Camp No. 1 at the top of Yosemite Logging Company's El Portal incline. (MHP.)

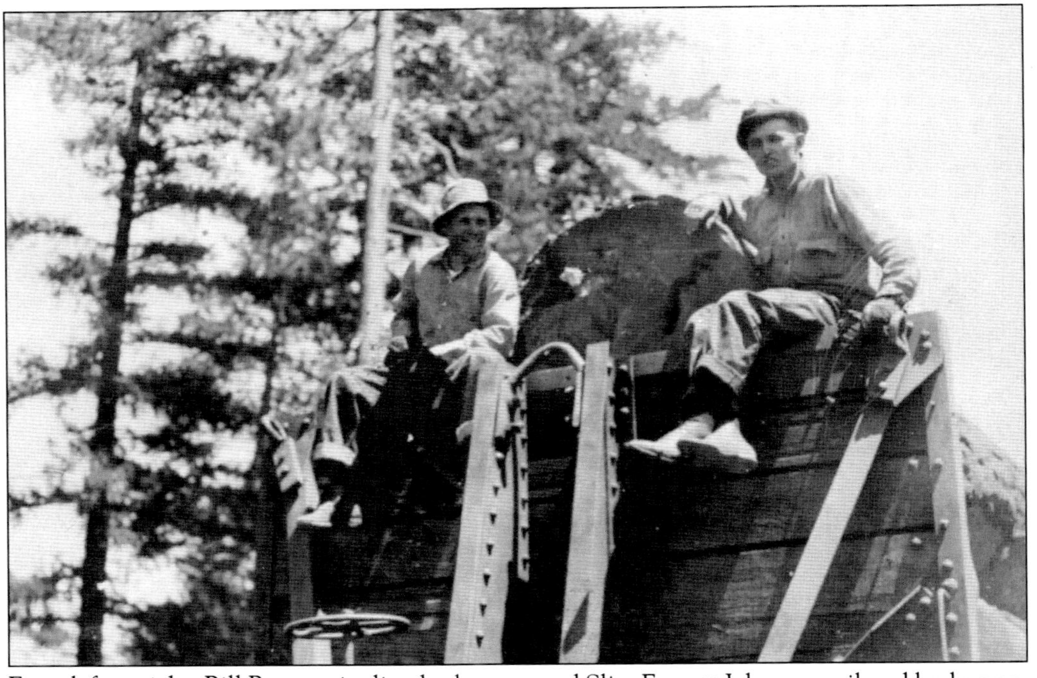

From left to right, Bill Renner, incline brakeman, and Slim Everett Johnson, railroad brakeman, are pictured at Camp No. 1 in 1920 at the top of the El Portal logging incline railroad. (MHP.)

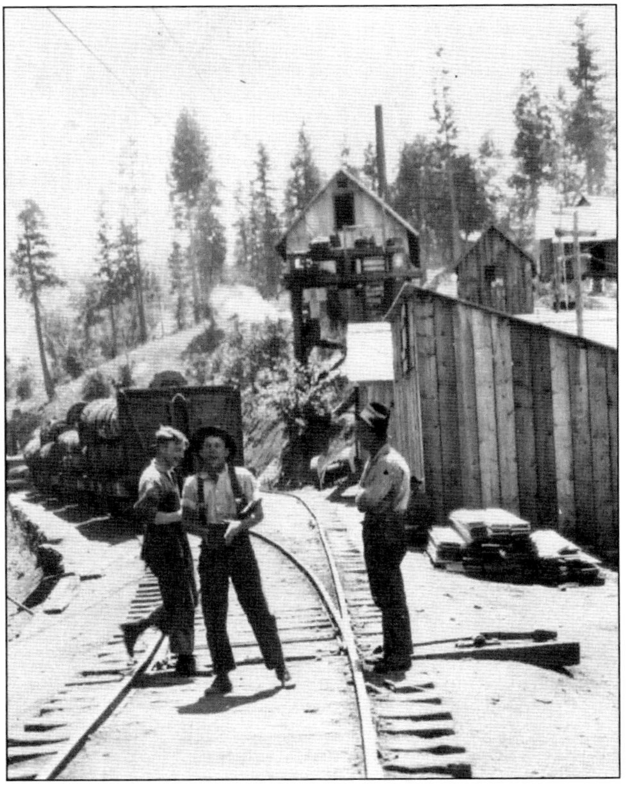

Yosemite Lumber Company employees are shown at Camp No. 1 at the top of the incline. The hoist house with a steam engine is located in the background. (MHP.)

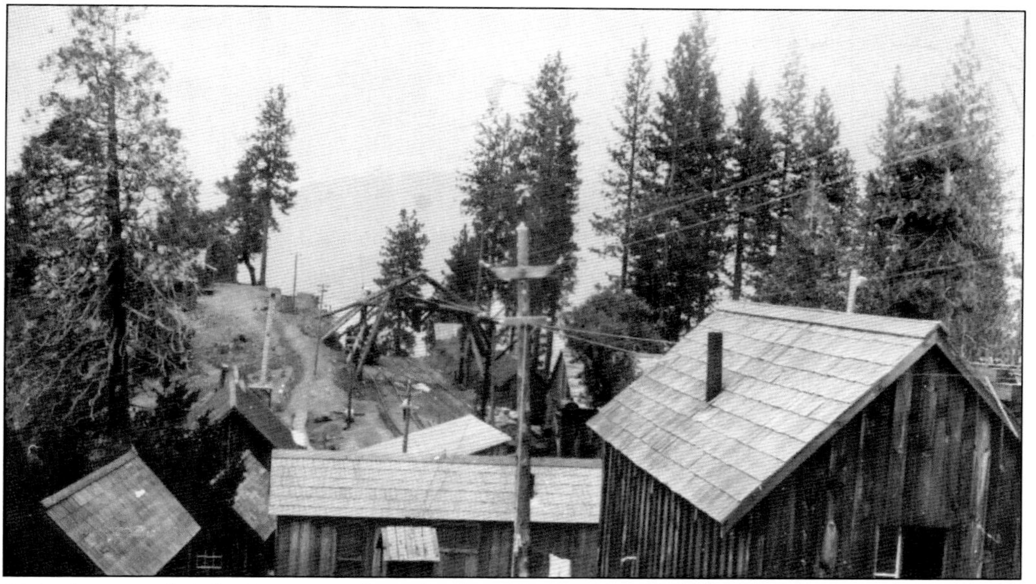

This photograph is looking west from the hoist house toward the top of the incline. The cook shack and bunkhouse are located in the foreground. (MHP.)

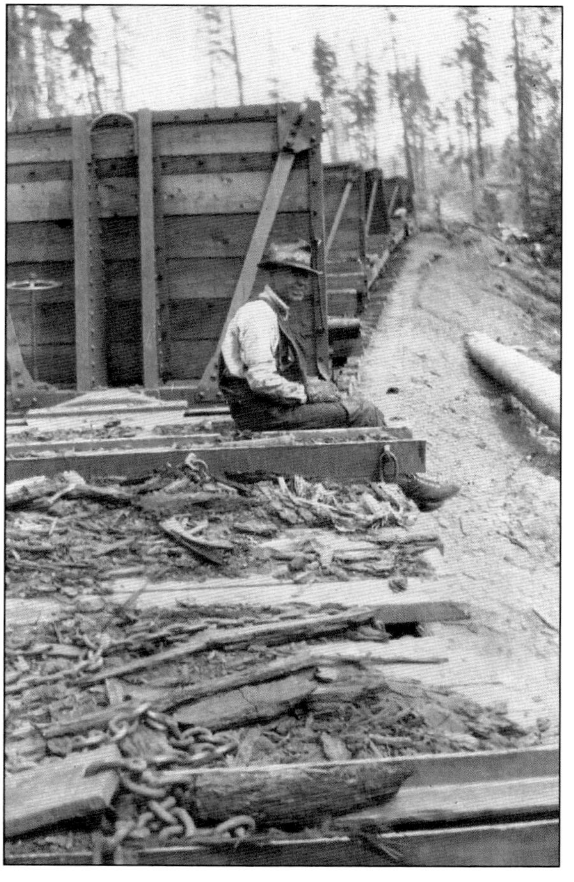

Bob Hoyt worked as a brakeman on a line of Yosemite Lumber Company cars in 1918 that were being hauled to the woods to be loaded. (MHP.)

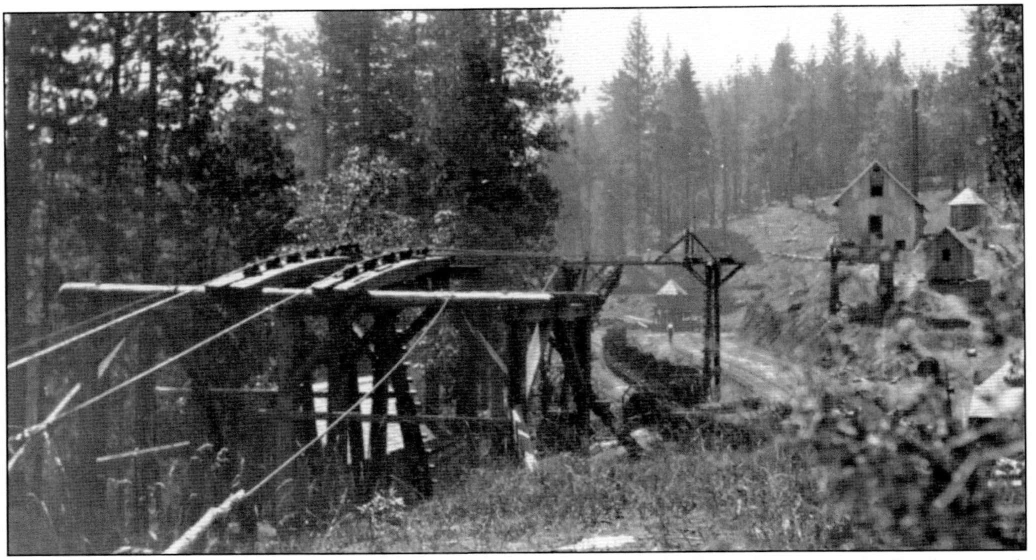

In 1913, gallows frame supporting haul cables are leading to the hoist house in the background. (MHP.)

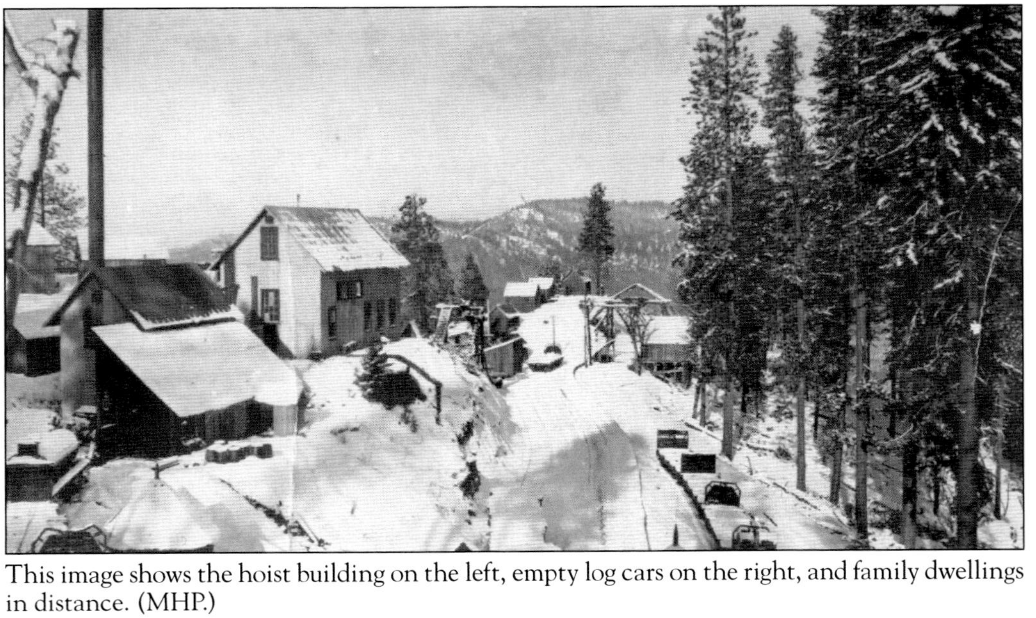

This image shows the hoist building on the left, empty log cars on the right, and family dwellings in distance. (MHP.)

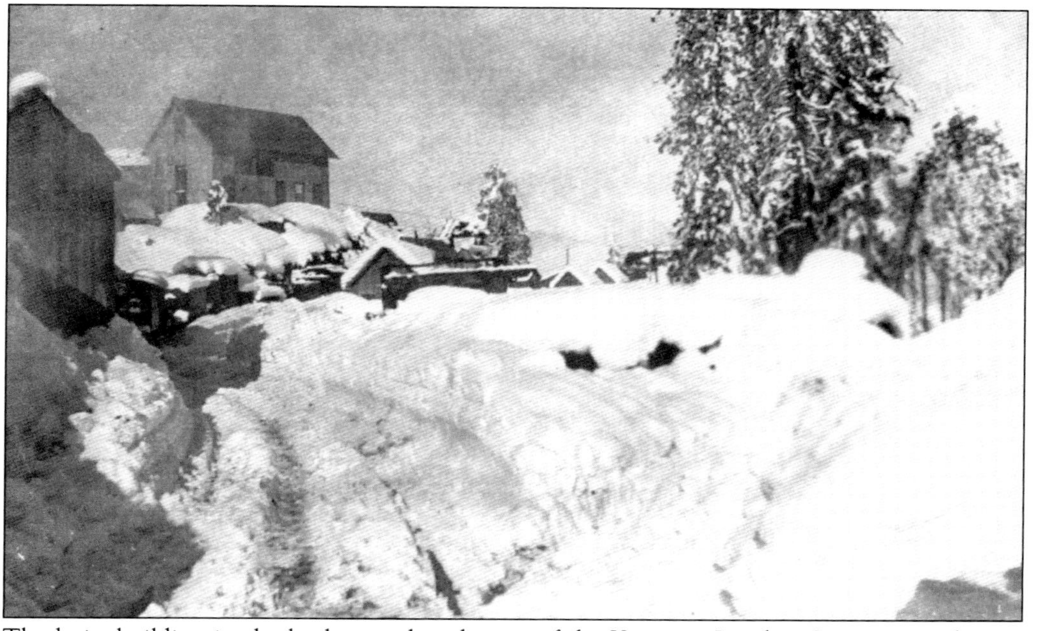

The hoist building in the background at the top of the Yosemite Lumber Company incline at Camp No. 1 is pictured in the winter of 1919–1920 (MHP.)

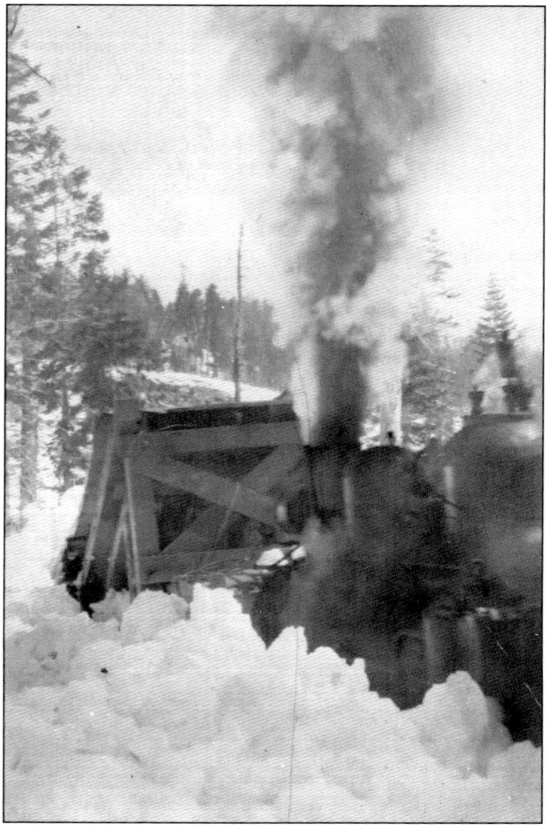

A Shay direct-drive steam engine was used to push a wooden snowplow to clear tracks in order to begin logging in the early spring of 1920. (MHP.)

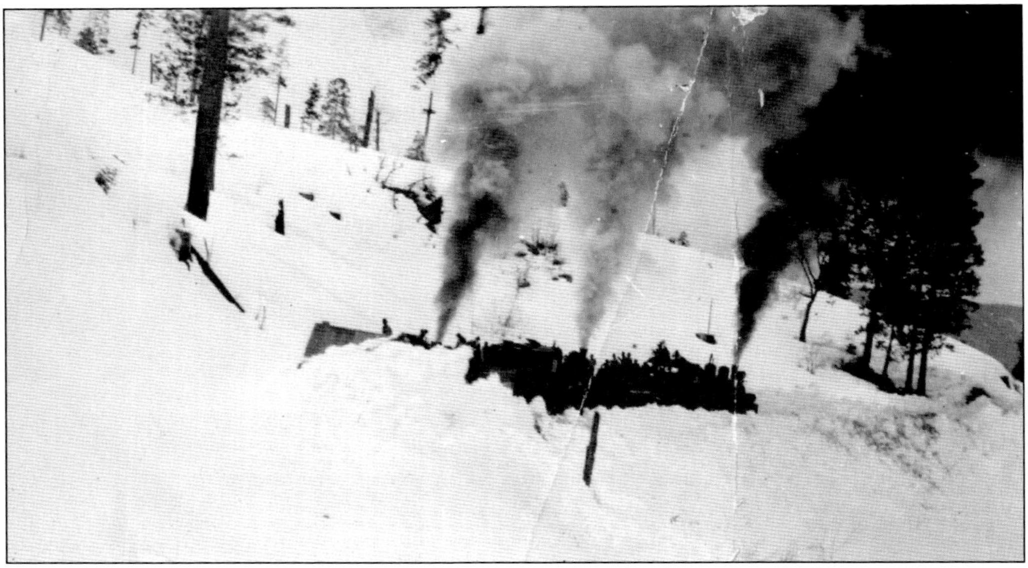

In 1920, three Shay locomotives plowed snow between Camp No. 1 and Chinquapin. Winters with heavy snowfall required early plowing to keep the timber flowing via the Yosemite Valley Railroad to the mill at Merced Falls. (MHP.)

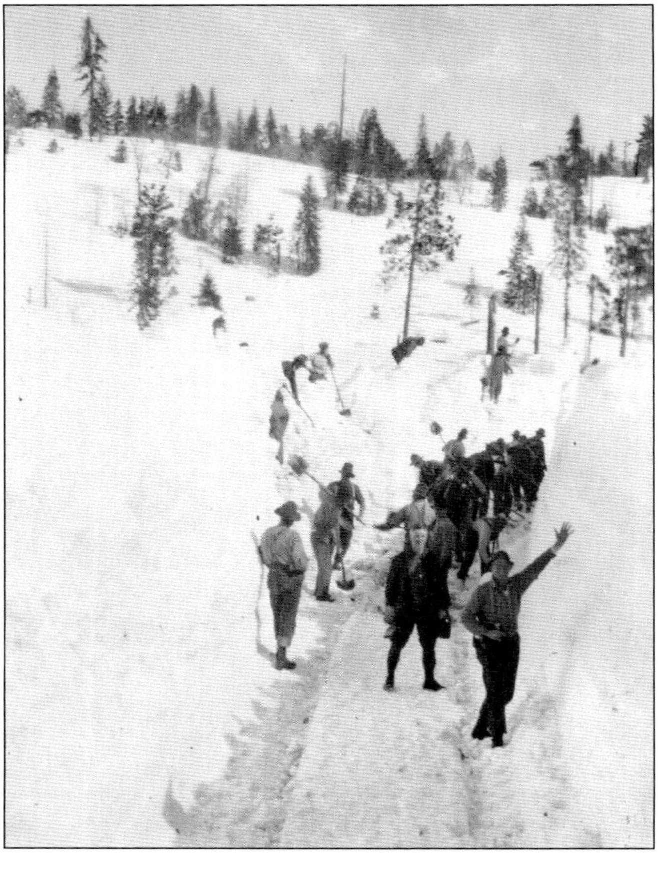

The final touch on the snow clearing was done by hand for the Yosemite Lumber Company in the spring of 1920. (MHP.)

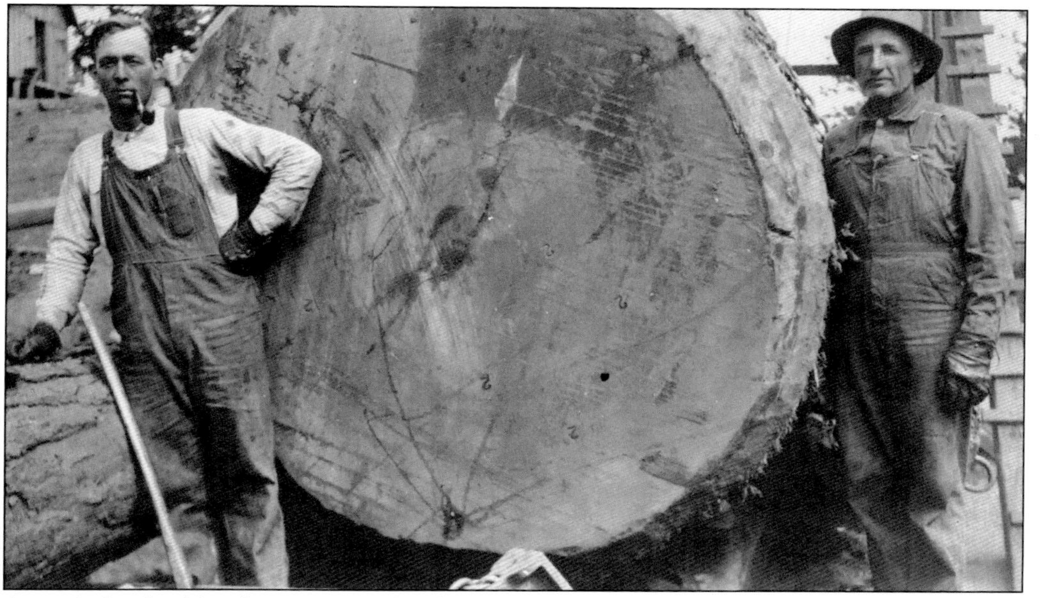

A single log load has been prepared to begin its descent via the Yosemite Logging Company incline railroad in 1915. (MHP.)

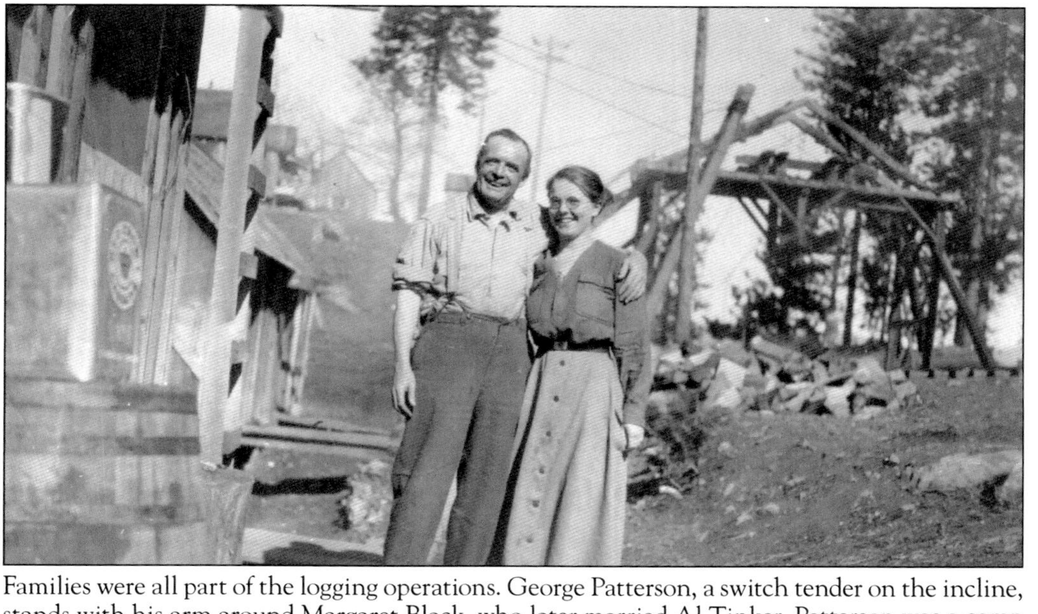

Families were all part of the logging operations. George Patterson, a switch tender on the incline, stands with his arm around Margaret Black, who later married Al Tinker. Patterson was a camp boss and later became superintendent of Yosemite Lumber Company at Camp No. 1 for the El Portal incline. (MHP.)

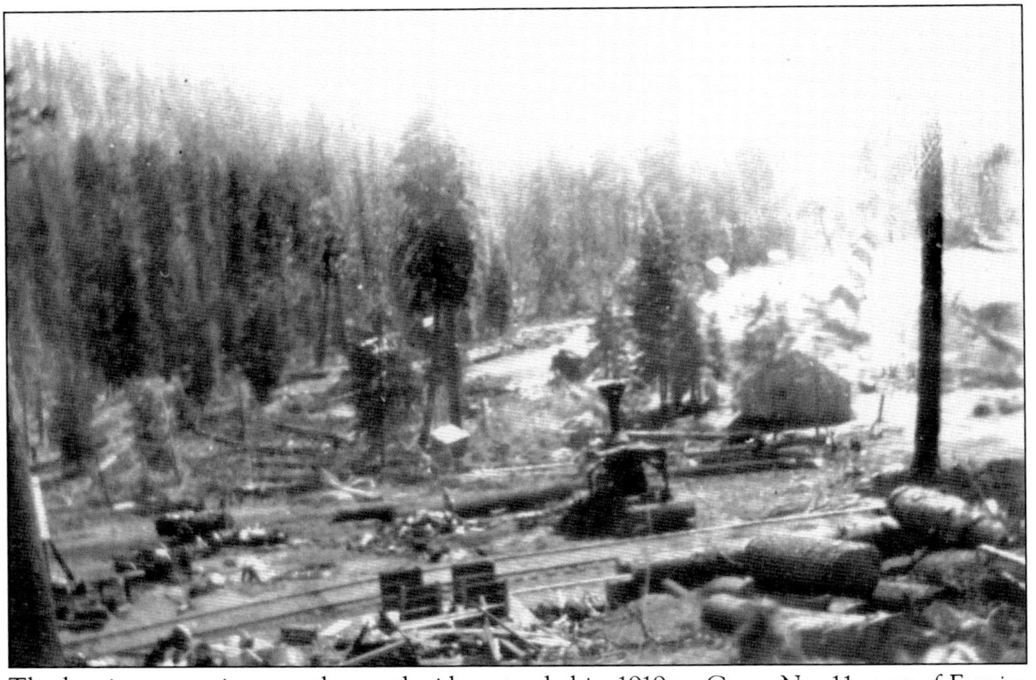

The logging operations on the south side extended in 1919 to Camp No. 11, east of Empire Meadows and within the boundaries of Yosemite National Park. The donkey engine was used to load the logs onto the bunk cars on their way to the incline. (MHP.)

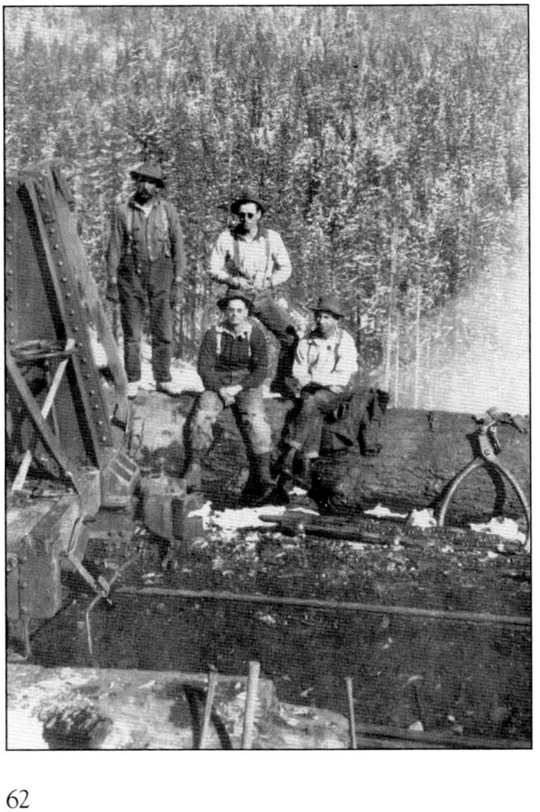

A crew stands at the landing where logs are loaded onto the log cars. The man sitting on the right was Paddy Connors, who studied for the priesthood before he became a logger. (MHP.)

Employees of the Yosemite Lumber Company were not always hard at work, but they were seldom far from the woods. The lumber company hosted a family picnic close to Chinquapin on July 4, 1920. (MHP.)

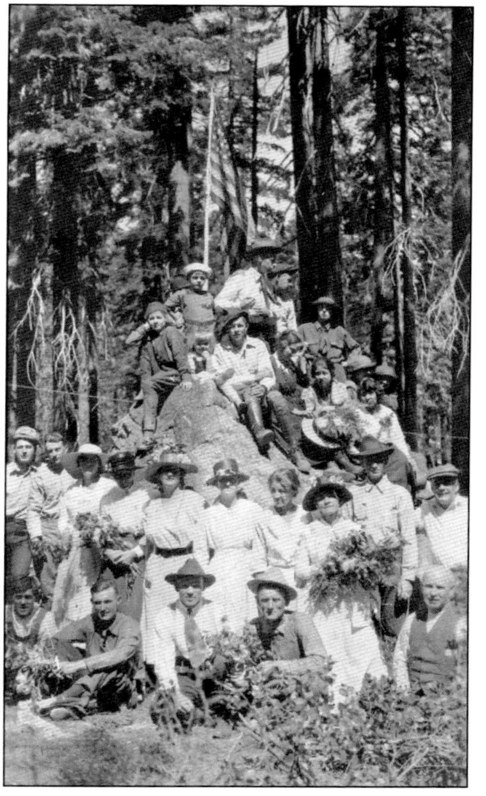

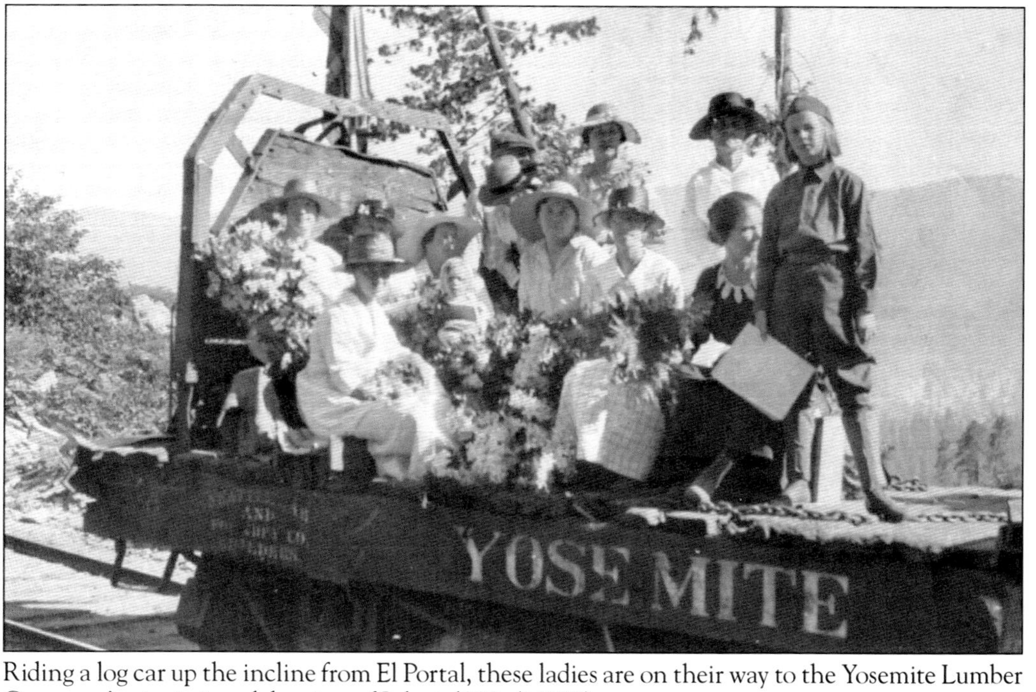

Riding a log car up the incline from El Portal, these ladies are on their way to the Yosemite Lumber Company's picnic in celebration of July 4, 1920. (MHP.)

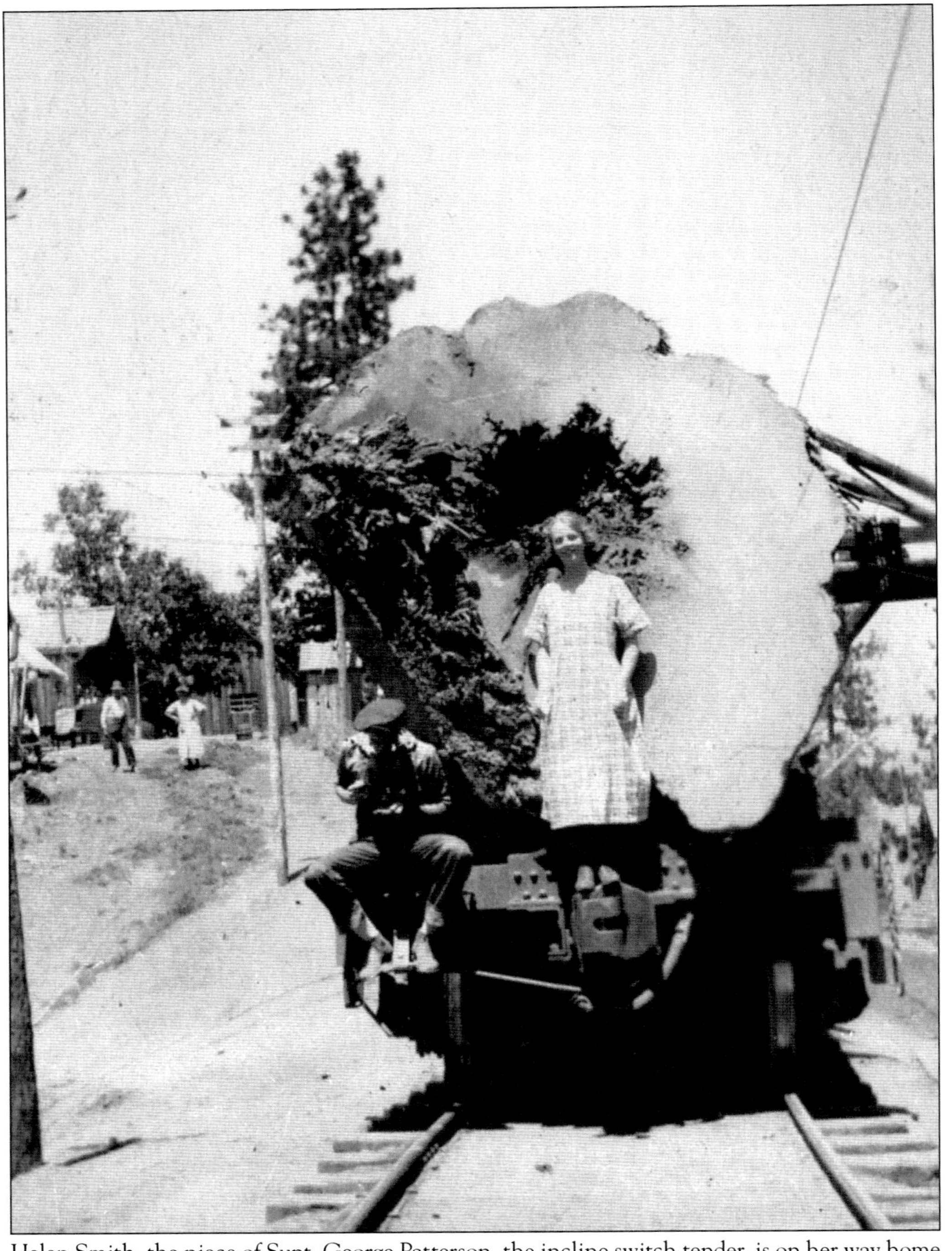

Helen Smith, the niece of Supt. George Patterson, the incline switch tender, is on her way home down the incline of the Yosemite Lumber Company. (MHP.)

Four

The Yosemite Valley Railroad Diversifies Further

The last of the El Portal Yosemite Lumber Company came in the fall of 1923. All of the equipment, Shay engines, track, and donkey engines were lowered down the incline to be stored until spring when the North Side Operation at the incline, which was 5 miles down river from El Portal, was installed. The new incline was built by converting the hoists from steam to electricity to lower the log cars to the Yosemite Valley Railroad. The San Joaquin Light and Power Company purchased the transmission lines and substation of the Mariposa Commercial and Mining Company at Bear Valley a few years after the powerhouse at Bagby burned in a brush fire in 1922. Power lines were extended up the Merced River to Indian Flat and across the river from the new incline. A substation was constructed to provide electricity to the incline as well as other facilities in the area. The Yosemite Lumber Company operated at the incline until the fall of 1927. It closed in 1928. The Sugar Pine Lumber Company operated during 1929 and 1930, starting in the spring of 1931 but closed early. During these breaks, the sawmill at Merced Falls was shut down also. The Depression must have had an effect on the ability of the various companies to operate. During the summer of 1935, the operation began again under the ownership of the Yosemite Sugar Pine Lumber Company, ending operations in the fall of 1942. Railroad logging in the Merced River Canyon never returned. Other operations ran in the river canyon, which affected the ability of the Yosemite Valley Railroad to survive. Also, a flood in 1937 damaged the tracks mainly near South Fork and El Portal, and the company was not able to repair the route completely. The railroad was mainly used for the logging company, and only occasionally would passenger cars reach El Portal. They would turn around at Rancheria Flat, below El Portal, and back the cars the rest of the way. However, the building of State Highway 140 in 1924–1926 made a significant difference in passenger travel.

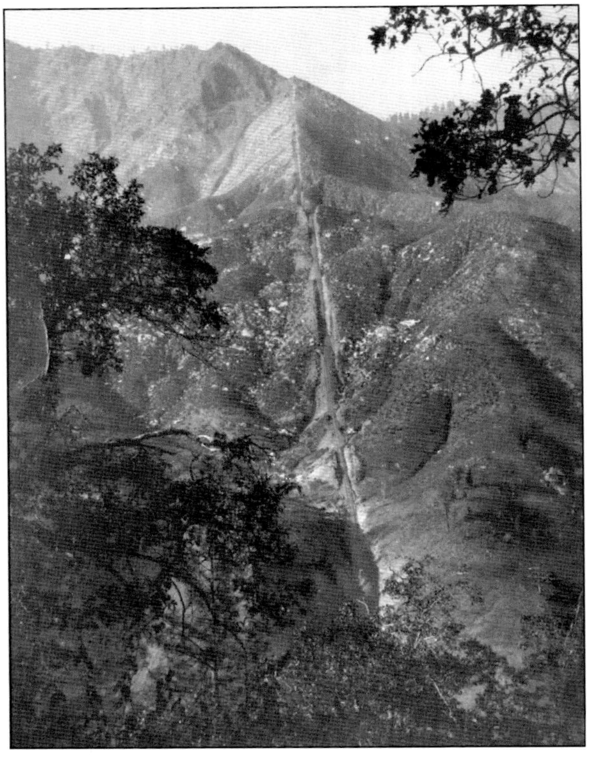

Here is the Yosemite Lumber Company logging incline railroad on the north side of the Merced River while it was under construction in the winter of 1923–1924. (MHP.)

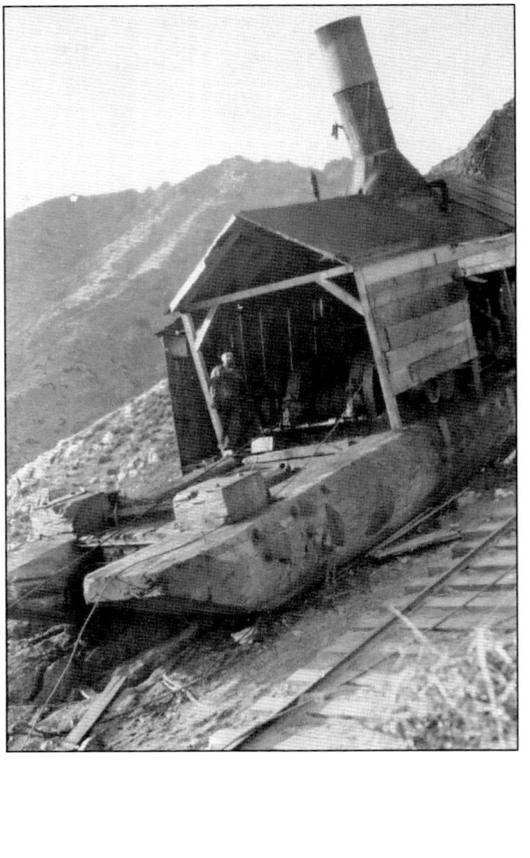

Yosemite Lumber Company's steam logging engine is dragging itself up the incline during construction of the incline. The engine was used to construct the incline railroad and later in the woods to load the cars. (MHP.)

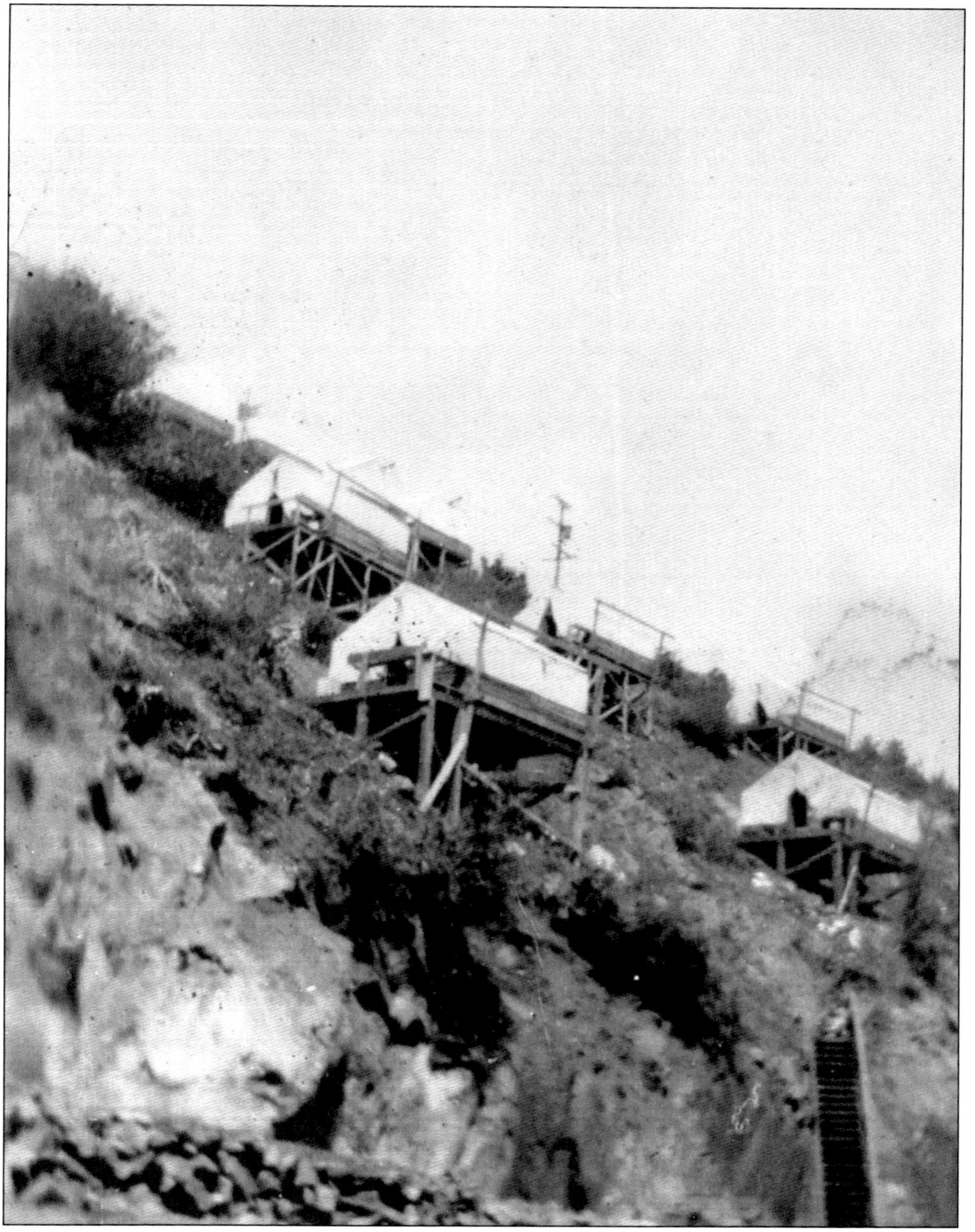

The 1923–1924 construction camp at the top of the incline did not waste any flat ground, as there was little of it without trees. (MHP.)

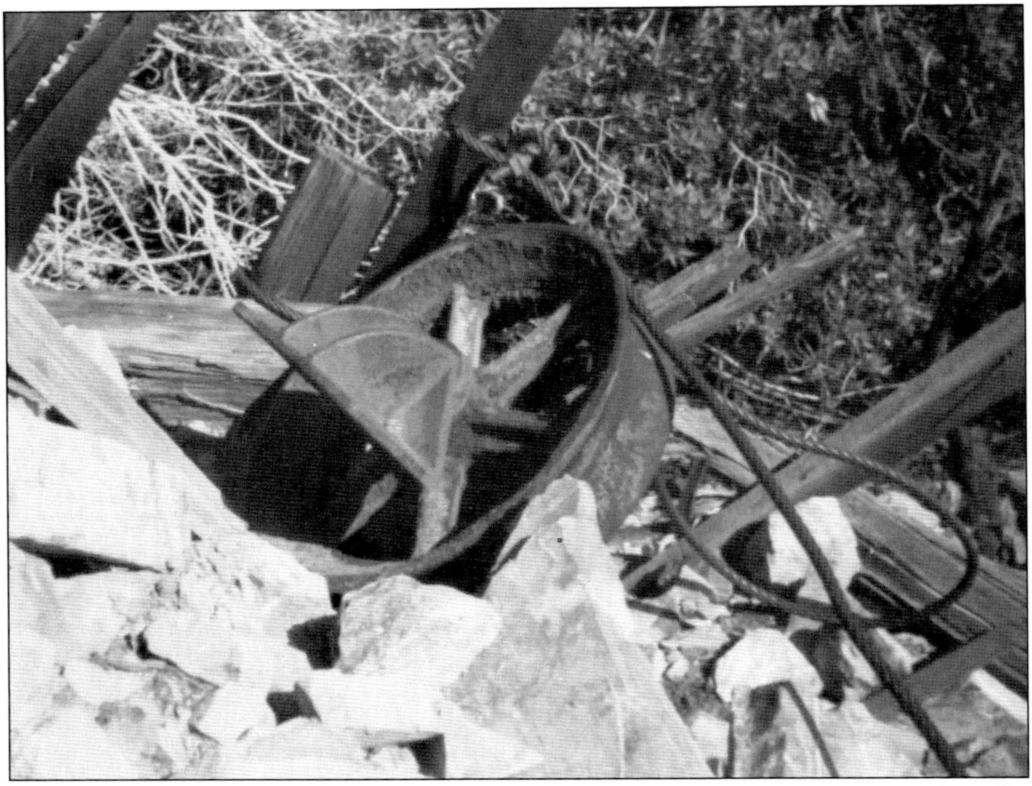

Here is a typical roller that was used to guide haul cable around corners on the incline. This roller cost $125, weighed 355 pounds, and was manufactured by Washington Iron Works. The groove in the roller guided the 1.75-inch cable on its path to lower and raise the log cars. (MHP.)

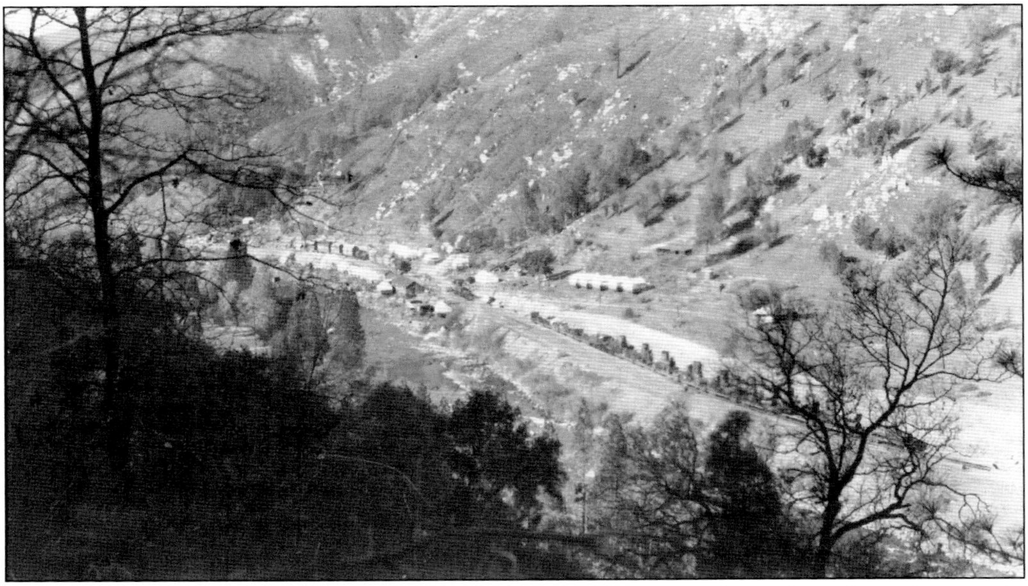

Pictured is the Yosemite Lumber Company construction camp at the incline along the river in 1923, which was during the installation of the north side logging incline railroad. (MHP.)

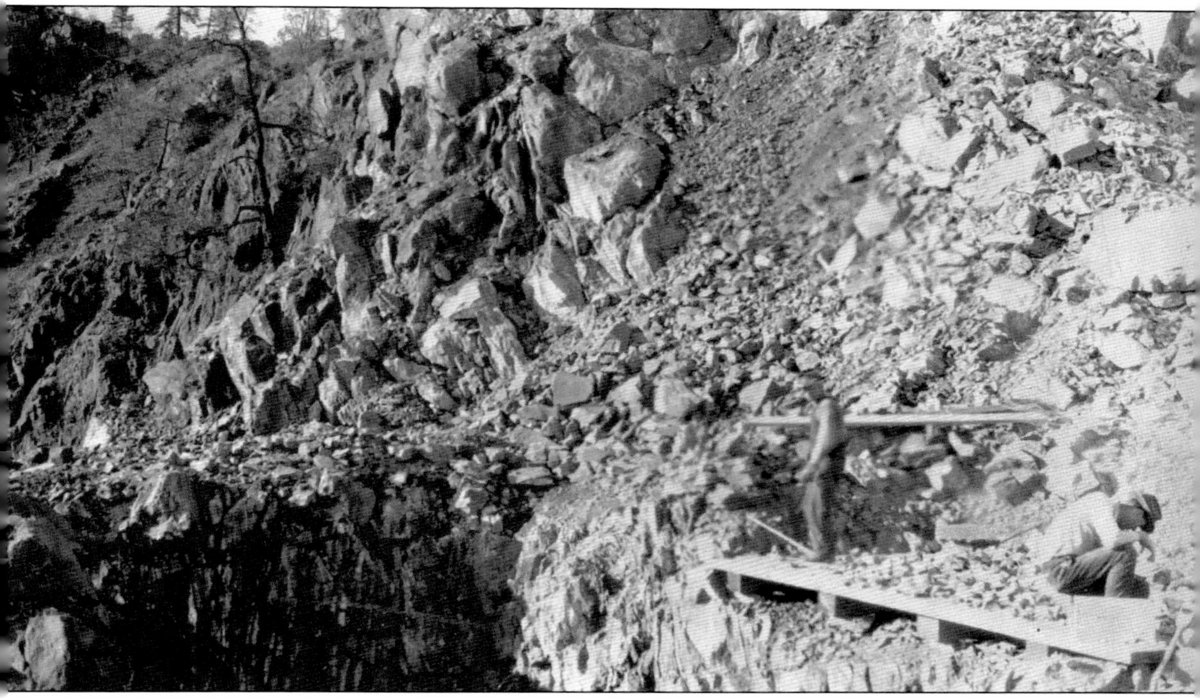

This image shows the construction of the electric hoist foundation at the top of the Yosemite Lumber Company incline railroad in 1923. The concrete foundation for the hoist house, as well as the incline route, can still be seen from Cedar Lodge on the Merced River. (MHP.)

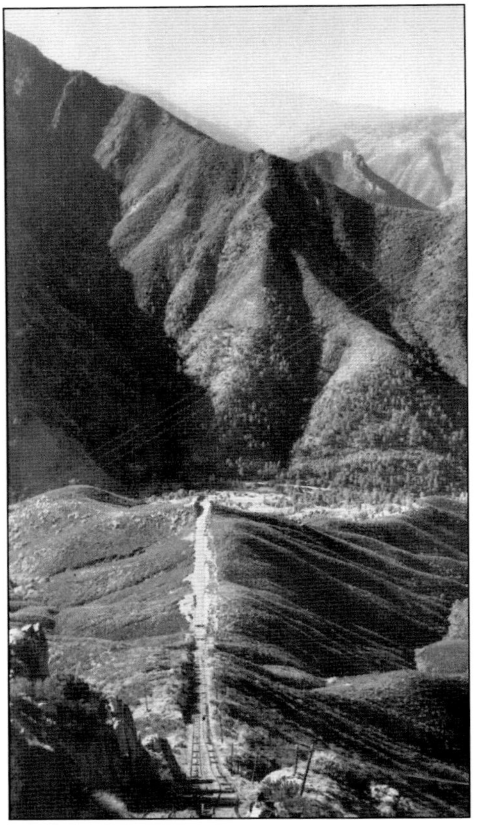

While looking down the incline toward the Merced River and Indian Flat, Highway 140 can be seen across the river. The opening of this state highway impacted the railroad as far as passenger travel was concerned, but the railroad continued to haul logs to Merced Falls. (MHP.)

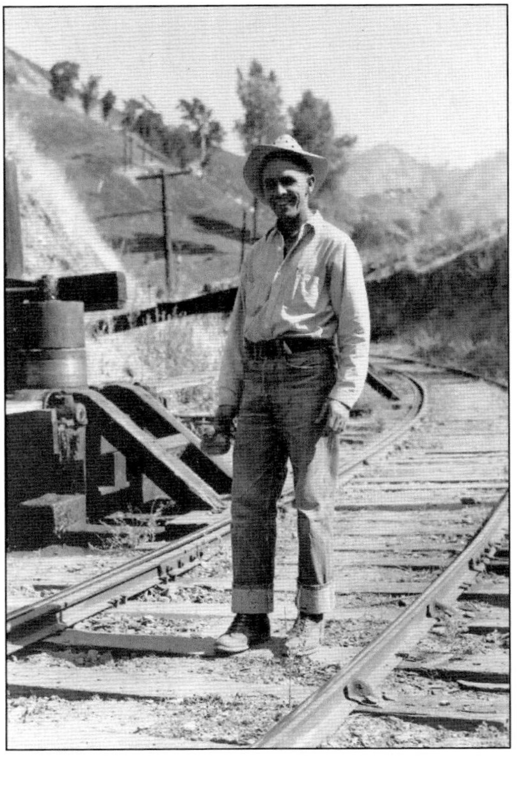

Jim Law lived in the canyon all of his life and worked for the railroad. He was also a foreman on both inclines. He authored the book *Memories of El Portal*. (MHP.)

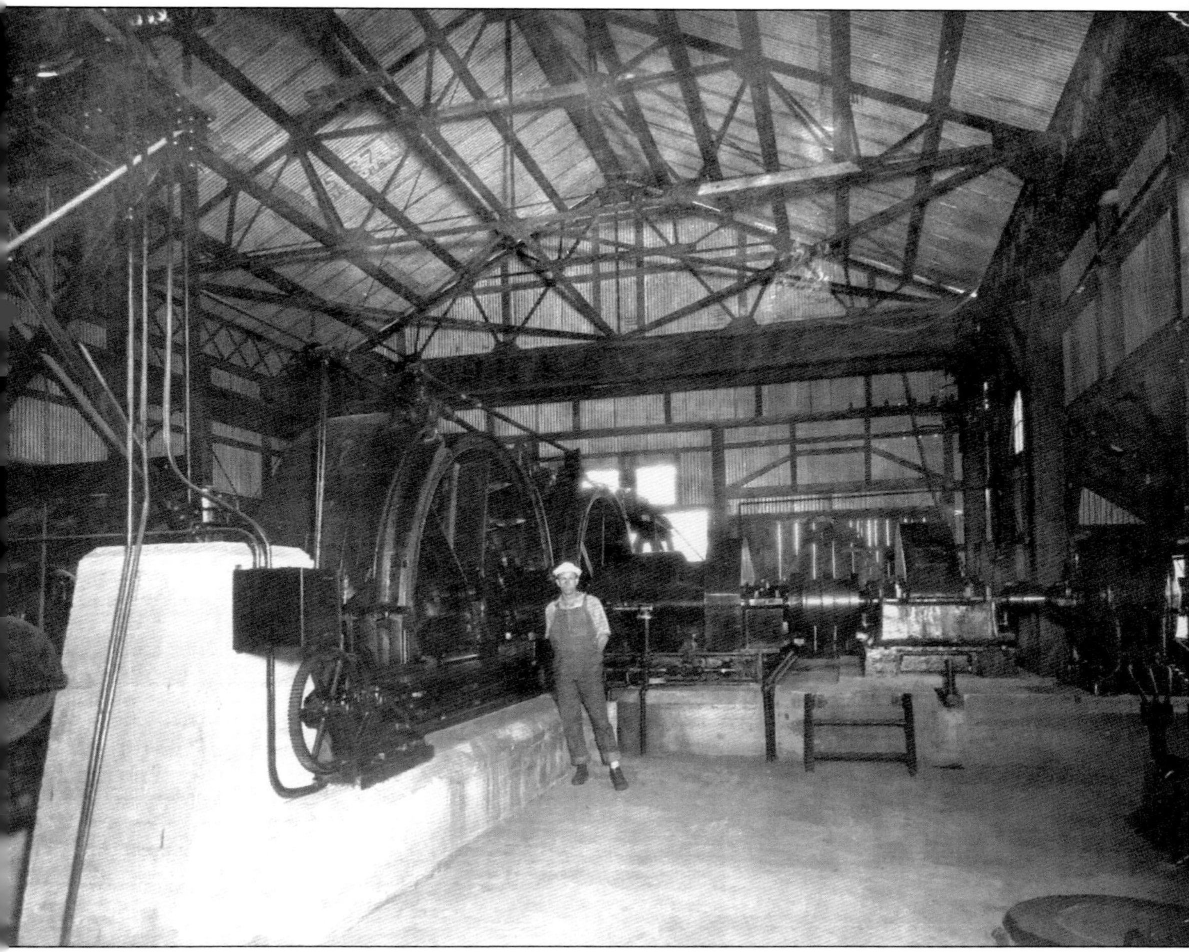

Engineer Roy Eldred stands with the finished hoist at the top of the incline. (MHP.)

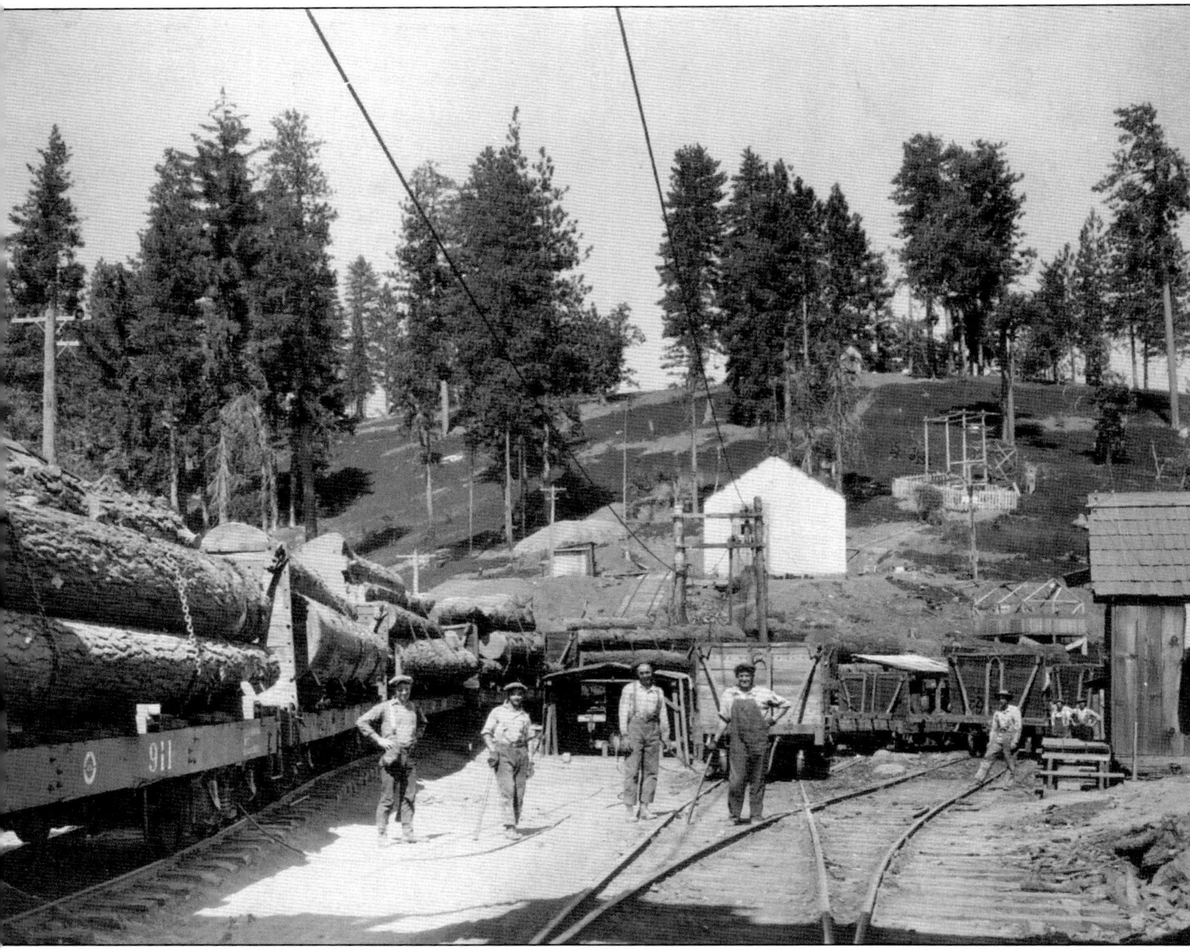

The incline railroad consists of two pitches. The Yosemite Lumber Company Camp No. 2, at the top of the second incline, is where the cars were loaded for the trip to the river. (MHP.)

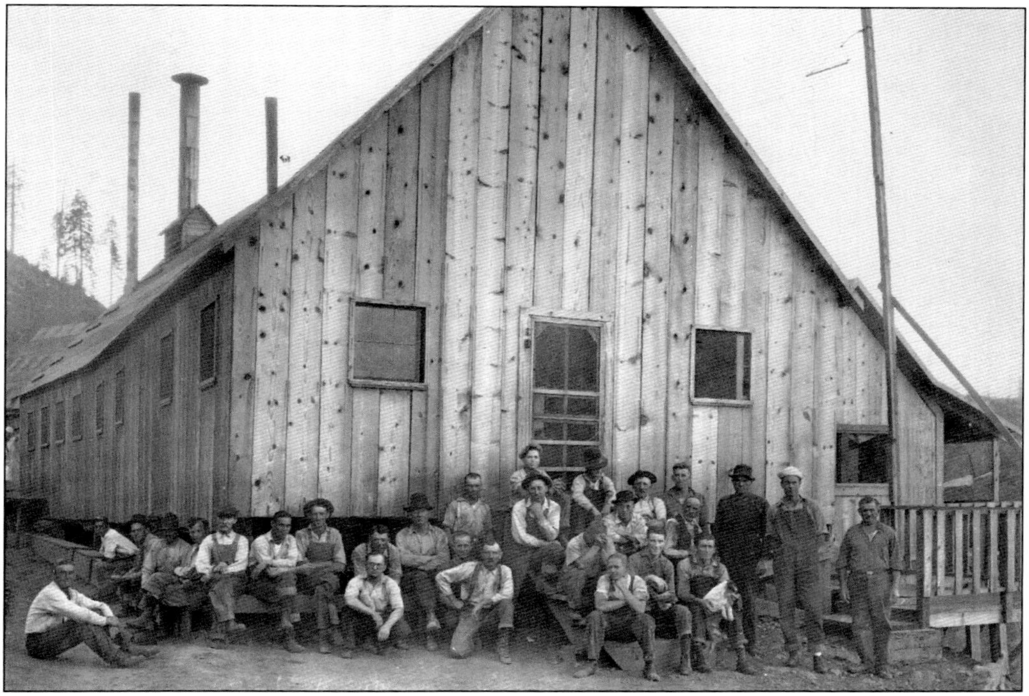

The Yosemite Lumber Company cookhouse was at Camp No. 1, which was located at the top of the first section of the incline railroad. (MHP.)

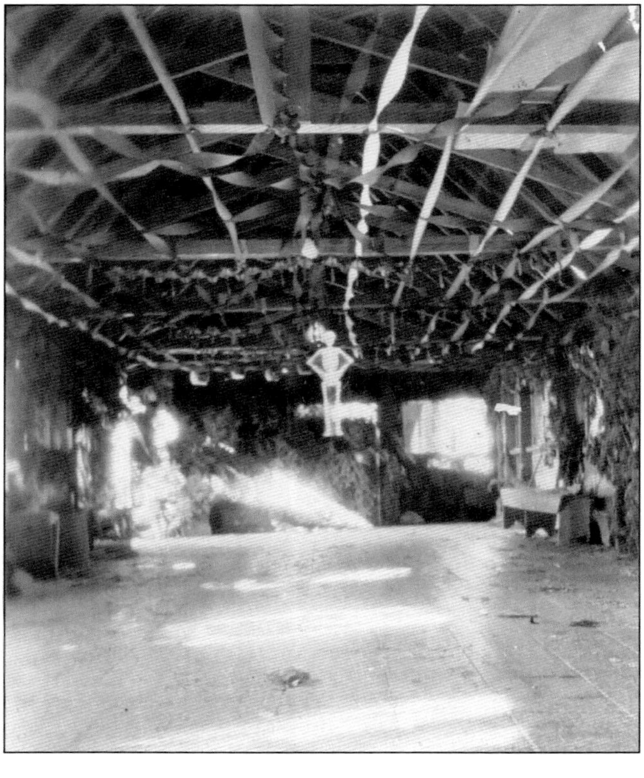

Another cookhouse at Camp No. 2 was used for parties. In 1925, a Halloween party was prepared for employees to enjoy. (MHP.)

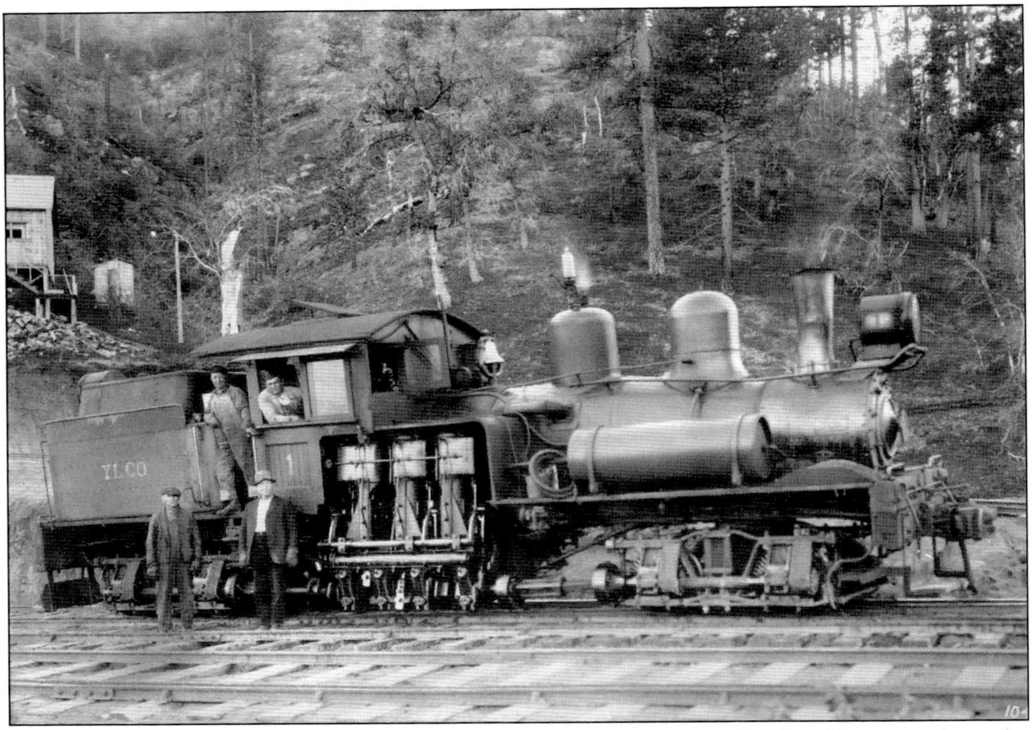

For the Yosemite Lumber Company, Shay locomotive No. 1 was used to haul logs cars from the foot of incline No. 2 to the top of the big incline. These Shay engines were used everywhere in the woods because of their great direct-drive power and were brought up the incline by the hoist works. Working Shay locomotive can be seen at Yosemite Mountain Sugar Pine Railroad in Fish Camp. (MHP.)

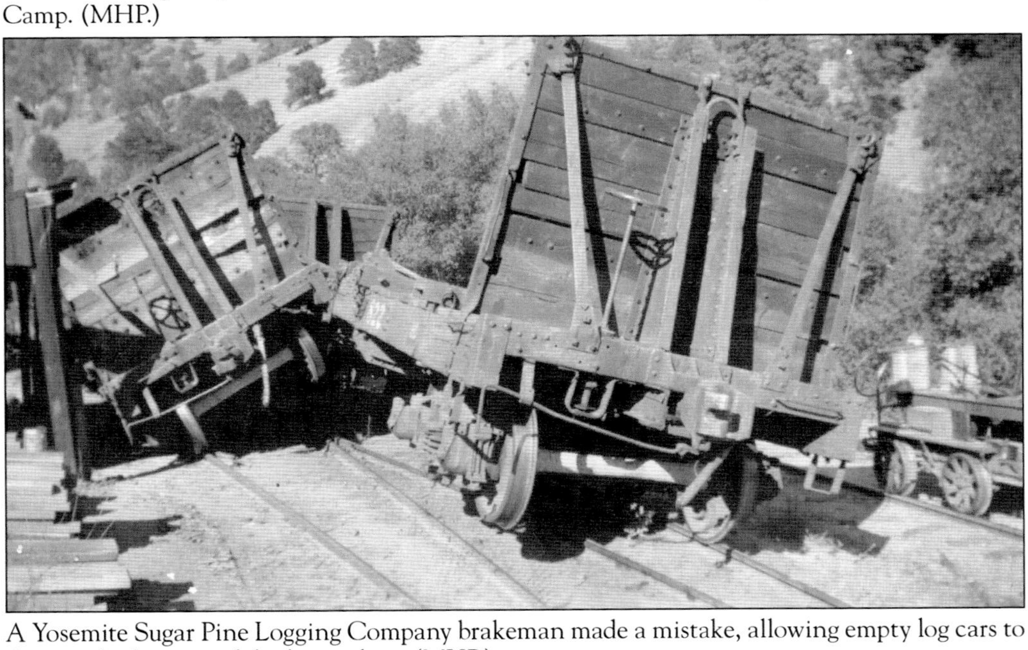

A Yosemite Sugar Pine Logging Company brakeman made a mistake, allowing empty log cars to drop to the bottom of the big incline. (MHP.)

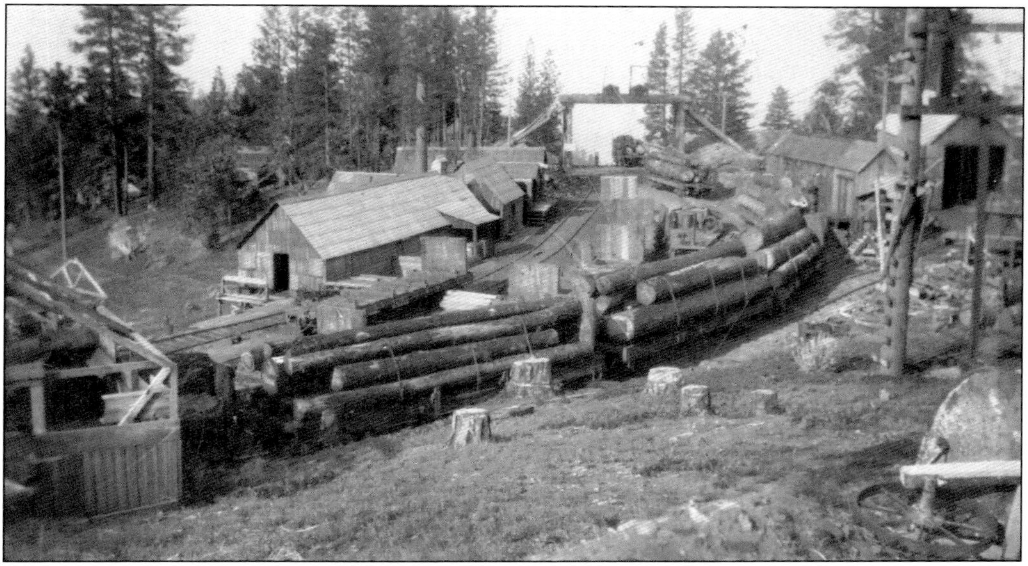

Pictured above is the Yosemite Lumber Company Camp No. 2 at the second incline in 1925 with loaded cars waiting to be lowered. (MHP.)

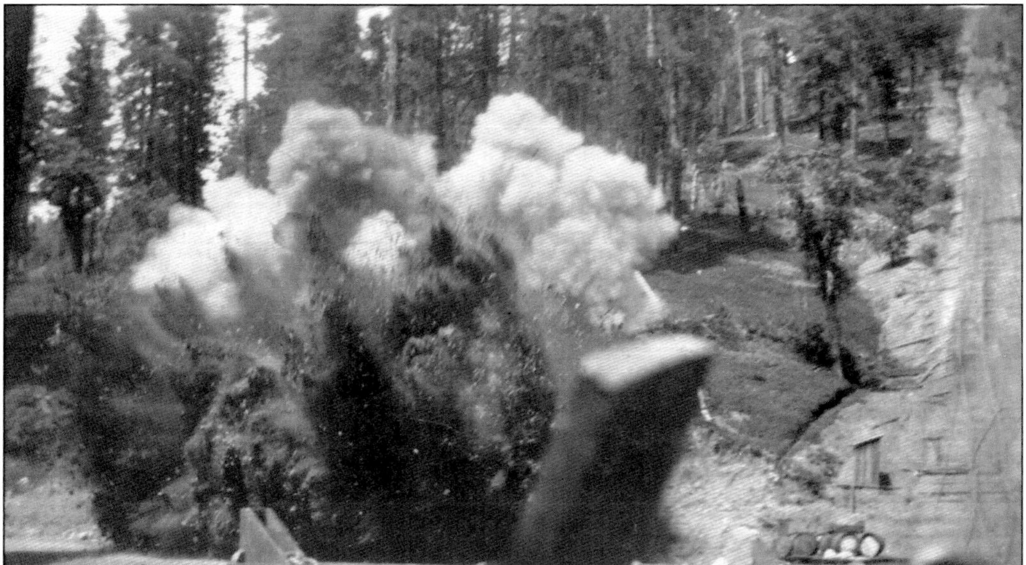

This photograph depicts blasting for the Yosemite Lumber Company railroad bed to Camp No. 18 in 1926. A railroad bed was constructed to Yosemite National Park, but no tracks were ever laid. These roadbeds became useful fire roads in later years. (MHP.)

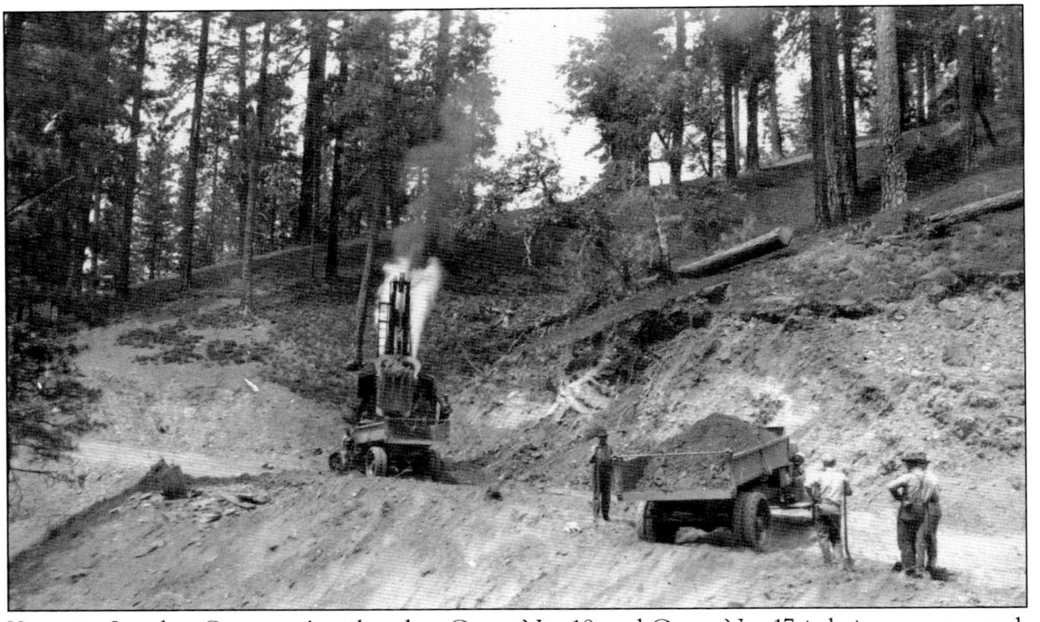

Yosemite Lumber Company's railroad to Camp No. 18 and Camp No. 17 is being constructed. This line began at the bottom of the second incline. (MHP.)

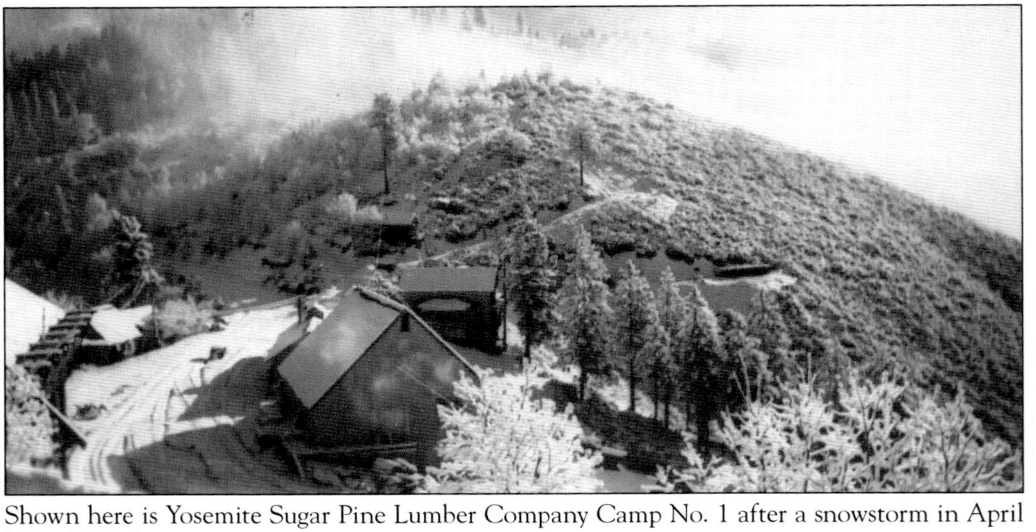

Shown here is Yosemite Sugar Pine Lumber Company Camp No. 1 after a snowstorm in April 1942. (MHP.)

Pictured is Yosemite Sugar Pine Lumber Camp No. 1 in 1935. (MHP.)

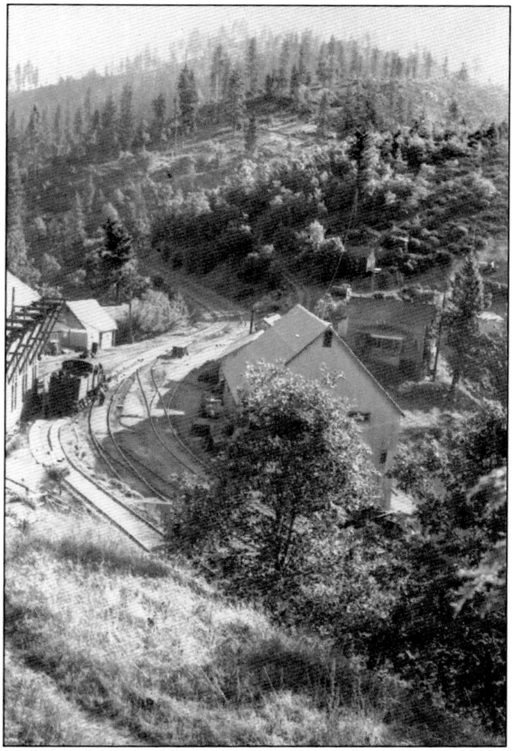

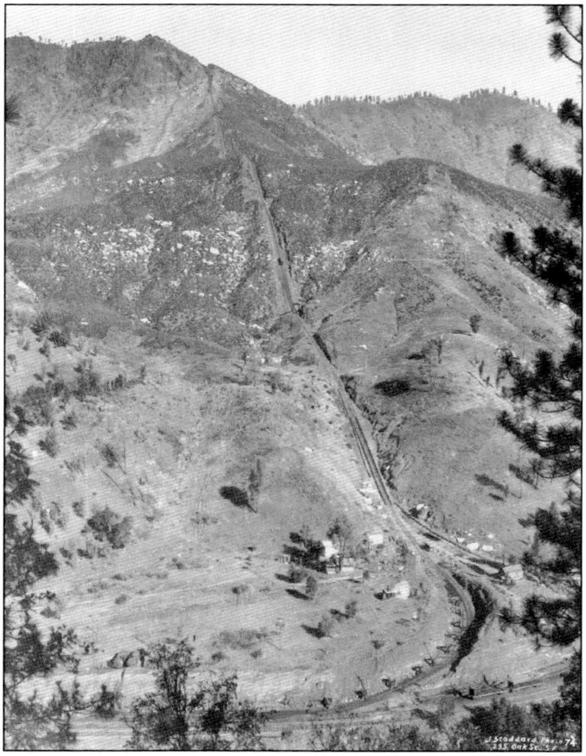

The completed and fully functioning north side incline served both the Yosemite Lumber Company and the Yosemite Sugar Pine Lumber Company until it closed. (MHP.)

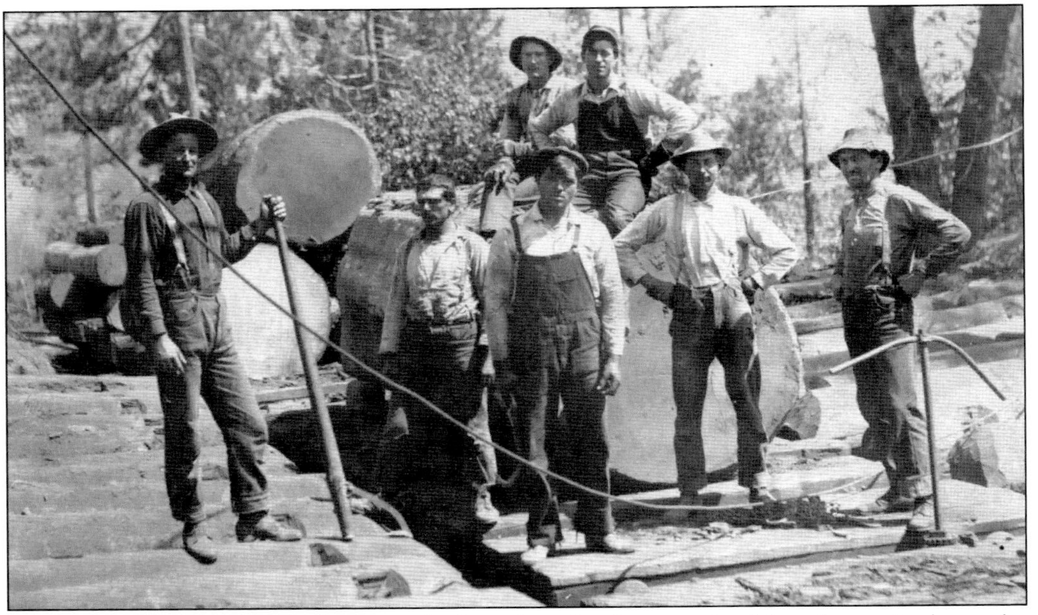

This crew is waiting on the logging platform for a bunk car to load logs for a trip down the incline. (MHP.)

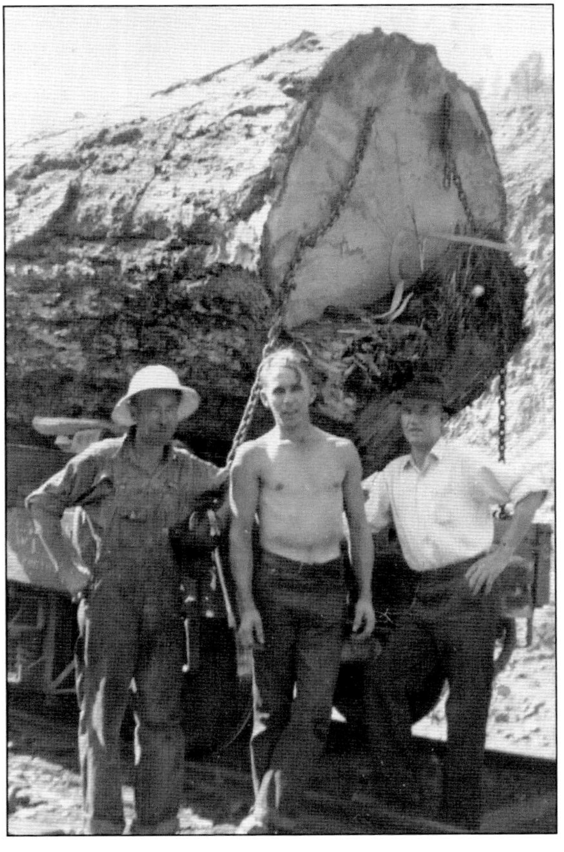

Jim Law (center) stands with two unidentified men in front of a one-log load at bottom of the incline. (MHP.)

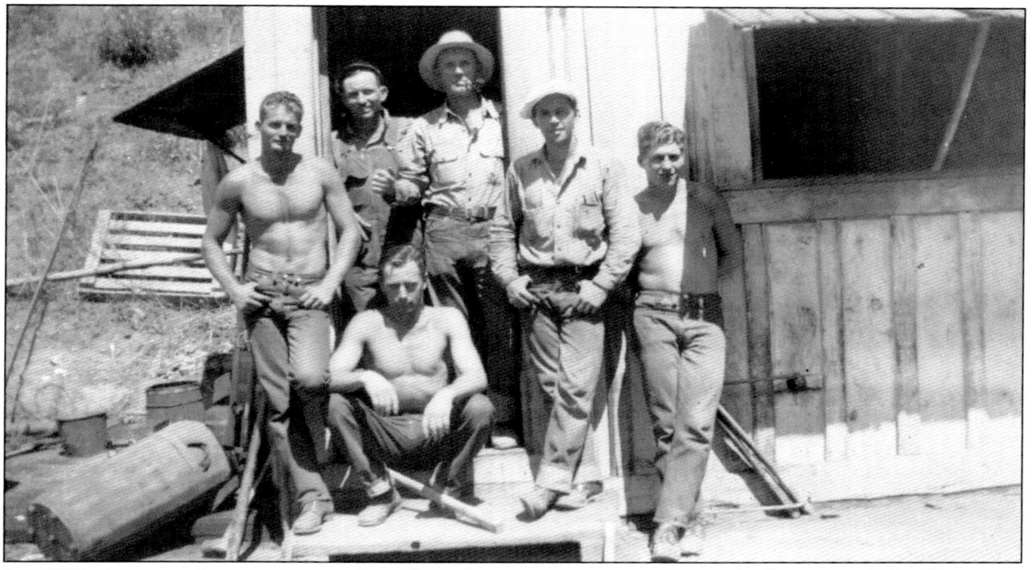

In 1938, this crew has just started work under new management at the bottom of the Yosemite Sugar Pine Lumber Company incline. Brakeman Jim Phillips is at far right. He was an El Portal resident, and after World War II, he had a business in Mariposa. (MHP.)

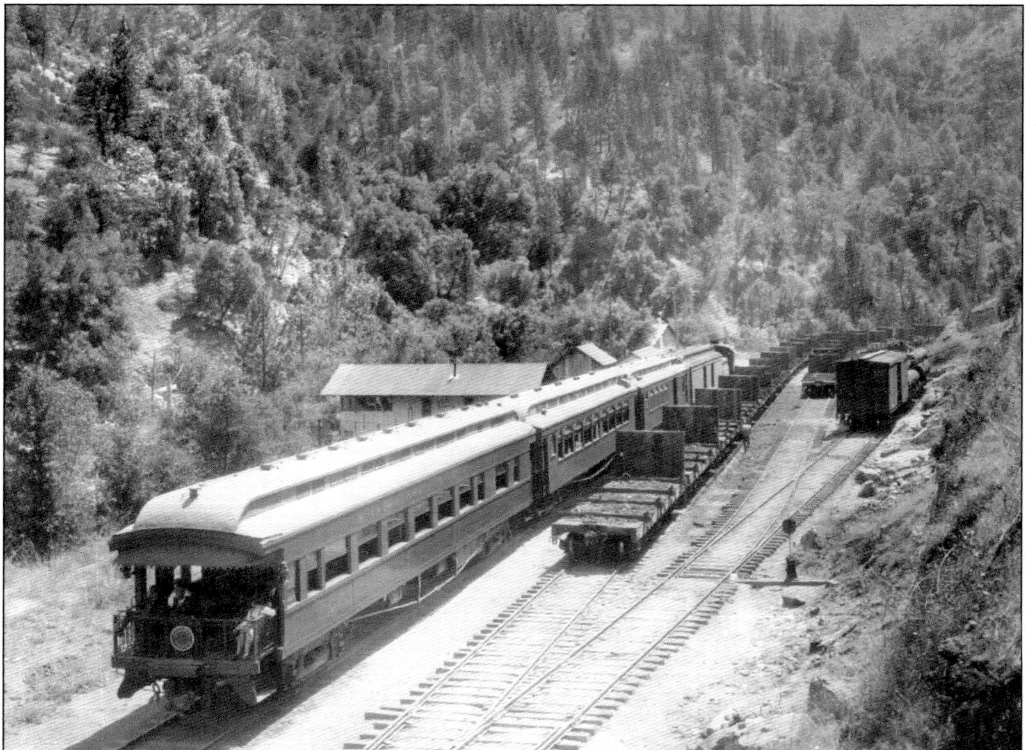

Log cars are waiting to be loaded at the bottom of the incline. A passenger train is passing on its way to Merced. (MHP.)

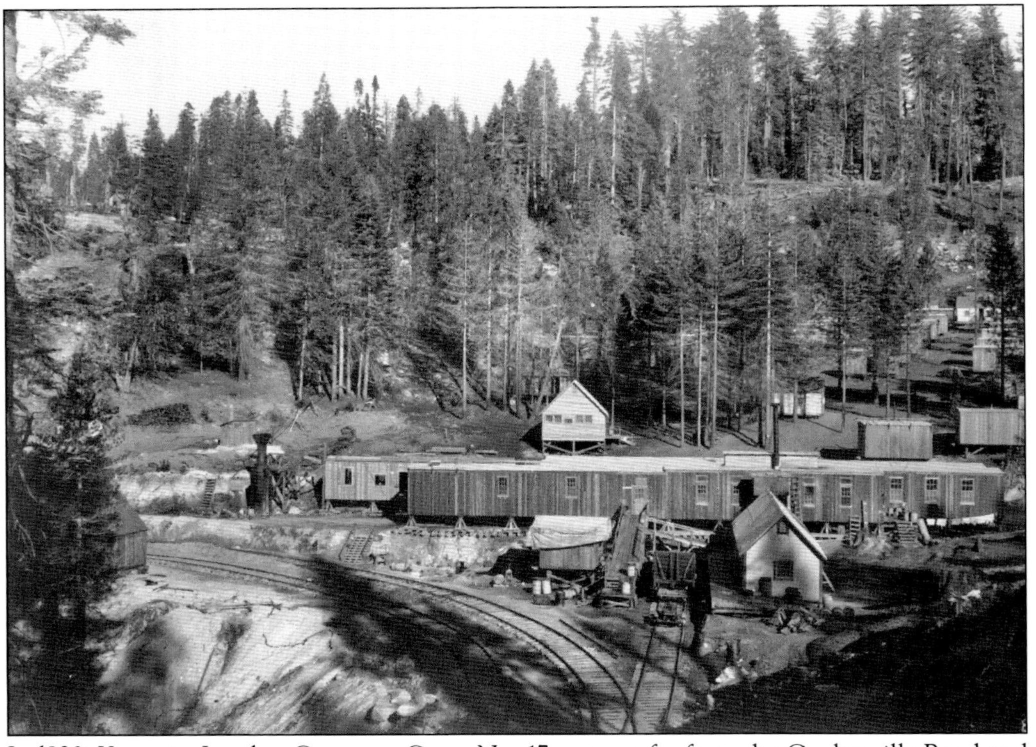

In 1930, Yosemite Lumber Company Camp No. 17 was not far from the Coulterville Road and was just outside Yosemite. (MHP.)

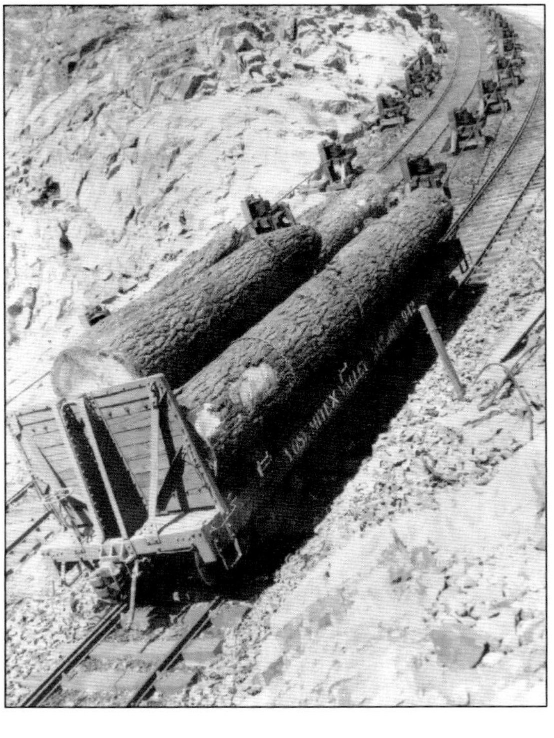

Pictured is a loaded log car about to reach the bottom of the Yosemite Lumber Company incline. (MHP.)

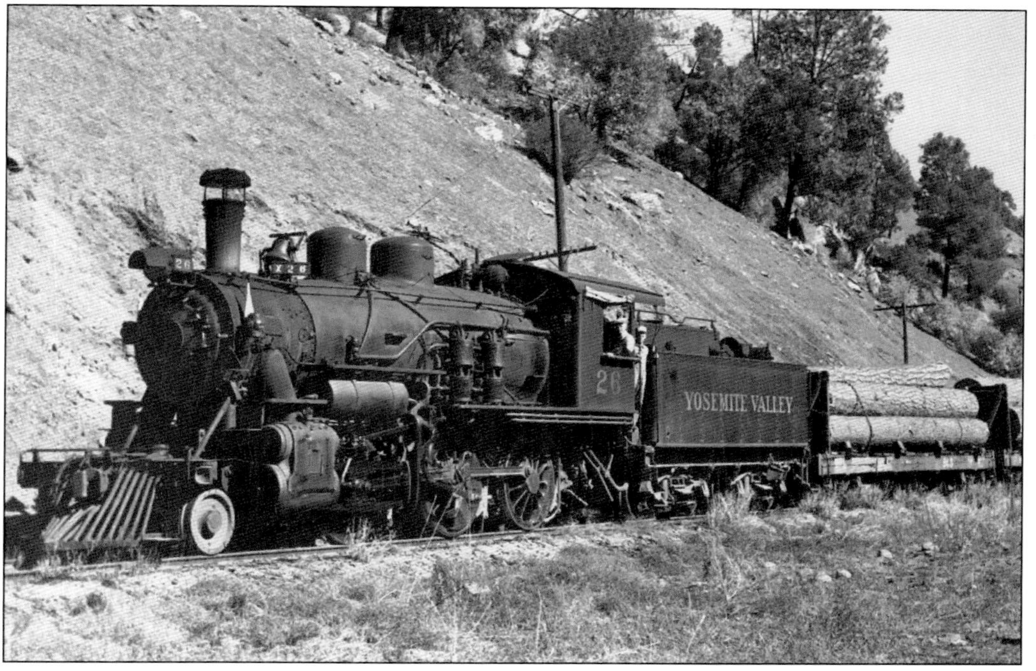

A loaded train of logs is on its way to the Merced Falls sawmill. (MHP.)

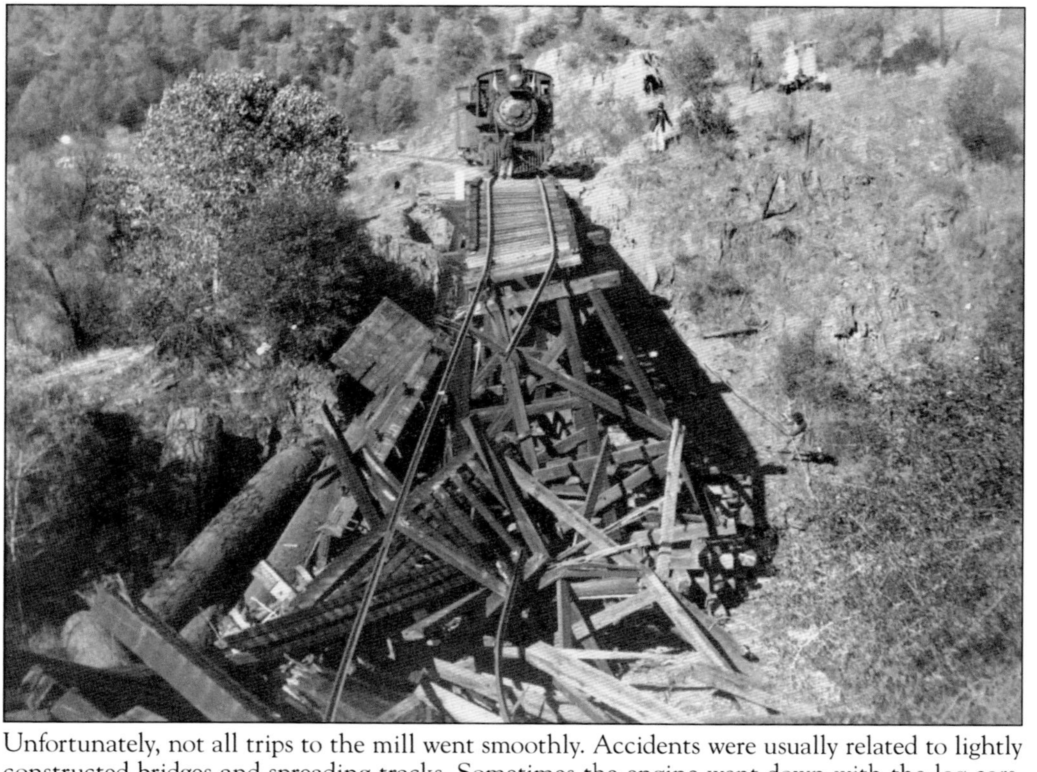

Unfortunately, not all trips to the mill went smoothly. Accidents were usually related to lightly constructed bridges and spreading tracks. Sometimes the engine went down with the log cars. (MHP.)

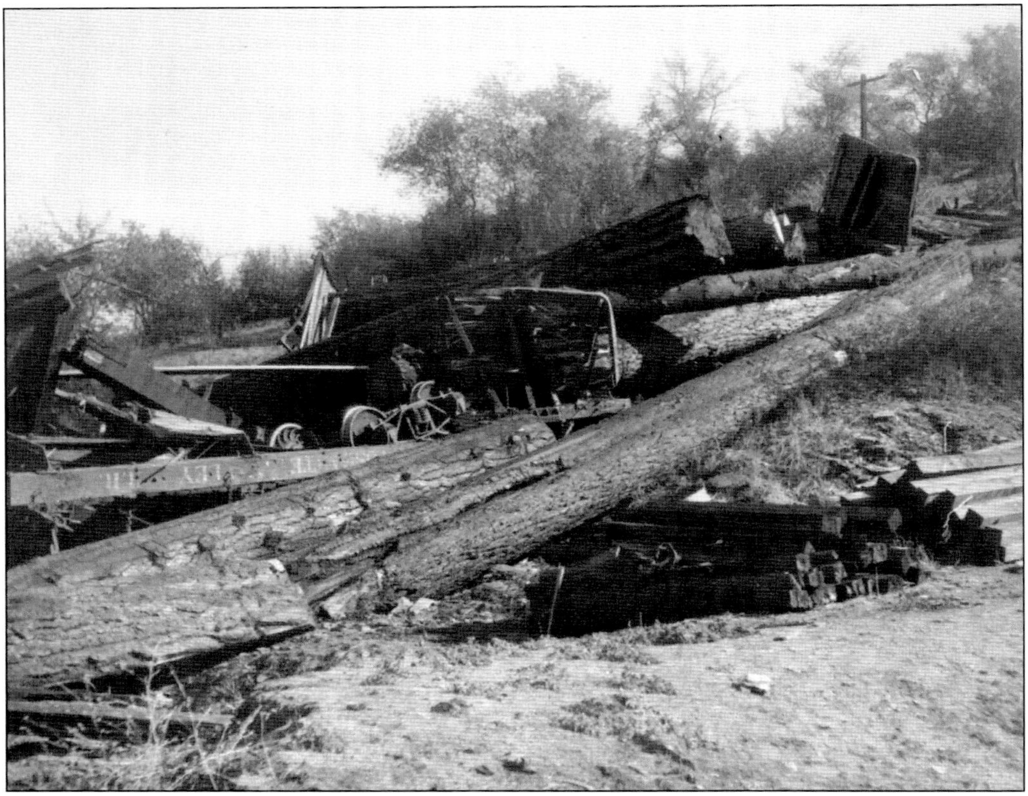

Heavily loaded log cars or problems with the trucks could cause rails to spread, which sometime meant entire loads could be lost. Other causes were washouts during heavy rain storms and the flooding Merced River. (MHP.)

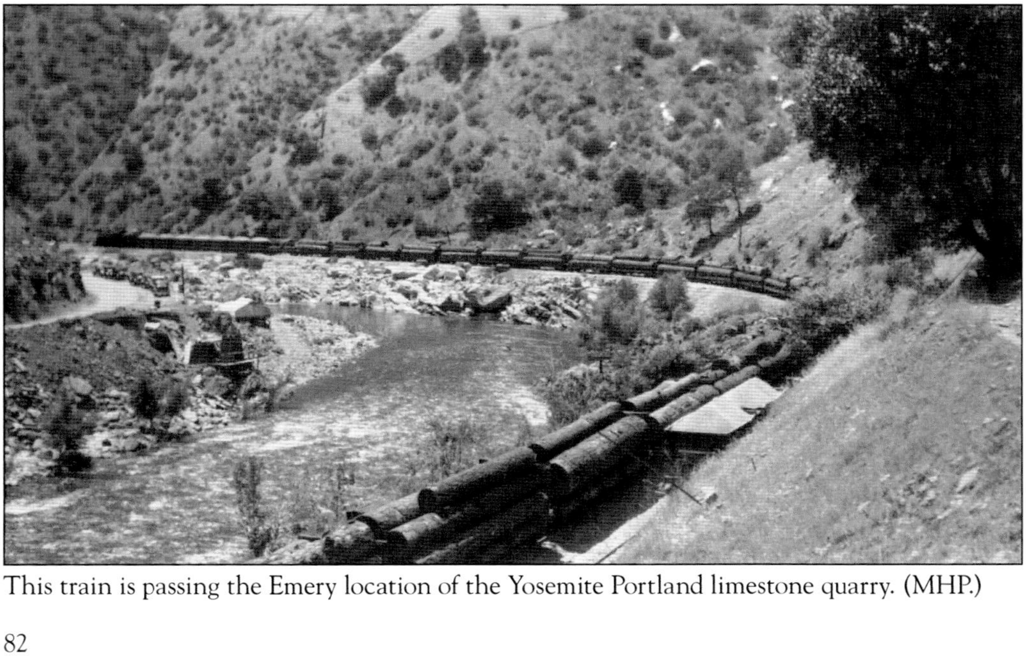

This train is passing the Emery location of the Yosemite Portland limestone quarry. (MHP.)

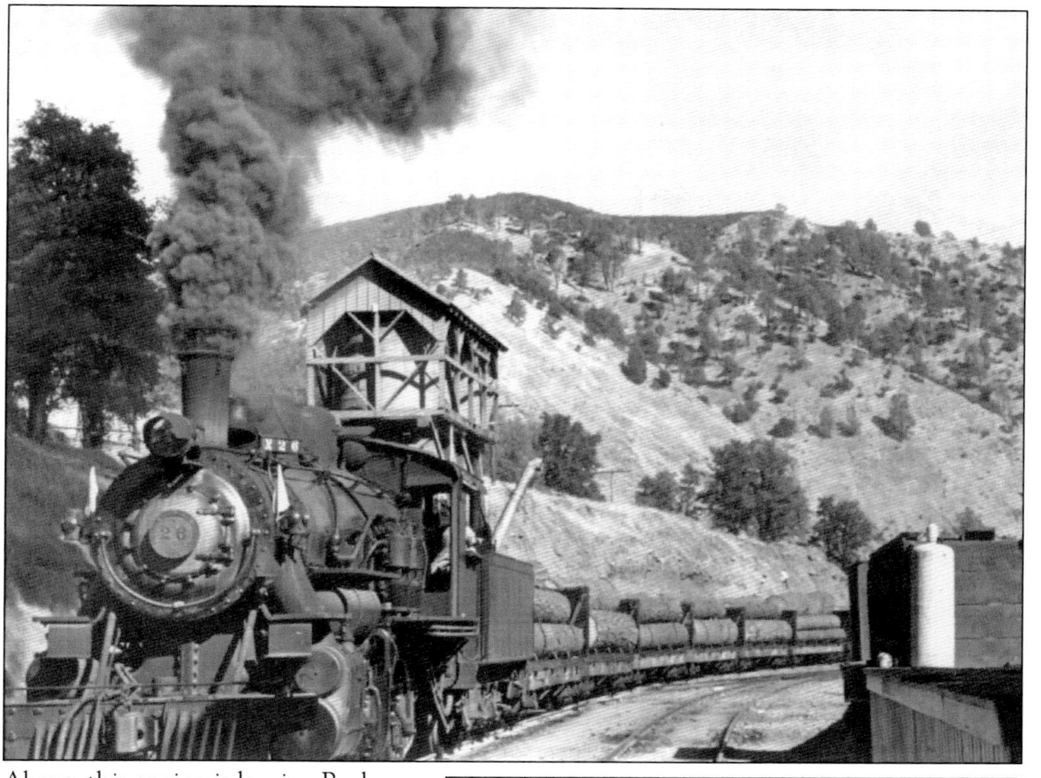

Above, this engine is leaving Bagby and is on its way to the Merced Falls mill. Bagby was a main stop between Yosemite and Merced. The water tanks that are pictured are now on display in El Portal. (MHP.)

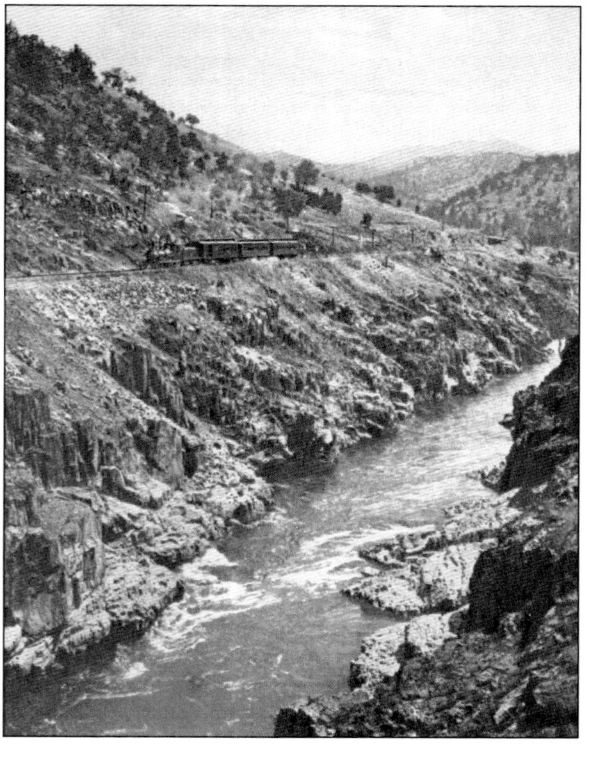

A log train travels along the lower canyon. (MHP.)

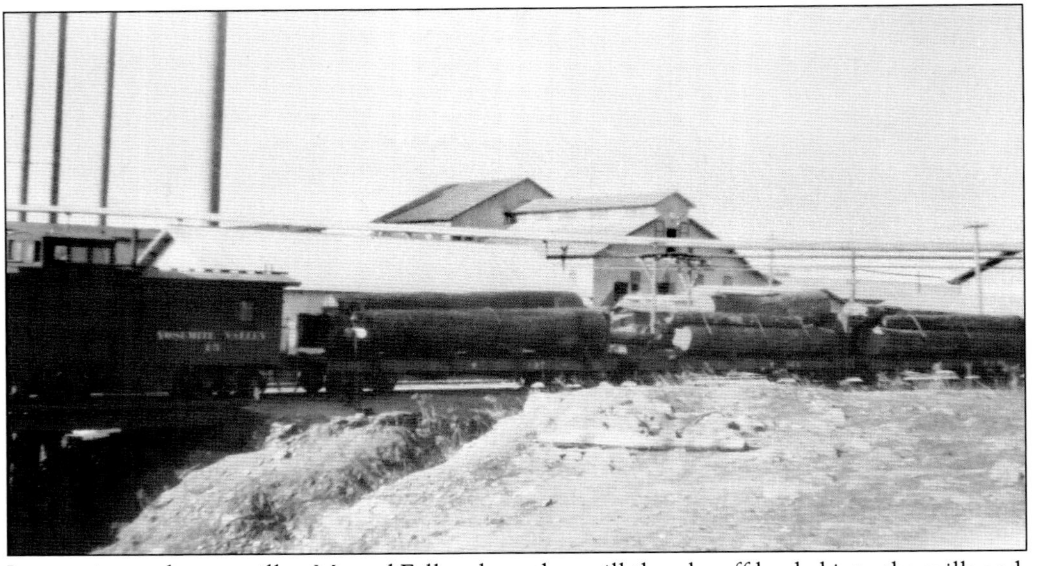

Logs arrive at the sawmill at Merced Falls, where they will then be off loaded into the millpond. (MHP.)

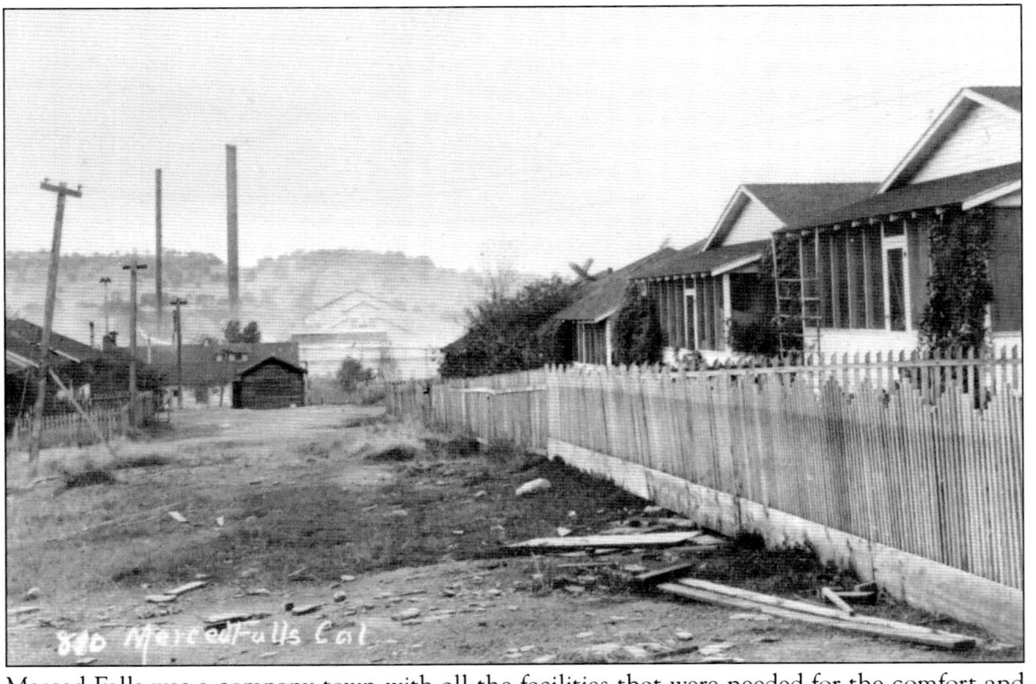

Merced Falls was a company town with all the facilities that were needed for the comfort and service of the families of the workers. There were row houses, a hospital, stores, a hotel, and a theater. (MHP.)

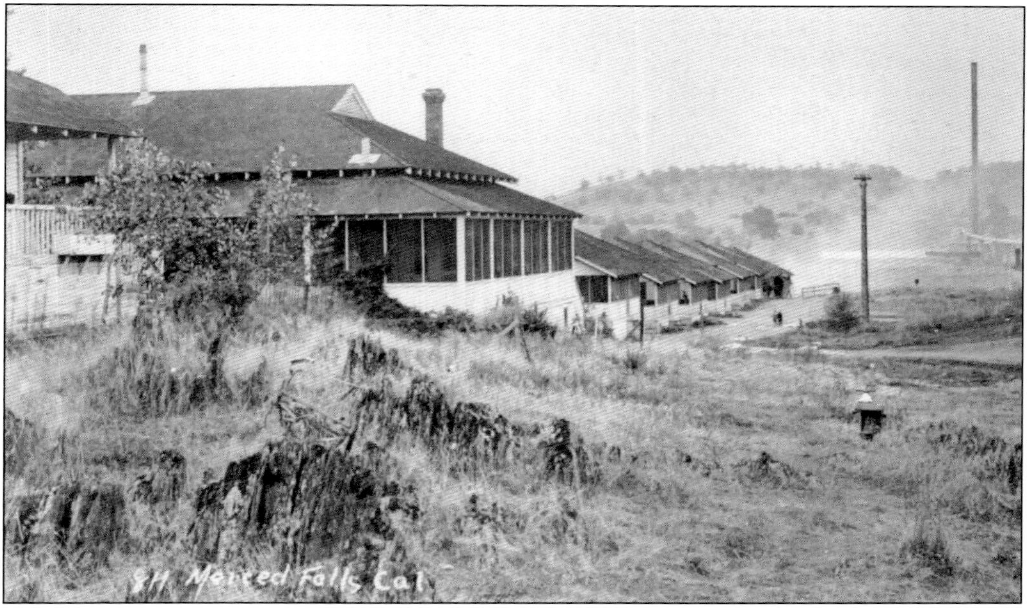

The hospital in Merced Falls looked toward the mill. The hospital stayed quite busy, as there were many mill accidents. (Winnie Williams.)

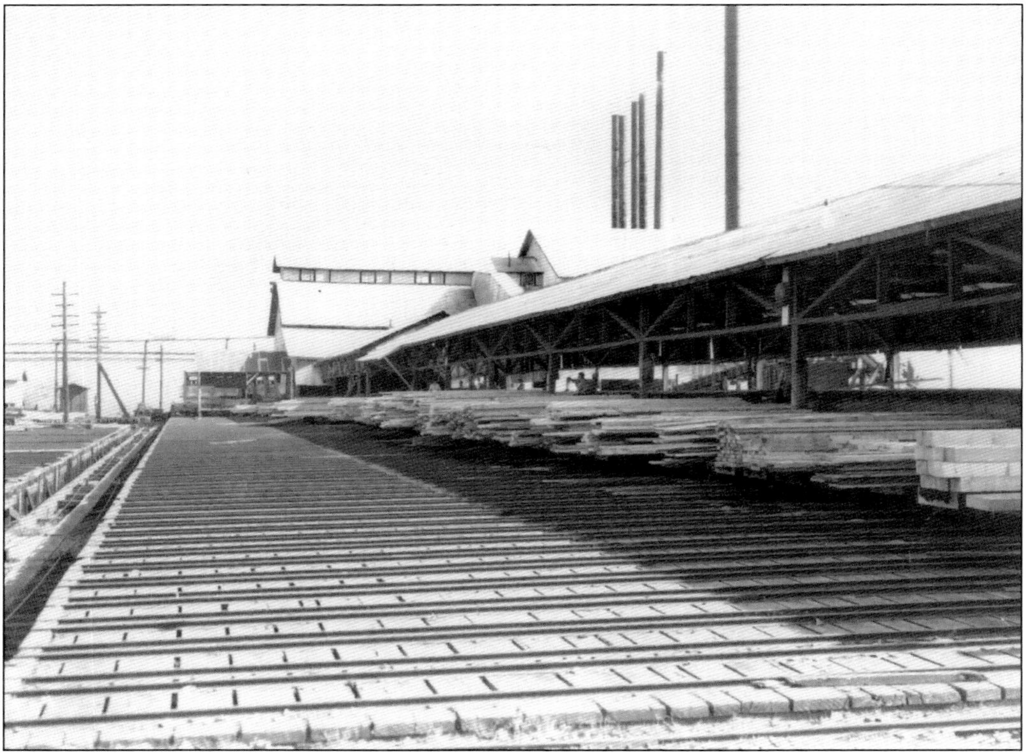

The sorting shed is pictured above, with the mill in background. The most desirable products of this mill were the large, clear planks of Sugar Pine, which were in great demand for construction of drain boards, sash, and doors. (Winnie Williams.)

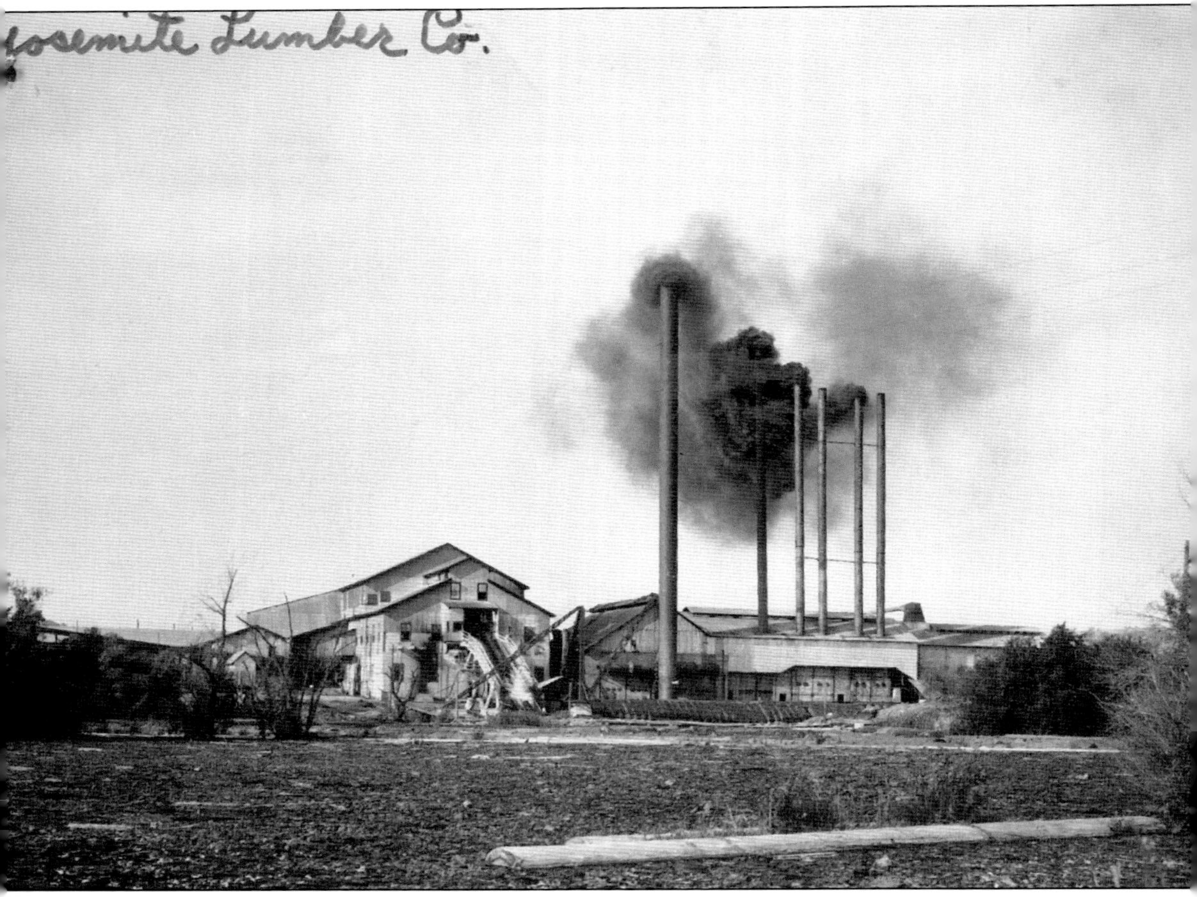

The Yosemite Lumber Company sawmill at Merced Falls is shown above at the height of its operation. The closing of the logging incline forced the mill to close in 1942. (MHP.)

Five

Yosemite Valley Railroad

Caught in Change

Events that occurred in the Merced River Canyon and the world determined the life span of the Yosemite Valley Railroad. The Yosemite Valley Railroad played an instrumental part in all of the following events and yet did not survive any of them: It helped Mariposa County surveyor Stonewall Jackson Harris acquire options on 10,000 acres of timber south of the Merced River between El Portal and Wawona; it assisted in the development the largest agricultural water storage dam project; it proved to be beneficial to those who mined for gold in Mariposa County; and lastly, it aided in making Yosemite National Park a major destination for visitors from around the world. For example, in order for the Merced Irrigation District to complete its 1.1-million-acre-foot water storage project on the Merced River just east of Merced Falls, the relocation of the rail route had to be made to accommodate the project and still provide for the new railroad. The railroad became an integral part of the construction of the project through the movement of materials and supplies to the site. The relocation of the railroad required tunnels to be built, which placed the roadbed above the level of the new Lake McClure. By 1924, the construction of the final leg of the Highway 140 is completed. It was feared that not enough visitors would use the train and that the newly popular private automobile and bus would be viewed as the answer. By 1926, the automobile could reach Yosemite Valley by an all-year low-elevation route. Again the railroad was affected. It was, however, the relationship between the Yosemite Lumber Company and the Yosemite Valley Railroad had allowed the railroad to continue until World War II. The harvesting of 20,000 acres of timber on the north side of the Merced River was drastically altered because of the beginning of World War II and the disastrous flood of the Merced River. Other shippers of mining products contributed some to the railroad's revenue, but these sources were short lived. The improvements brought about in Yosemite Valley like the Ahwahnee Hotel and the consolidation of the various concessionaires into the Yosemite Park and Curry Company, which also occurred in 1924, spelled the eventual end of this rail line.

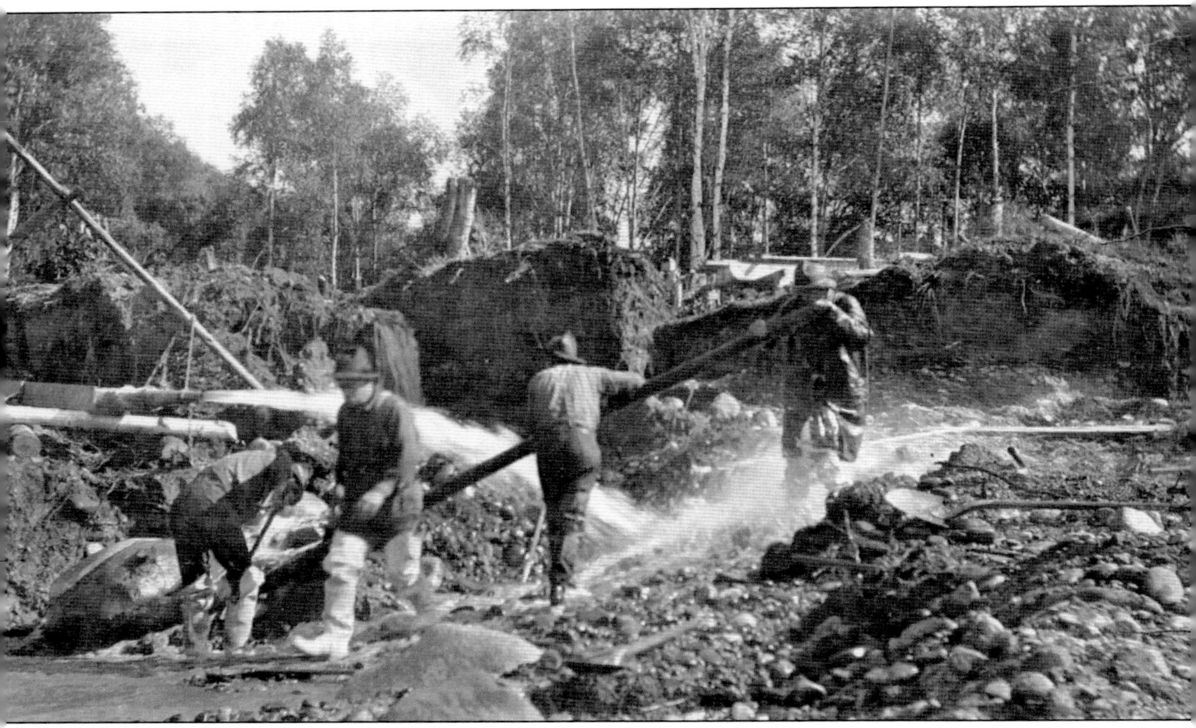

From 1849 until the building of the railroad and beyond, there was a strong tradition of gold mining on the Merced River. (MHP.)

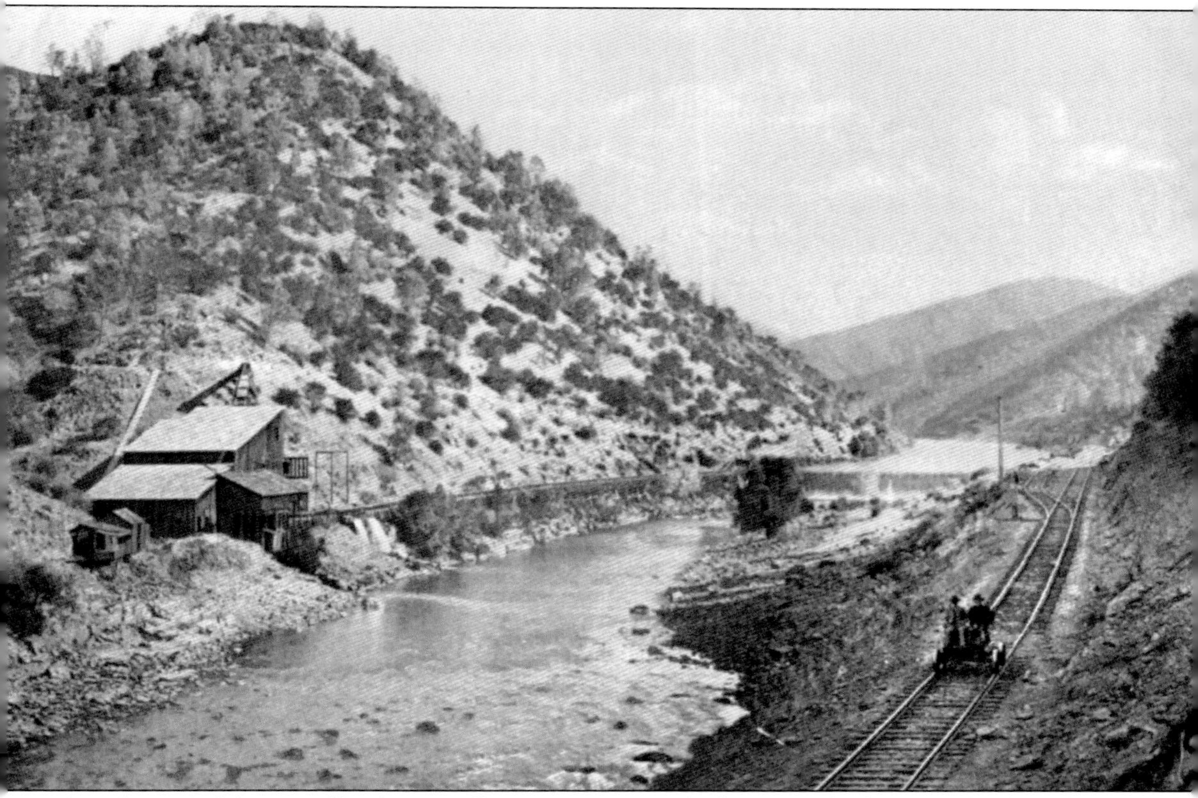

At White's Gulch, west of Bagby, a small power station was built to provide electricity for the mill working in that area. The railroad had to skirt the millpond while moving east. (MHP.)

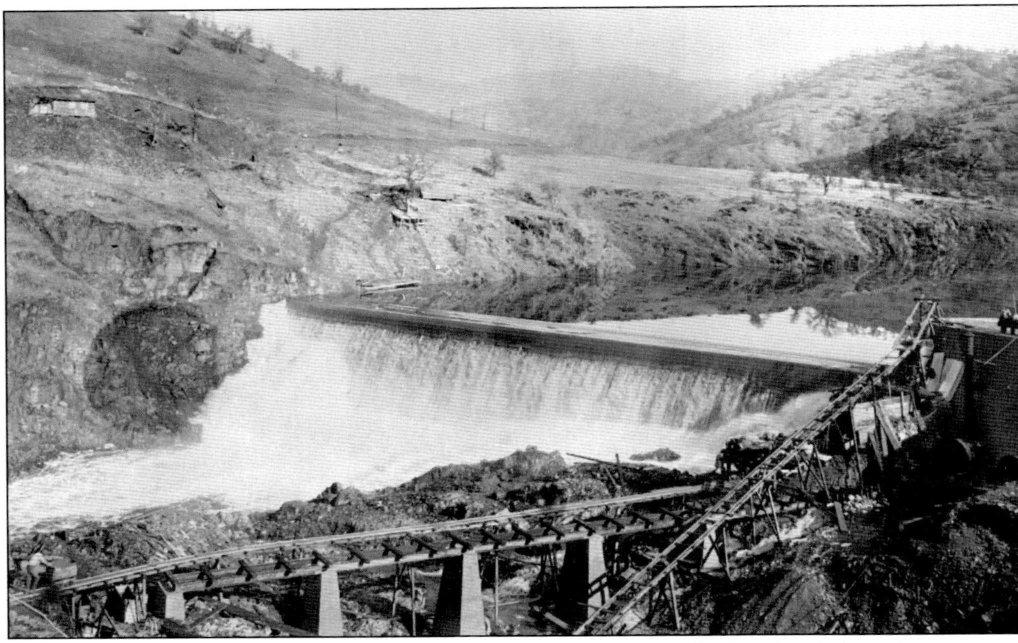

Farther west, near Merced Falls, the Exchequer Mining Company built a check dam that was used for mining. It was near this site that the Merced Irrigation District (MID) began the development of a major dam, which was designed to provide irrigation water to the farms of Merced County and to generate electricity. (MHP.)

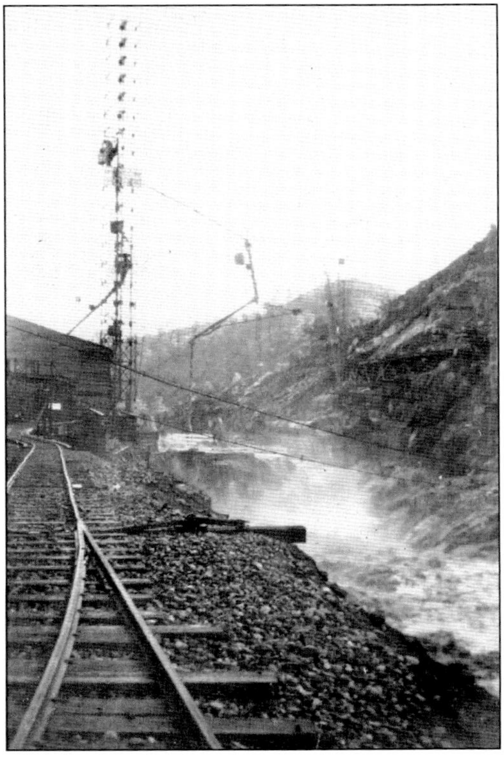

For the construction of the MID dam to begin, it required the relocation of the railroad. During the construction, a tunnel in the dam allowed the train to continue to El Portal. (Gerald Williams.)

The rail bed was raised above the high-water mark of the new Lake McClure. Pictured is the west end of Tunnel No. 1. The subsequent rising of the dam flooded this tunnel but only after the end of the Yosemite Valley Railroad operations. (Gerald Williams.)

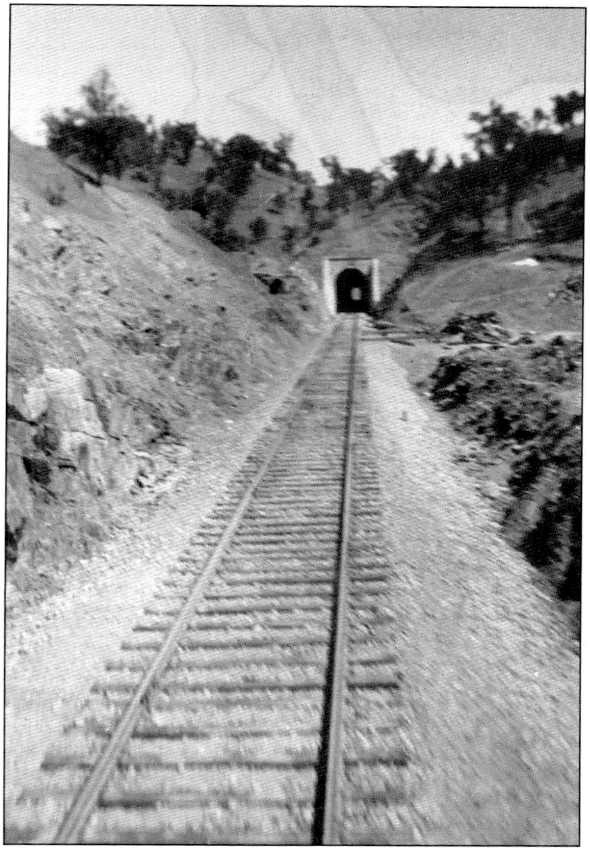

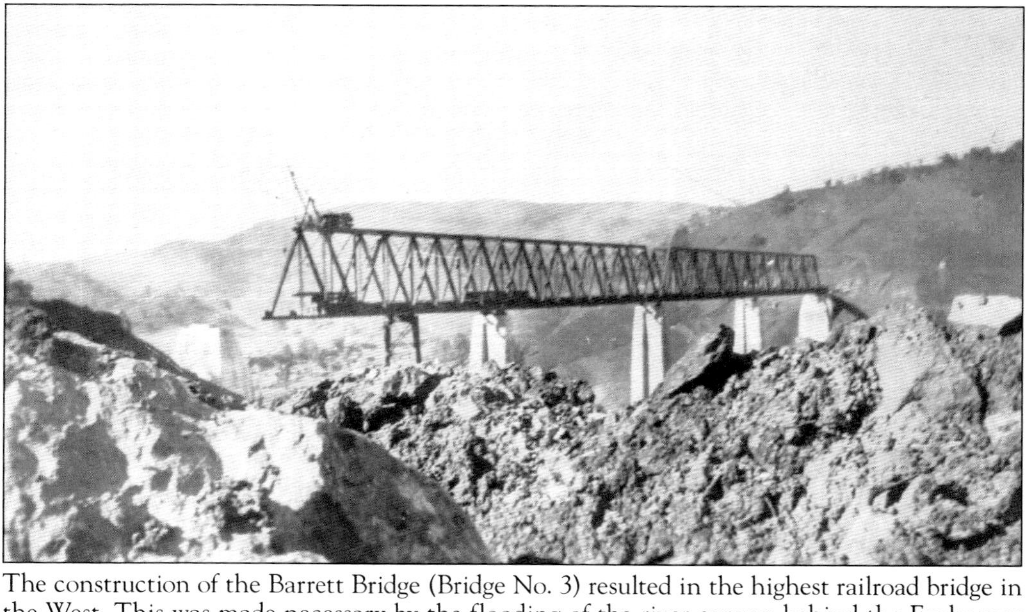

The construction of the Barrett Bridge (Bridge No. 3) resulted in the highest railroad bridge in the West. This was made necessary by the flooding of the river canyon behind the Exchequer Dam. (Gerald Williams.)

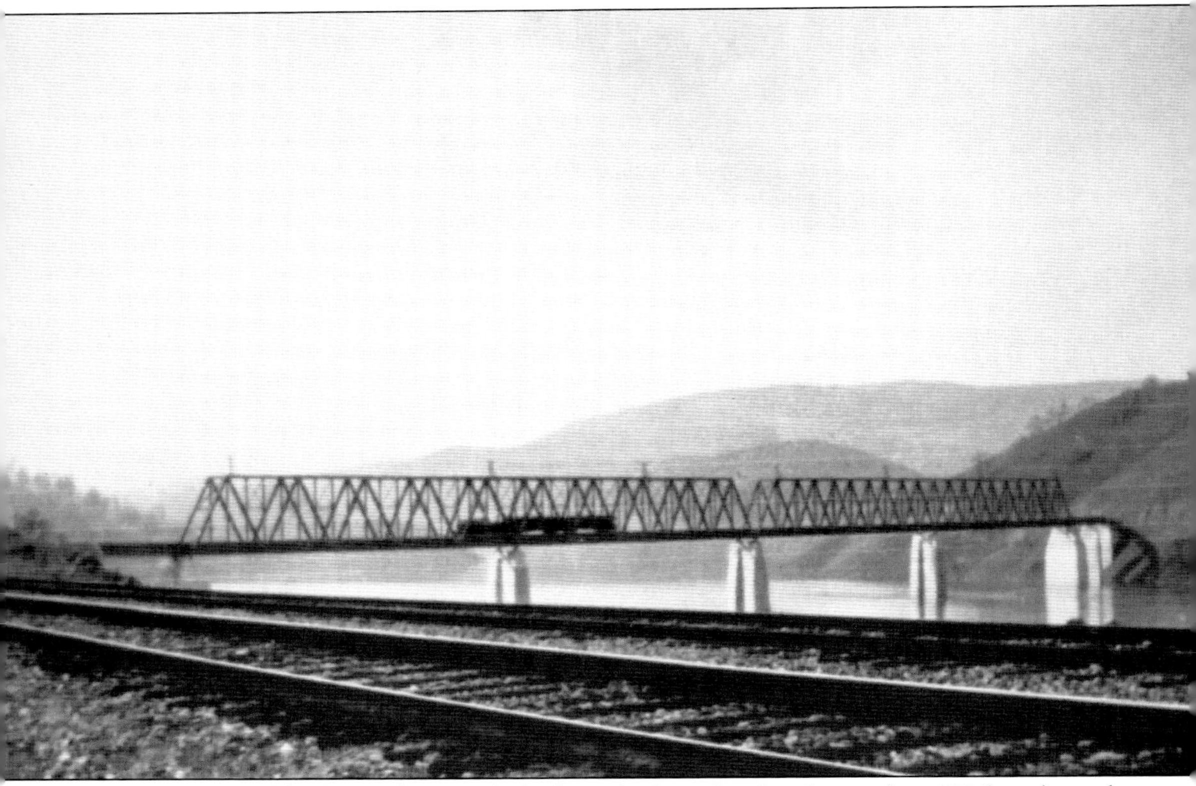

The completed bridge, with its tracks laid, resulted in a height of more than 220 feet above the river bed, but this was not noticeable once the lake was full. This bridge carried the railroad to the south side of the river. (Gerald Williams.)

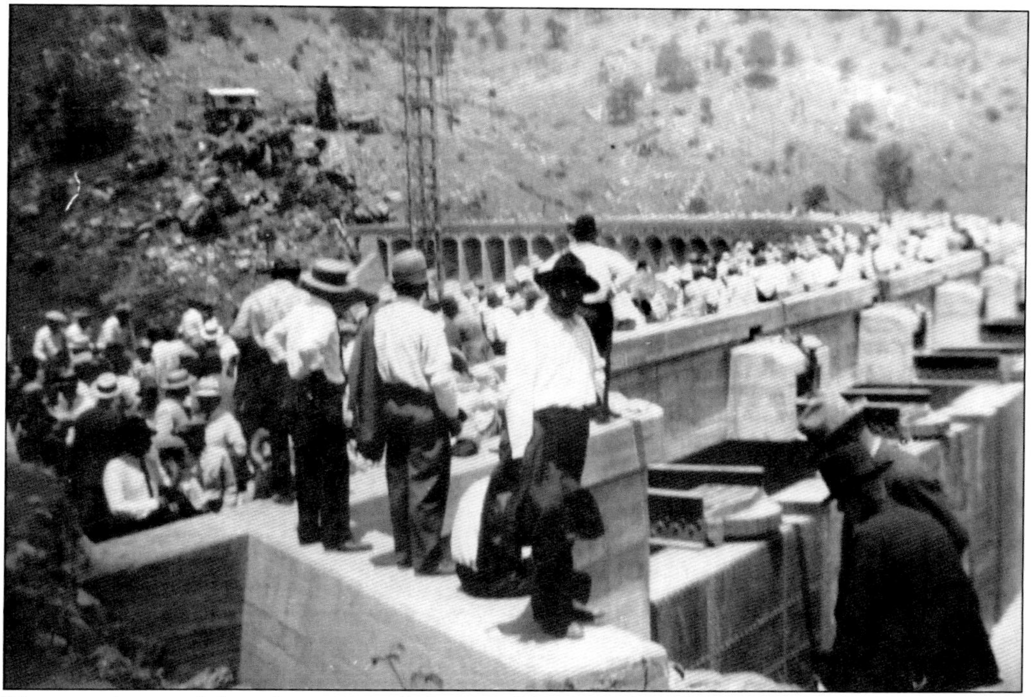

The completion of the relocation and closing of the tunnel in the dam resulted in a dedication of the completed project without an interruption of service. (MHP.)

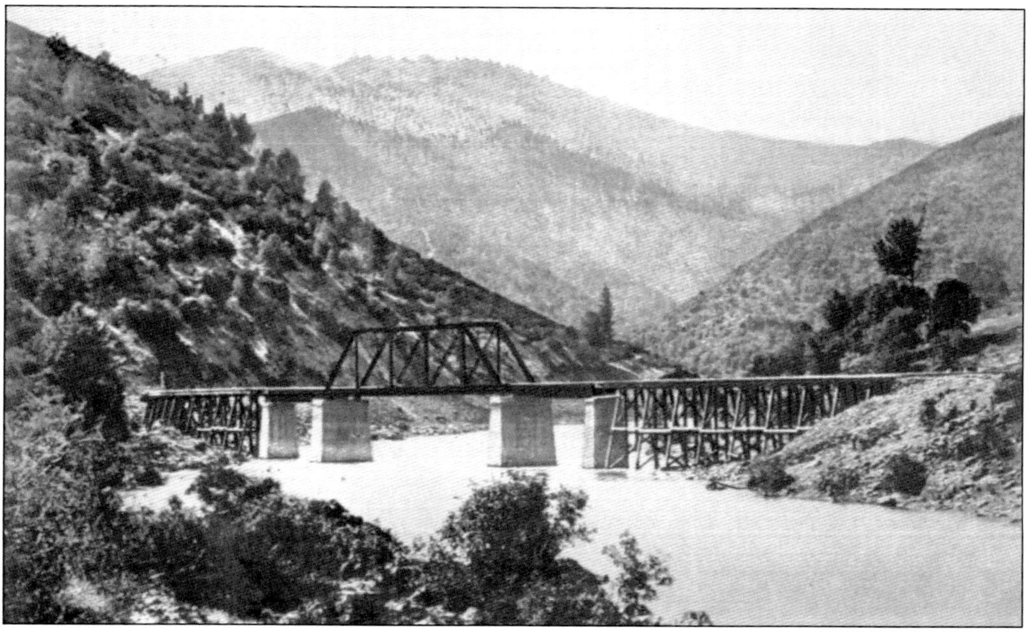

The bridge just west of Bagby returned the rail line to the north side of the river, where it would continue on to El Portal. (Gerald Williams.)

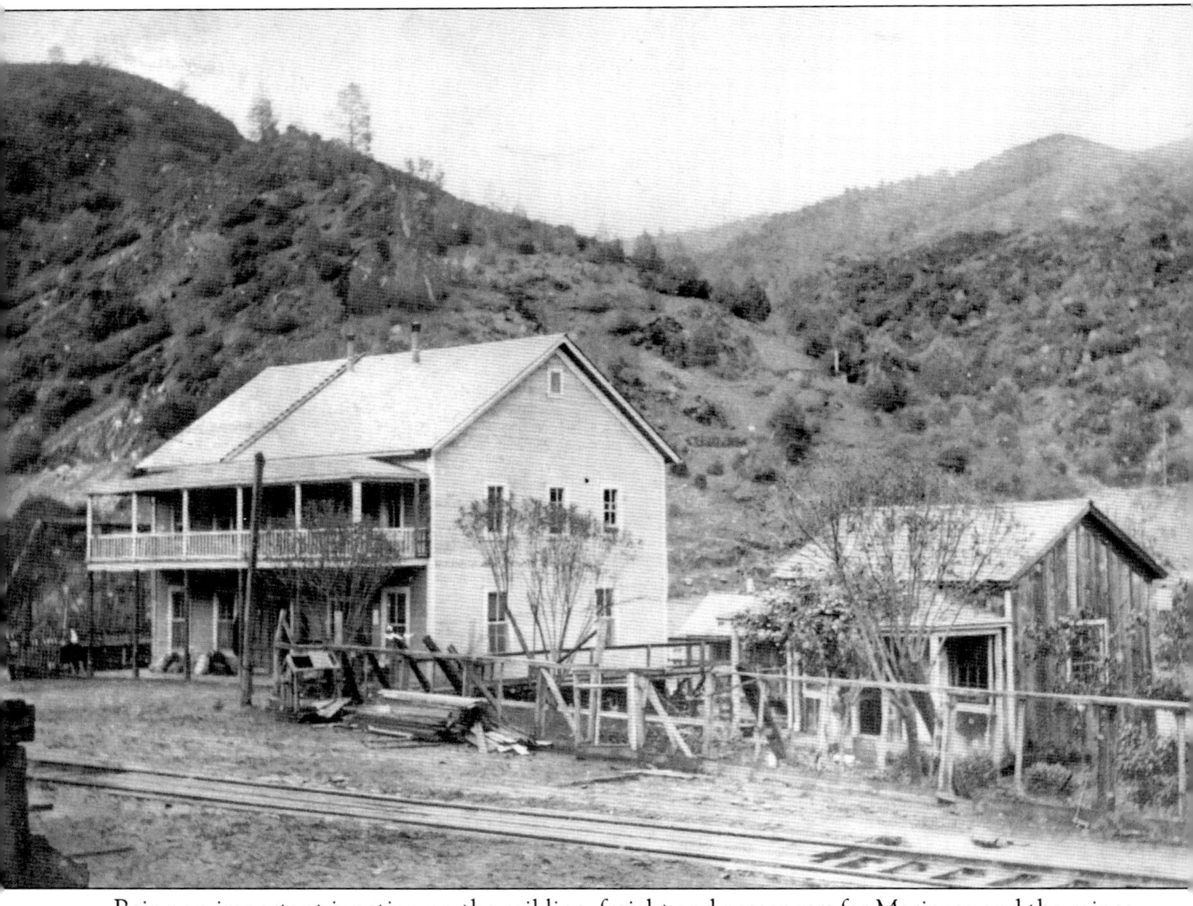

Being an important junction on the rail line, freight and passengers for Mariposa and the mines in between could be off-loaded in Bagby. The Bagby Hotel was known for its pioneer hospitality and pie. (MHP.)

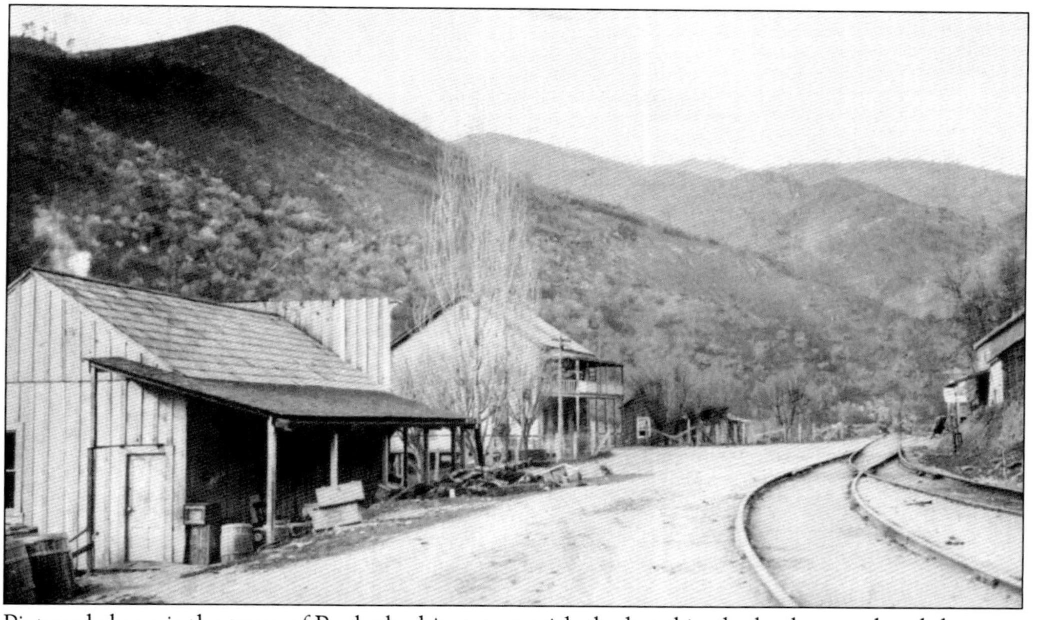

Pictured above is the town of Bagby looking west, with the hotel in the background and the store on the left. Bagby becomes the milling center for the Pine Tree and Josephine Mines, and many workers lived in the vicinity. (MHP.)

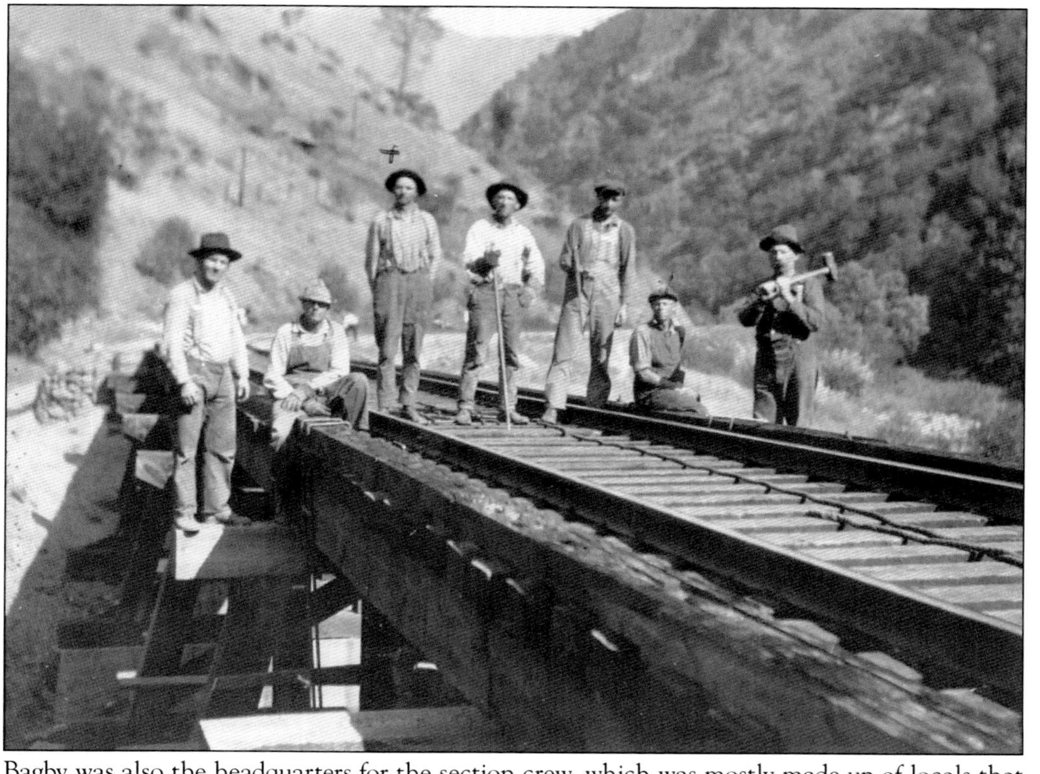

Bagby was also the headquarters for the section crew, which was mostly made up of locals that were often between jobs in the mines. (Gerald Williams.)

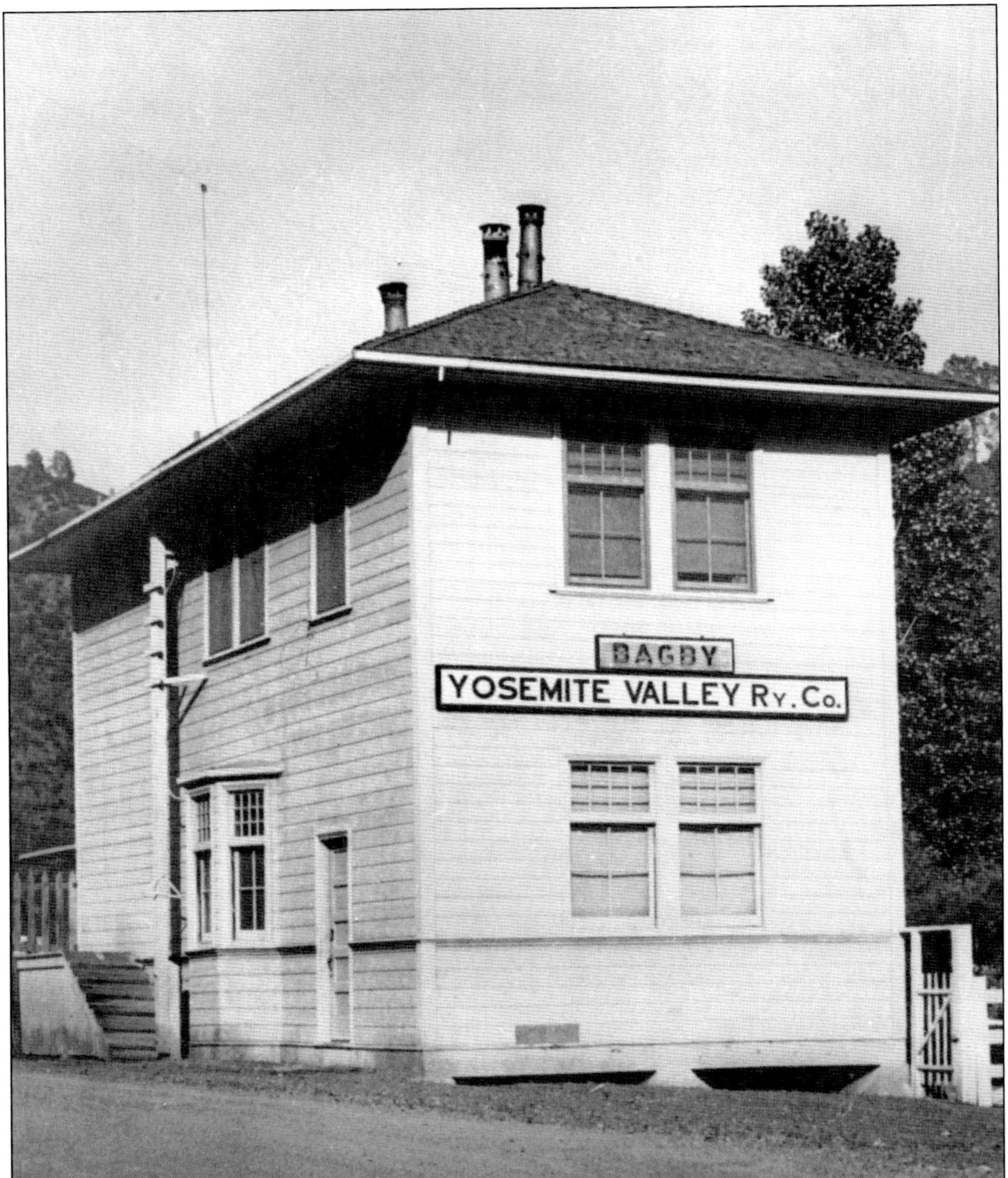

This third and final station at Bagby was constructed around 1925 after the previous station burned in a fire. Today this building is the office of the Yosemite Association in El Portal and is part of a railroad display created by the park service. (MHP.)

Between Bagby and Briceberg is the Mountain King Mine. Isolated at first, the railroad brought frequent passenger and freight services. Schoolchildren from the mine families rode the train to Briceberg to attend school. (Photograph by F. A. Judkins.)

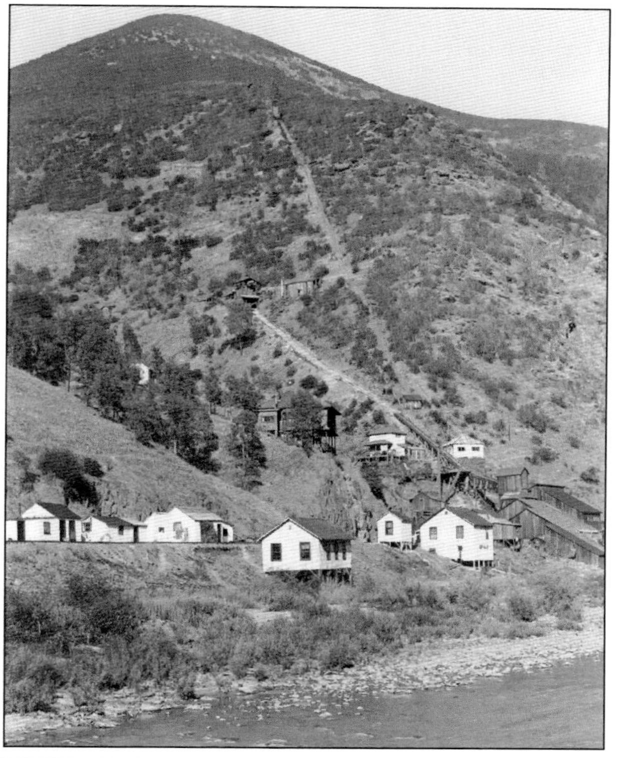

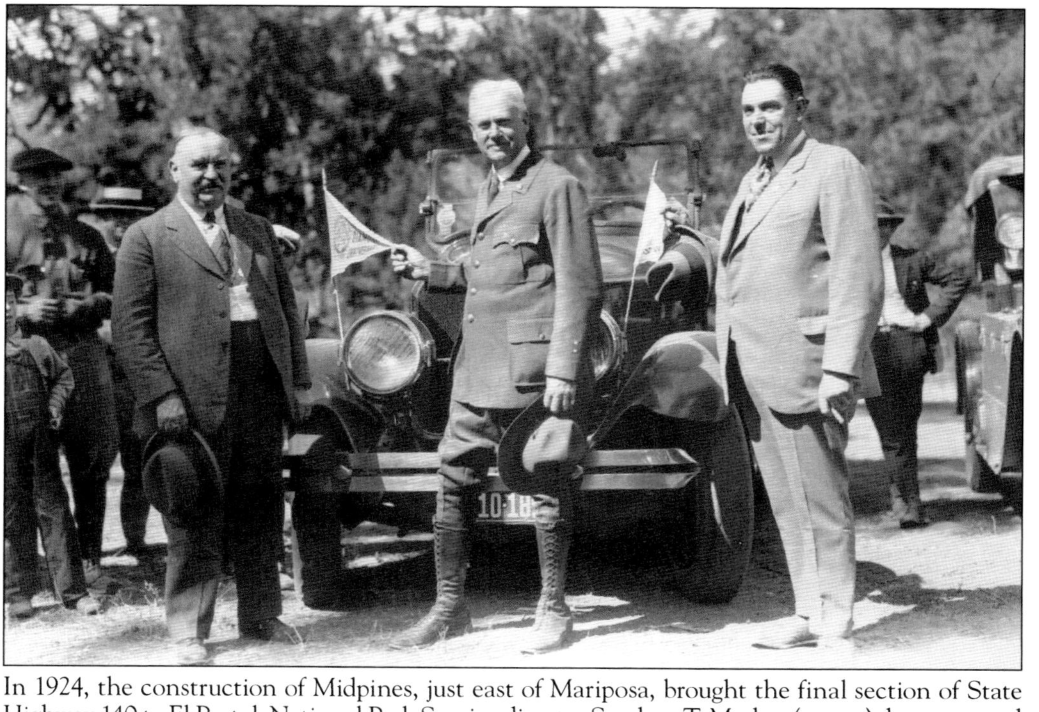

In 1924, the construction of Midpines, just east of Mariposa, brought the final section of State Highway 140 to El Portal. National Park Service director Stephen T. Mather (center) demonstrated the value of the all-year highway to the park by participating. (Yosemite Museum.)

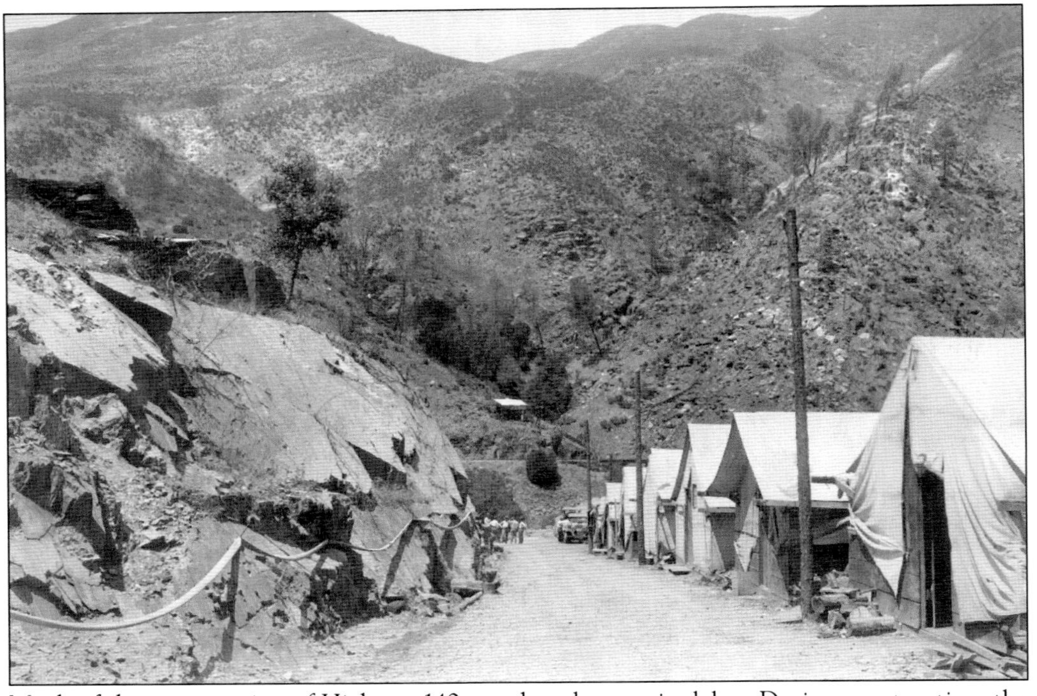

Much of the construction of Highway 140 was done by convict labor. During construction, the workers were placed in tent camps along the Briceberg Grade right-of-way. Another camp was located at South Fork along the highway. (Bertha Schroeder.)

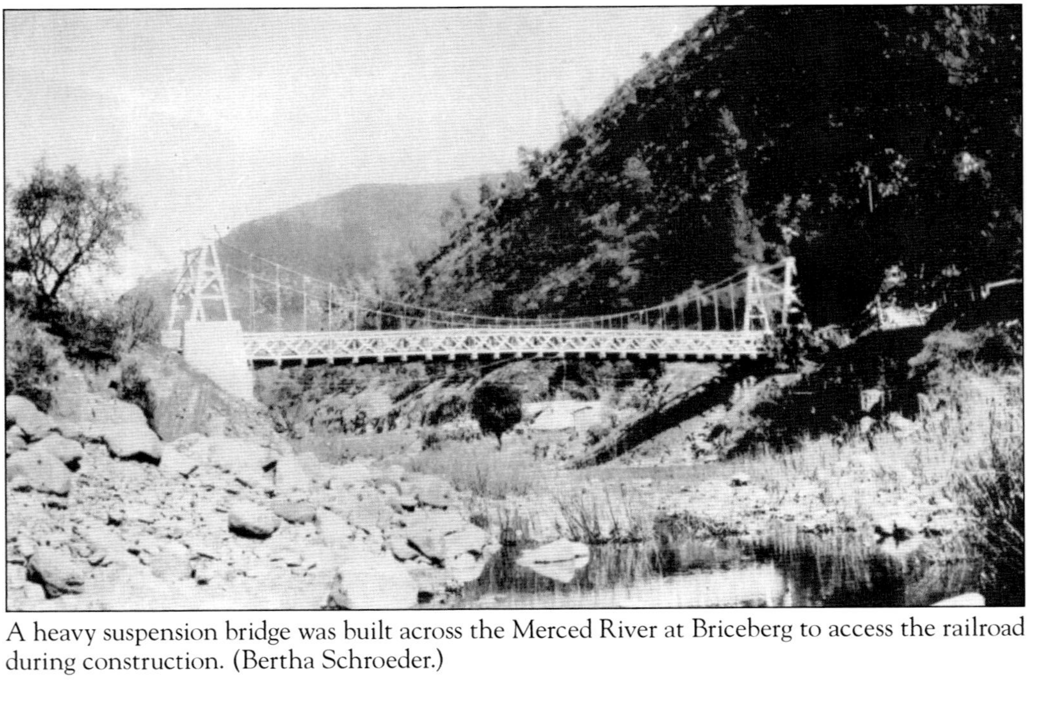

A heavy suspension bridge was built across the Merced River at Briceberg to access the railroad during construction. (Bertha Schroeder.)

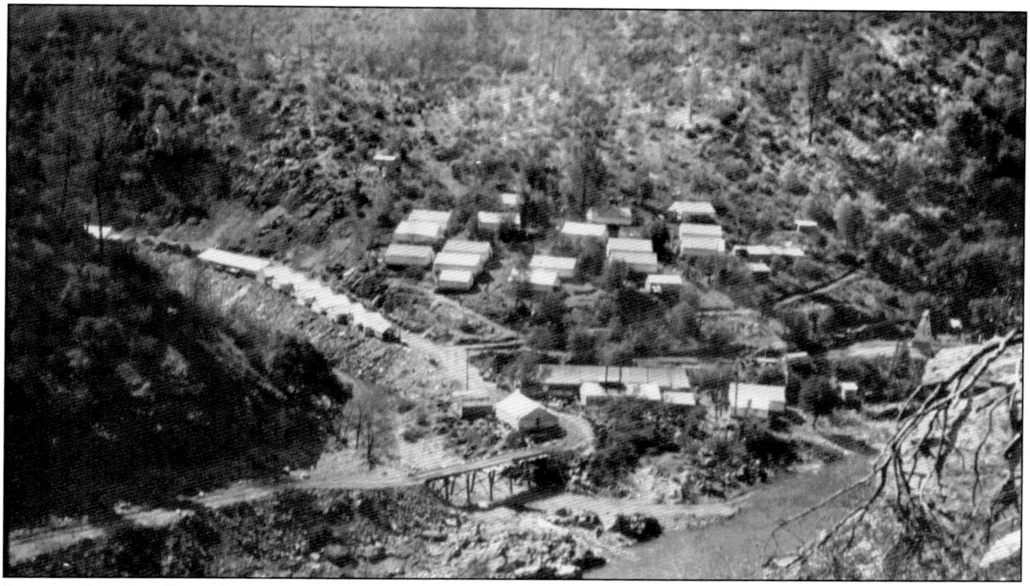

Pictured is the Briceberg construction camp with the temporary bridge across from Bear Creek. Briceberg eventually became a stop on the Yosemite Valley Railroad and an important tourist stop on the new highway. (Bertha Schroeder.)

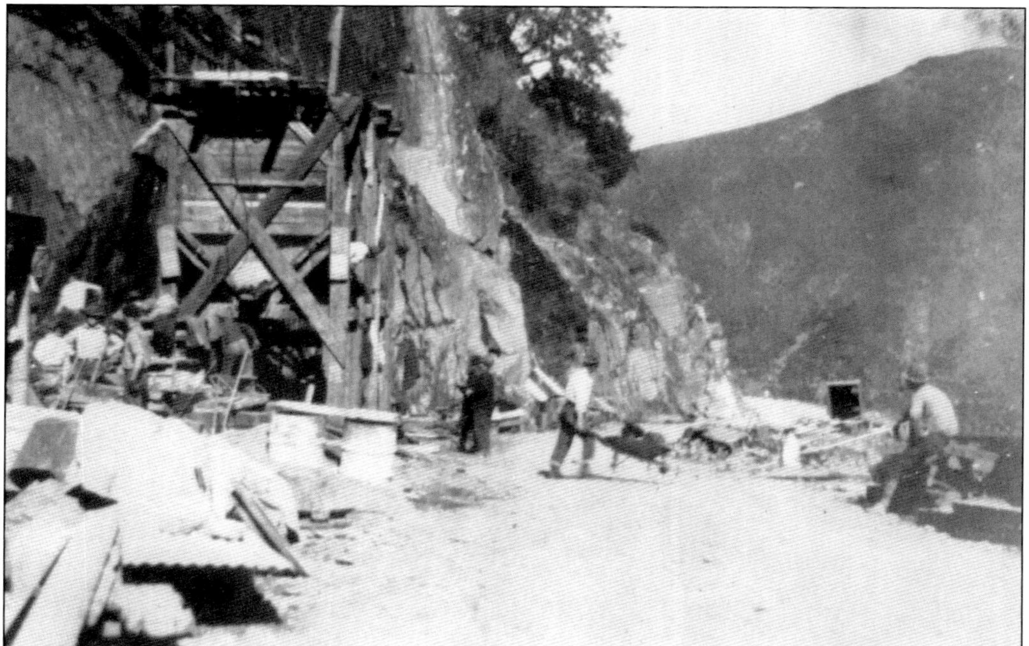

The highway along the river required many retaining walls. Skilled rock workers built these walls, with the help of the convicts. (MHP.)

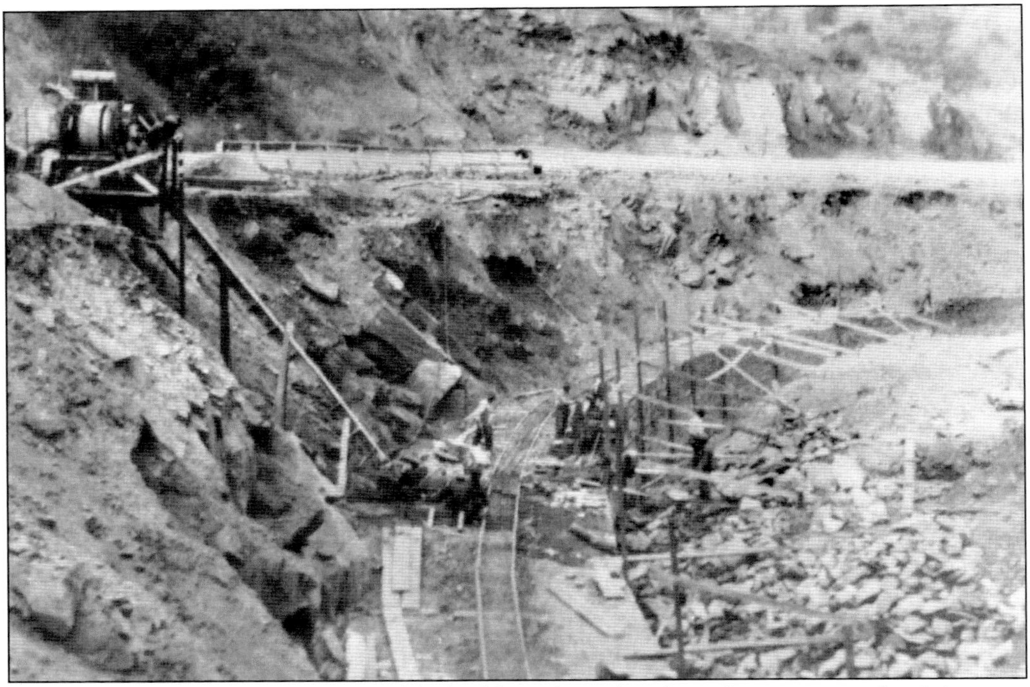

Many of the difficulties encountered by building the railroad on the opposite side of the river also challenged the highway builders. Cement plants supplied with local materials were used to build the walls. (MHP.)

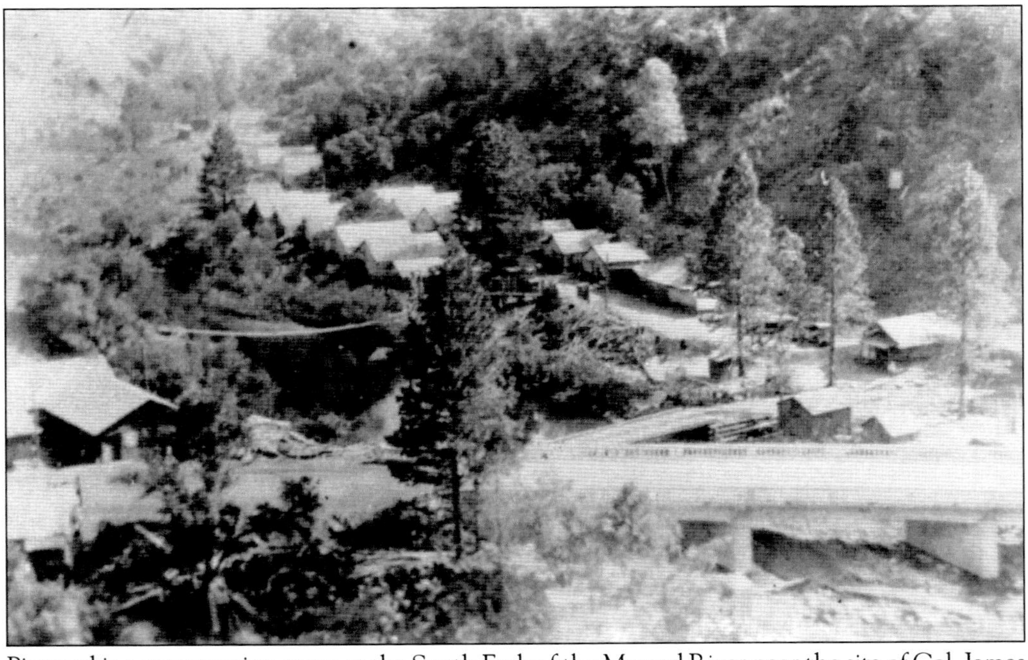

Pictured is a construction camp at the South Fork of the Merced River near the site of Col. James Savages Trading Post from the gold rush days. A major bridge was constructed across the South Fork. (Gerald Williams.)

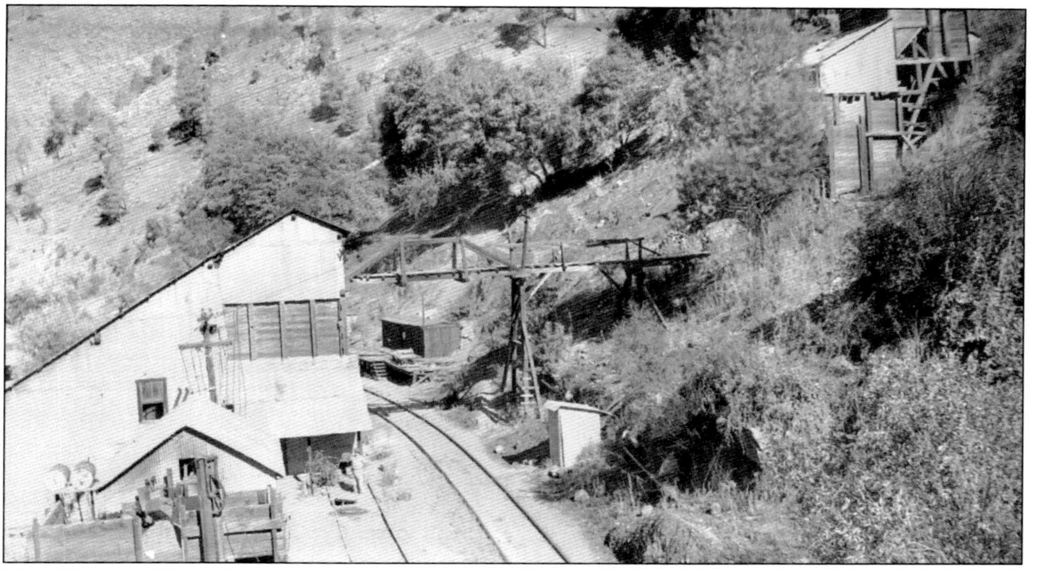

The Clearing House Mine continued to operate during the life of the railroad. A series of floods damaged the operation until its closing after 1950. The mill building is located along the river bank with the train tracks running between the buildings. This photograph is looking southwest toward Merced. (MHP.)

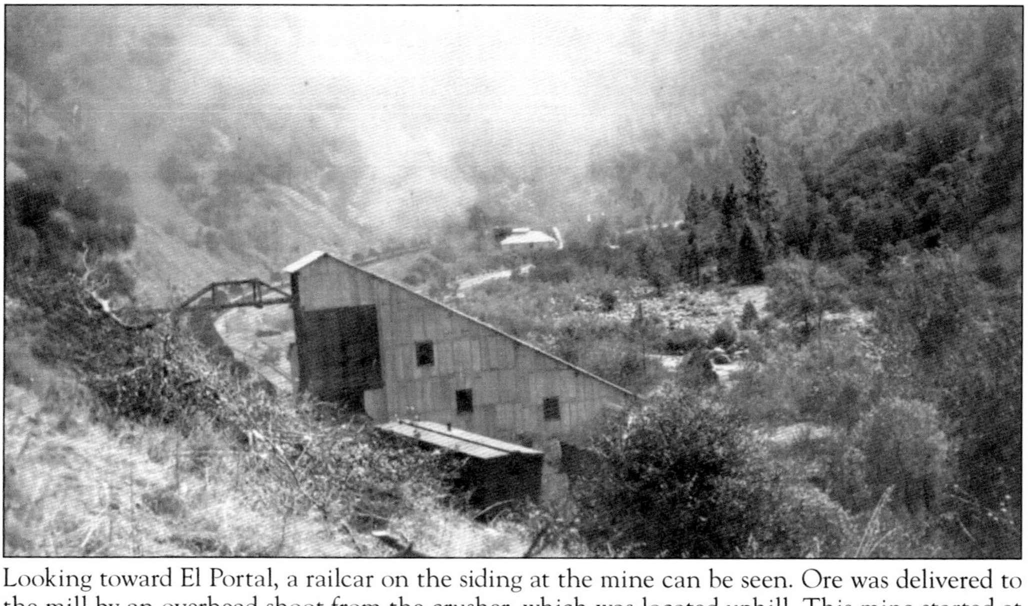

Looking toward El Portal, a railcar on the siding at the mine can be seen. Ore was delivered to the mill by an overhead shoot from the crusher, which was located uphill. This mine started at the Original Mine, which began long before the railroad. (MHP.)

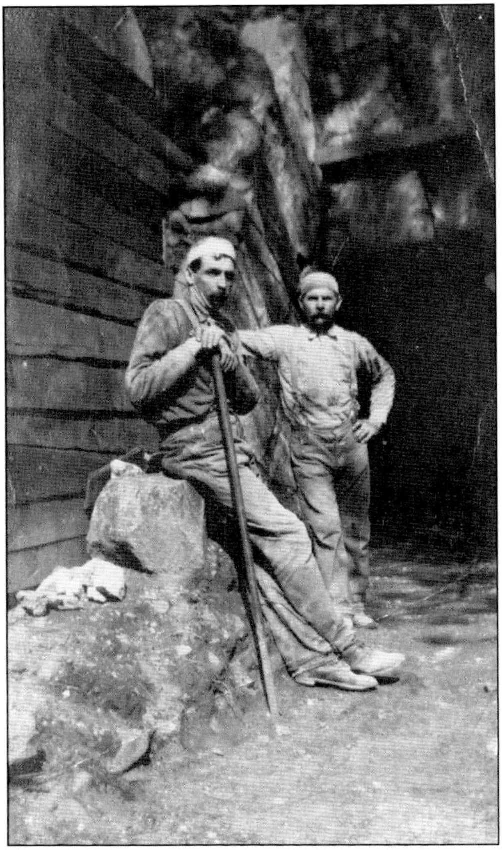

Miners Bob Halstead and Bill Grinfell stand at the entrance to the Clearing House Mine. (MHP.)

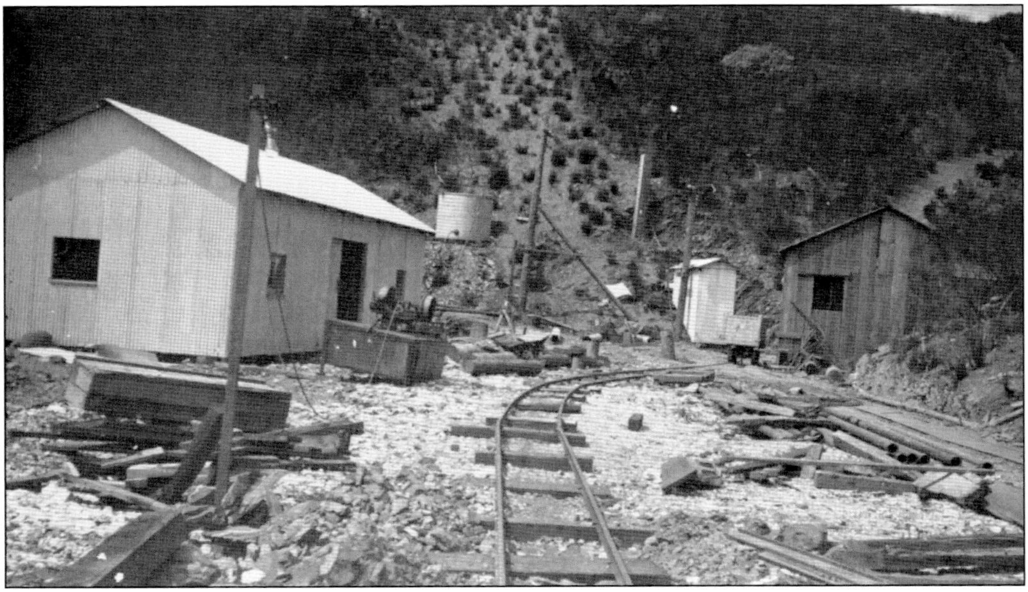

Pictured is the assay office and blacksmith shop at the Original Mine (later the Clearing House Mine) in 1913. (MHP.)

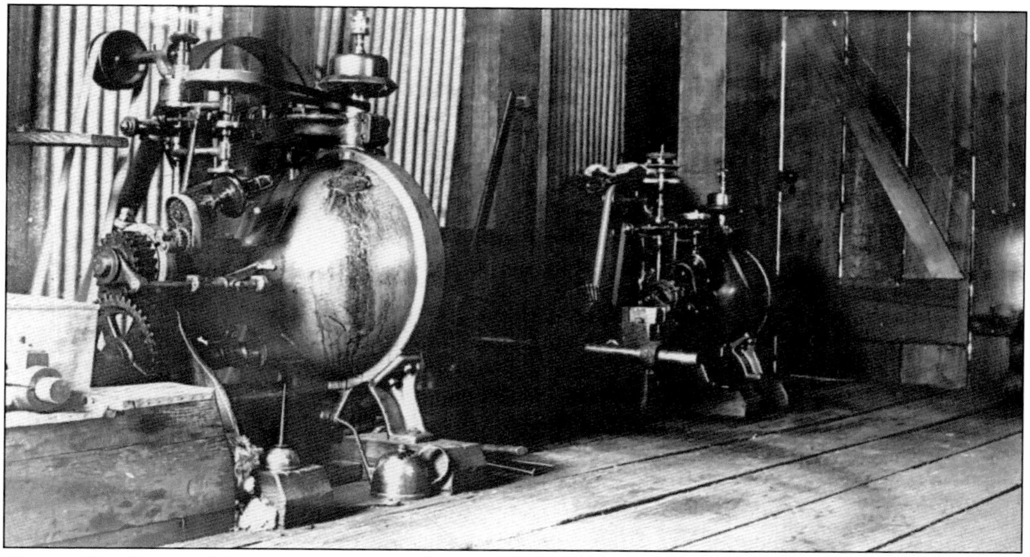

Pictured is the machinery governor at Original Mine (later the Clearing House Mine) in 1913. The cement collar for the penstock for the generator can still be seen in the river at low water. (MHP.)

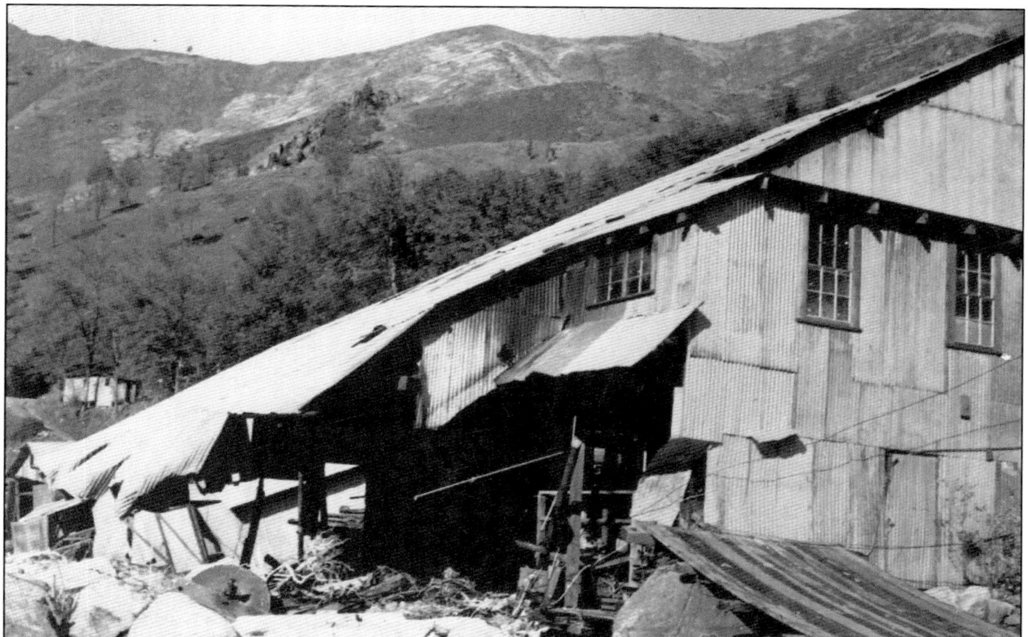

Damage is apparent on the lower part of the mill building after the flood of 1937. (MHP.)

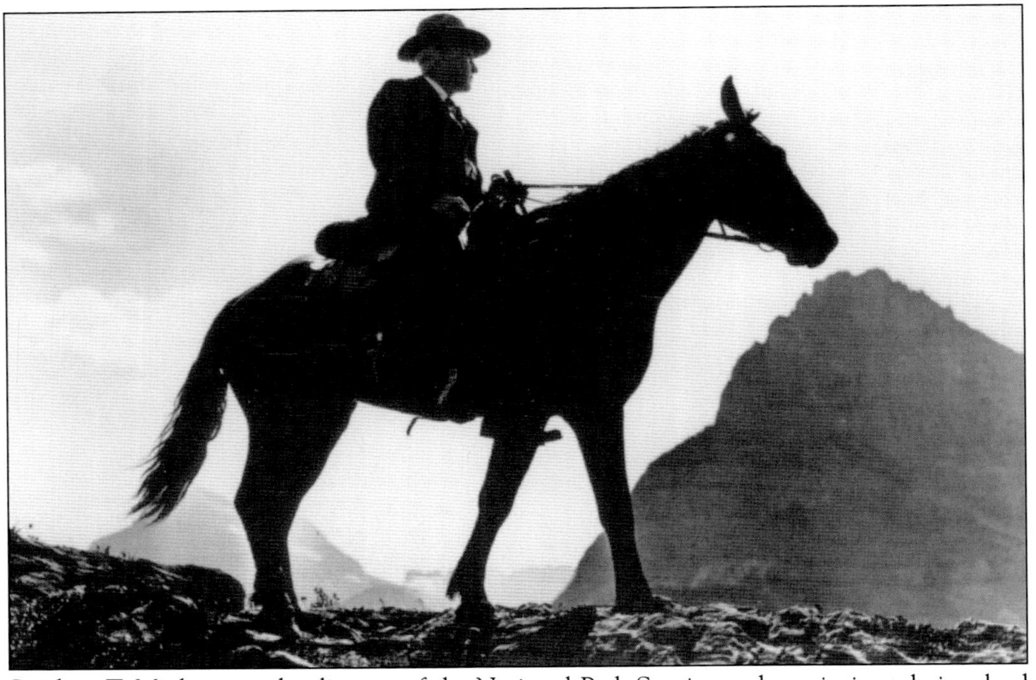

Stephen T. Mather was the director of the National Park Service and was intimately involved in the development of Yosemite National Park. His desire to have a first-class hotel in Yosemite Valley led to the building of the Ahwahnee Hotel. Crafted to be virtually fireproof, the six-story building is one of the crown jewels of the park. (MHP.)

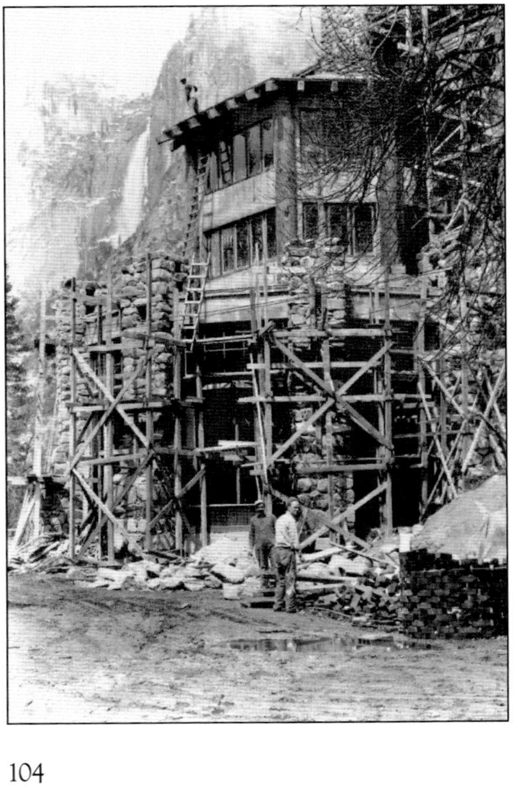

The hotel was constructed of steel and stone and what appeared to be wooden beams but were actually made of concrete. There was, of course, some wood in the building. Constructed by the newly consolidated Yosemite Park and Curry Company, the hotel fully fulfilled Mather's dream. (MHP.)

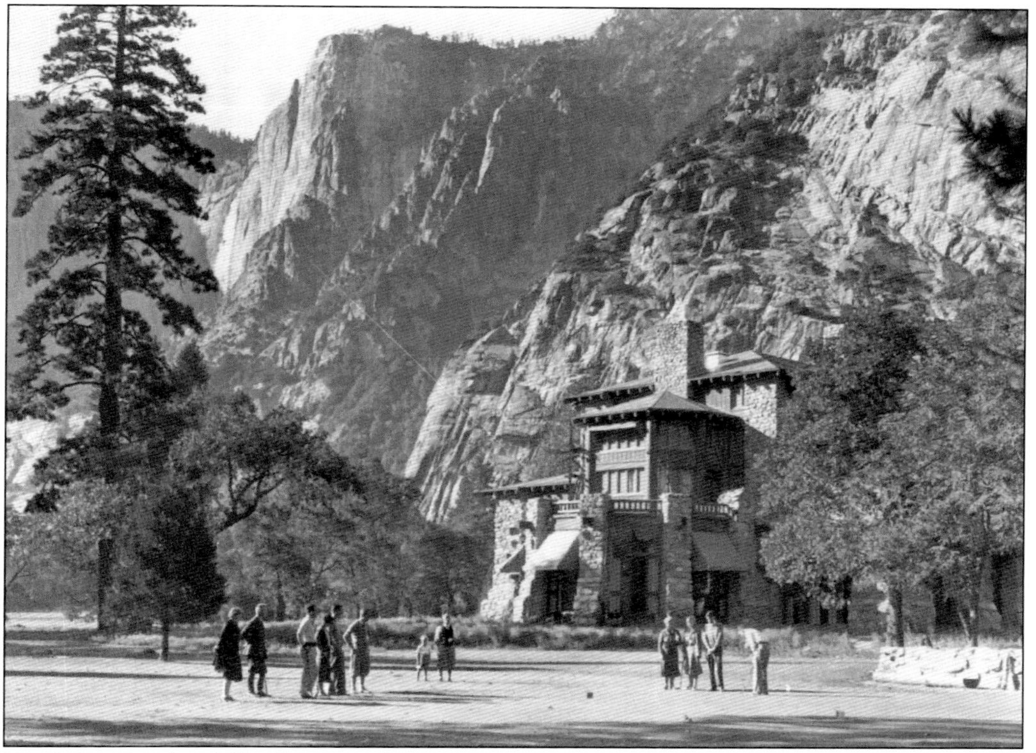

Nestled under the cliffs of the Royal Arches, the hotel and grounds have served the public since 1926. (MHP.)

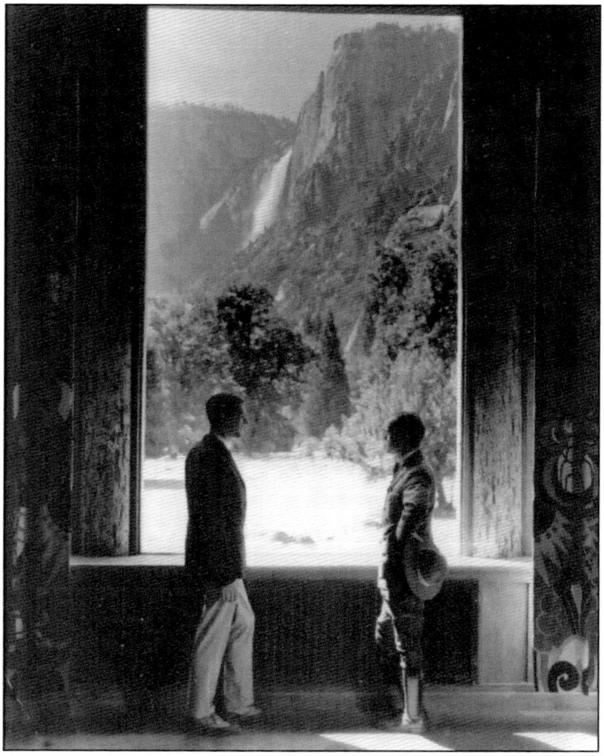

Donald Tresidder (left), president of the Yosemite Park and Curry Company, and W. B. "Dusty" Lewis, superintendent of Yosemite National Park, pose at the window of the dinning room of the Ahwahnee Hotel, with Yosemite Falls in the background. (MHP.)

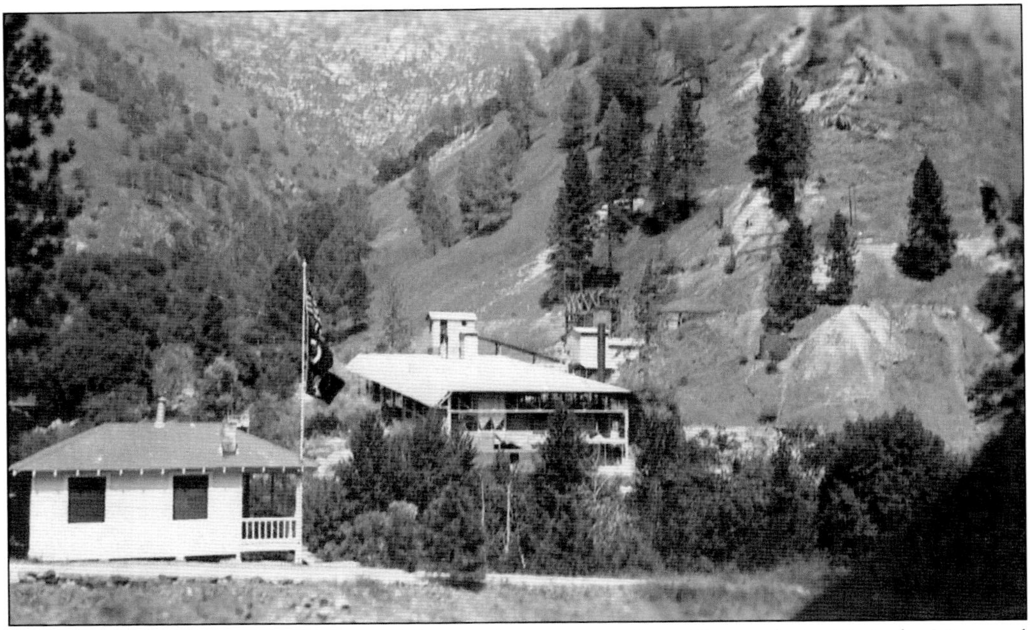

In 1910, a barium mine was located 1.5 miles downstream from El Portal. By 1930, the National Pigments and Chemical Division of the National Lead Company took over the mine property, including the housing property in El Portal, which was owned by the railroad. By this time, there were two mines, one on the north side and one on the south side of the river. In 1958, the park acquired much of the El Portal property for its housing and administrative site. The office is located in the foreground, with the processing and bagging plant in background. (MHP.)

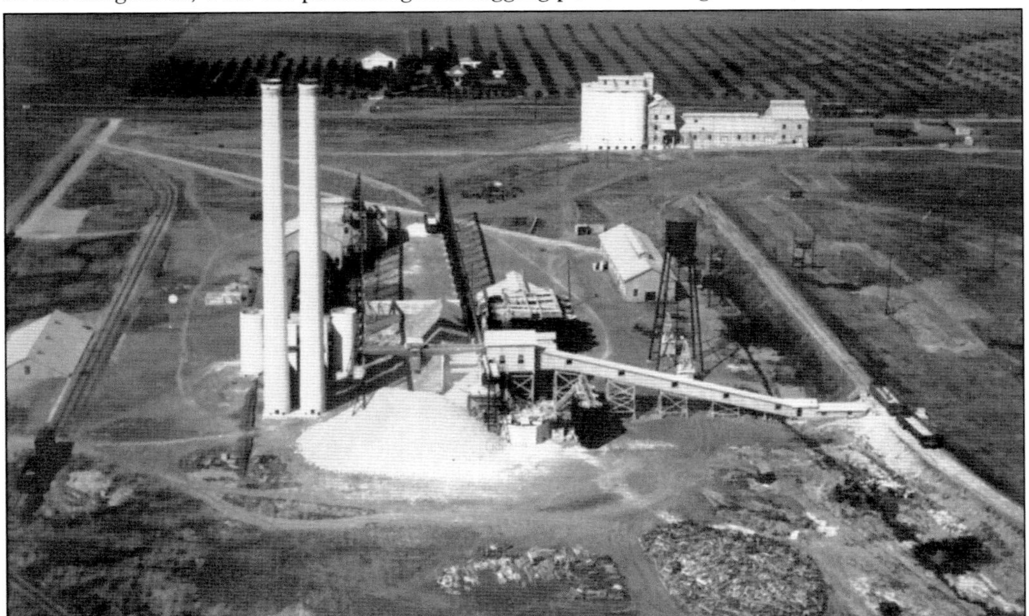

At Emory, 11 miles west of El Portal, a limestone quarry was established. The development of the ore required the Yosemite Valley Railroad to transport the prepared material 67 miles to a processing plant in Merced. (MHP.)

For many years, the twin smokestacks of the Yosemite Portland Cement plant, located near Merced, were landmarks. In 1944, Henry J. Kaiser purchased the quarry and closed it down to eliminate competition for his operations in Columbia, South America. (MHP.)

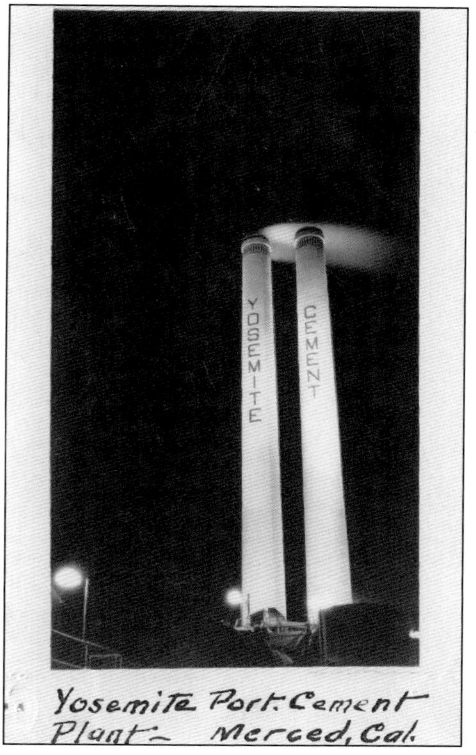

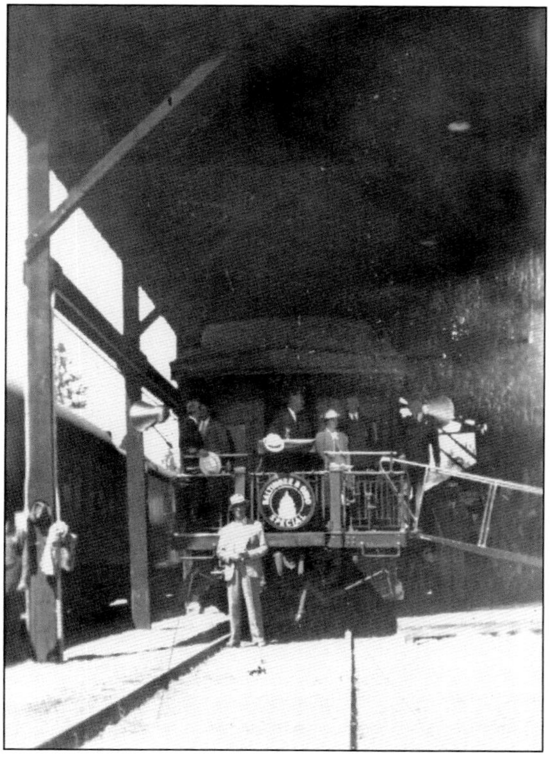

U.S. president Franklin Delano Roosevelt arrives at the El Portal train shed during his 1938 visit to Yosemite National Park. (Bob Babcock.)

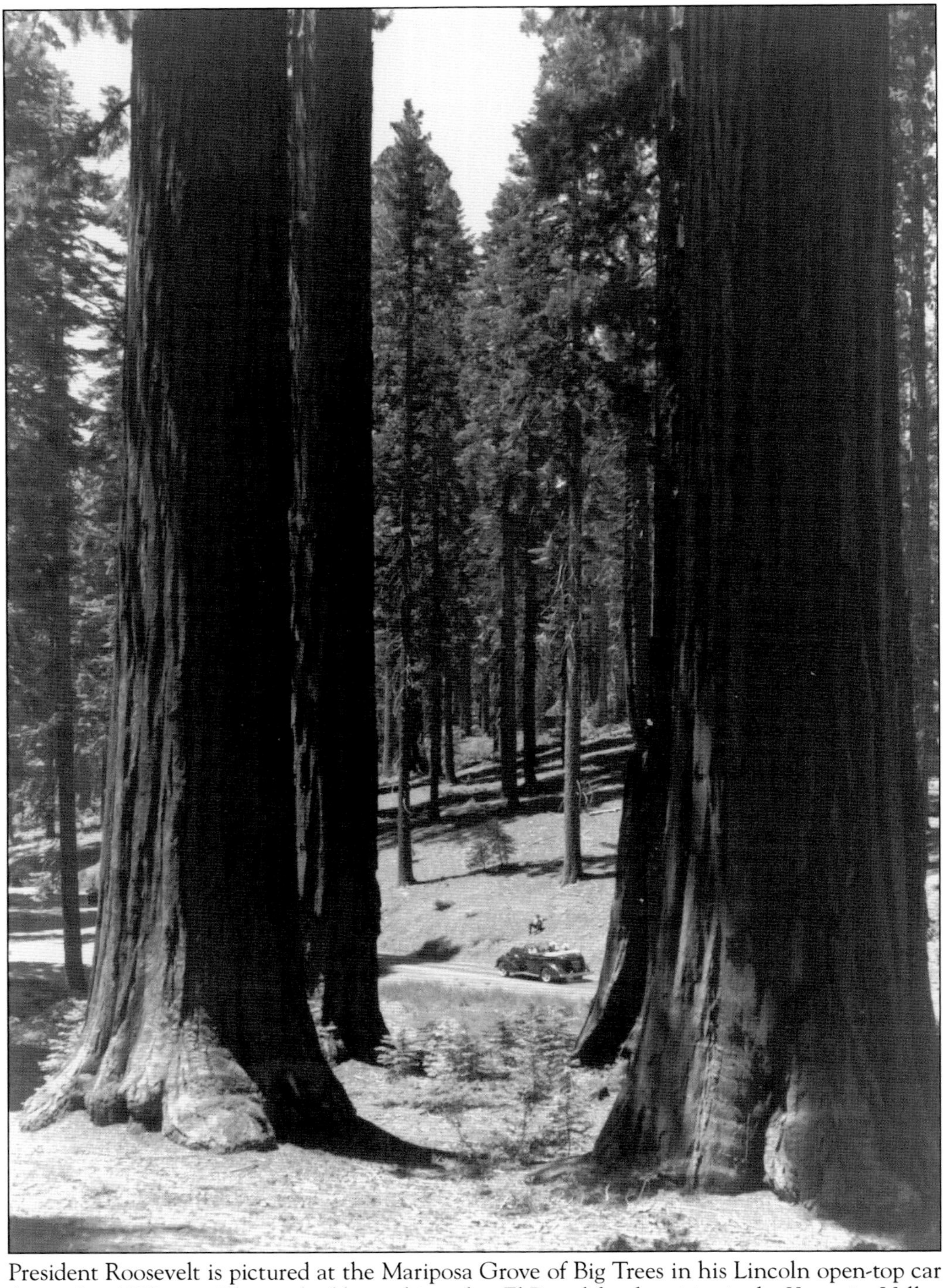

President Roosevelt is pictured at the Mariposa Grove of Big Trees in his Lincoln open-top car during his 1938 visit. The car had been shipped to El Portal for the visit via the Yosemite Valley Railroad. (Bob Babcock.)

Six

Merced River Canyon and El Portal

End of the Yosemite Valley Railroad

As the variety of activities in and around El Portal increased, so did the number of permanent residents. A school was started for the families, as well as a post office and store. While the railroad was primarily involved with industrial uses such as lumber, mining, and freight, excursion trips were sold to rail fans. The highway project prompted the building of the El Portal Motor Inn, the Shell Station, and the motel of Menzies and Bradshaw on the riverside of the highway. Unfortunately, in 1937, a major flood wiped away or damaged the motel and gas station, as well as a large section of track downriver, sections of the highway, bridges, and facilities at the Clearing House Mine and the Yosemite Cement Quarry. World War II brought a virtual halt to visitation to Yosemite National Park and slowed down many of the industrial sites in the river canyon. Many of the young men who worked at the various sites enlisted in the military or worked in war-related industries near San Francisco. With the end of the war, most of the activities in the river canyon did not return; thus the railroad ceased to run. The rolling stock and property were sold, and tracks were removed. The return of the tourists by 1950 began a rapid growth in visitation to Yosemite and the building of new motels in the river canyon, which were all the result of automobile travel. After the opening of State Highway 140 in 1926, the railroad continued to offer passenger service. Advertising in travel publications helped some, but there was a gradual decline in traffic as the highway and automobiles improved.

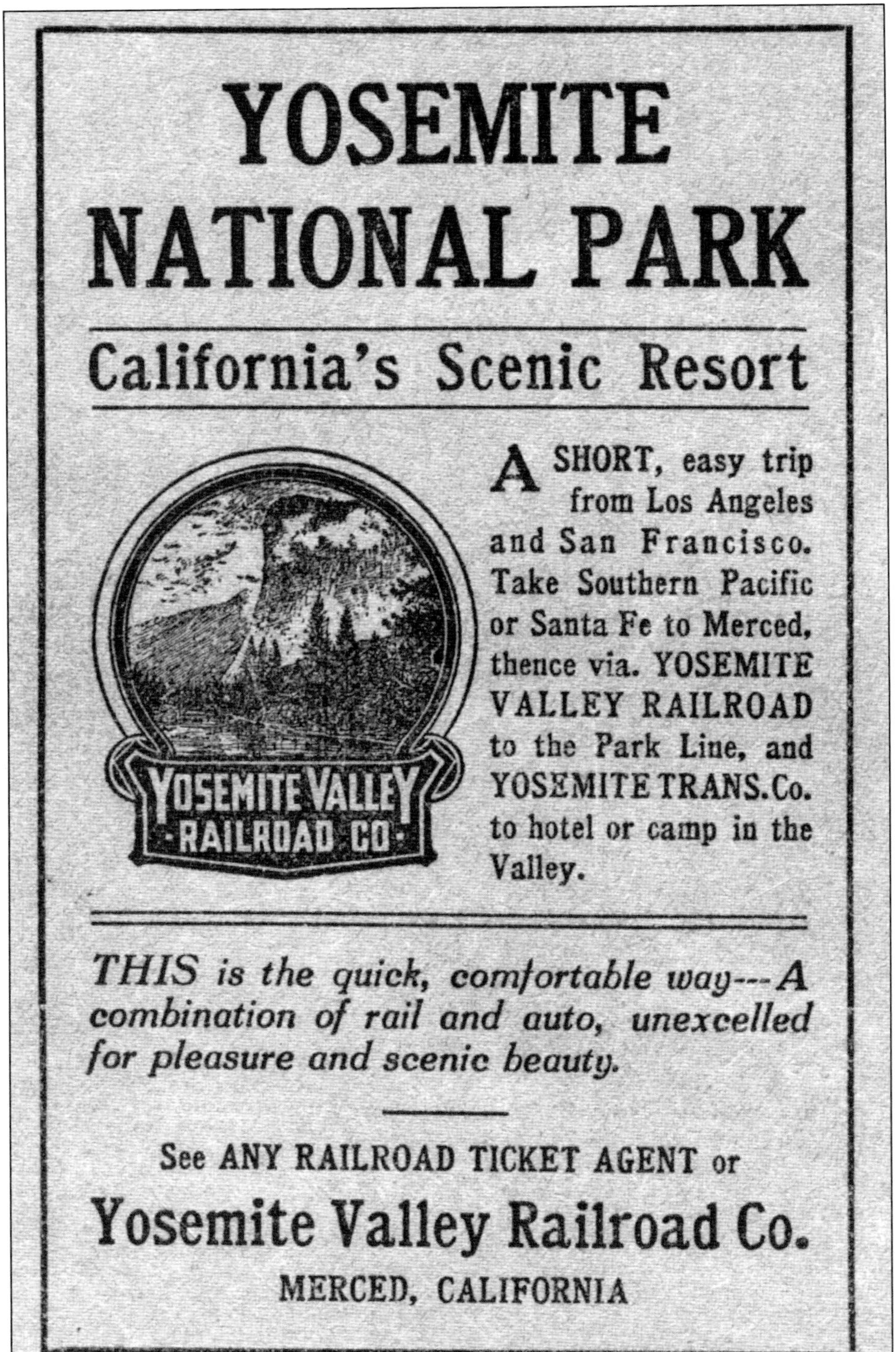

Promoting the beauty of Yosemite National Park, this flyer for the Yosemite Valley Railroad Company encouraged people to take advantage of "California's Scenic Resort." (Author's collection.)

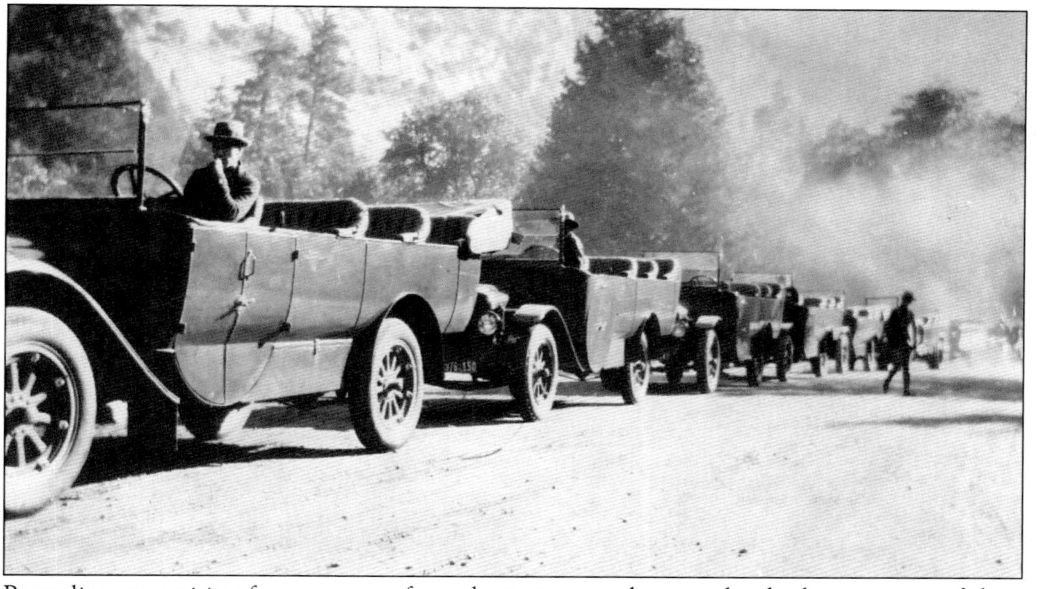

Buses line up, waiting for passengers from the train to make to make the last segment of their trip to Yosemite Valley. (MHP.)

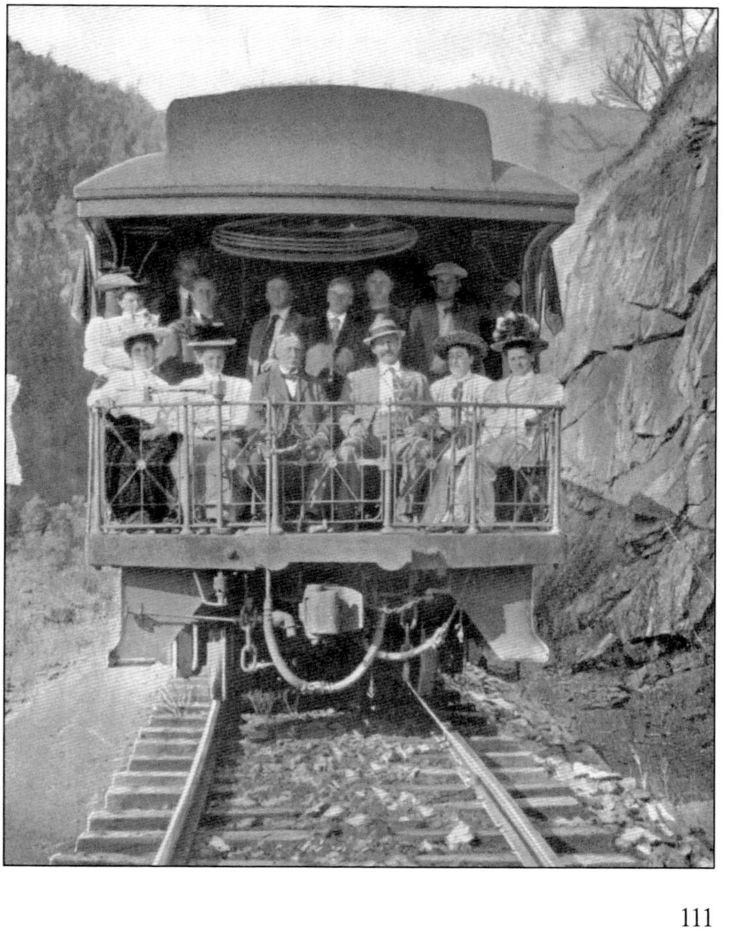

Observation cars were added to the train as a way to lure passengers. Covered sheds were used to protect the passengers from the elements, with the experience of entering Yosemite Valley having seen the beauty of the Merced River Canyon as an added attraction. (MHP.)

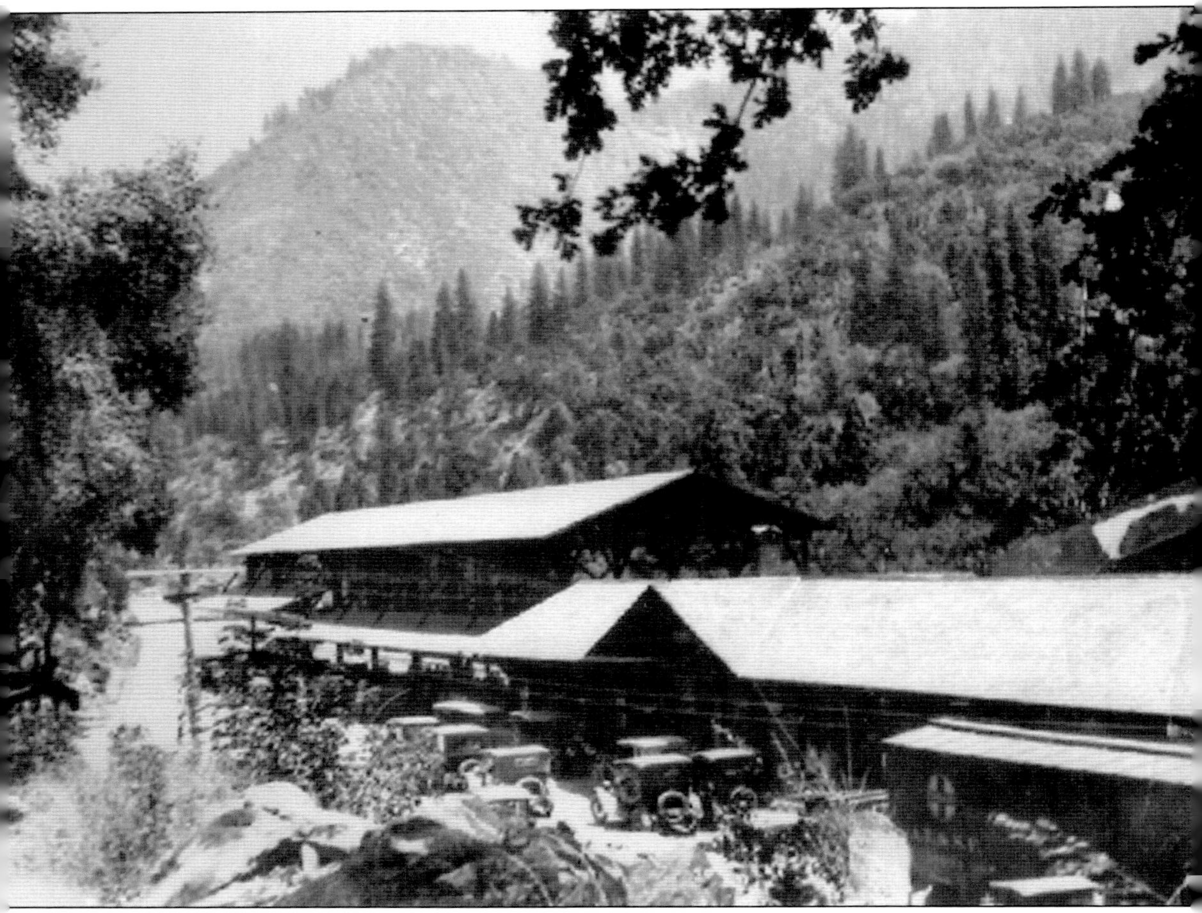

Passenger travel by railroad was greatly influenced by improvements to Highway 140 and automobiles. If it had not been for the lumber and mineral shipments, the railroad would have ended earlier. Pictured here is a busy day at the El Portal train shed in the late 1920s. (MHP.)

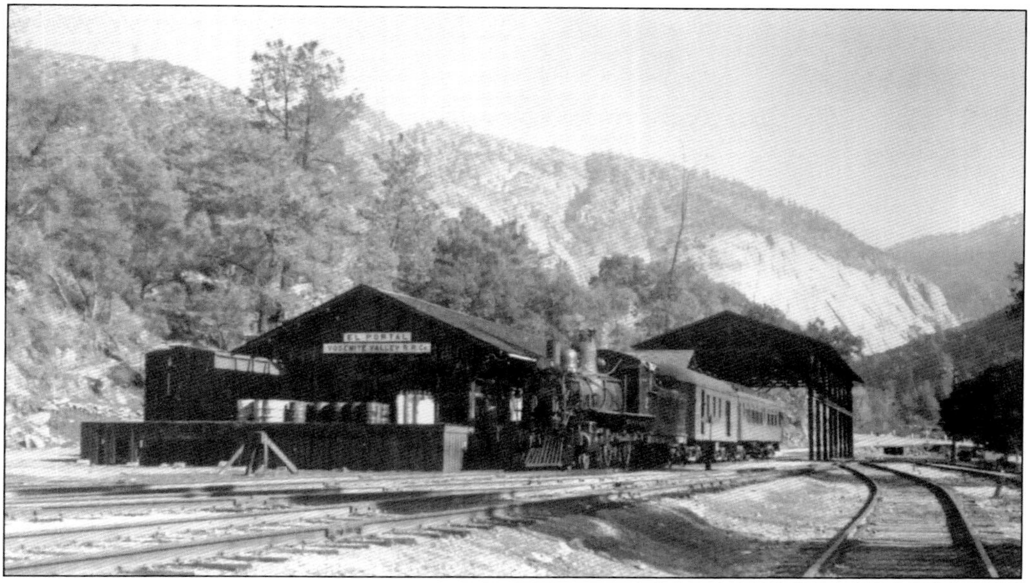

The log cars were dropped off at the incline, and the mail and passenger cars continued to El Portal. (MHP.)

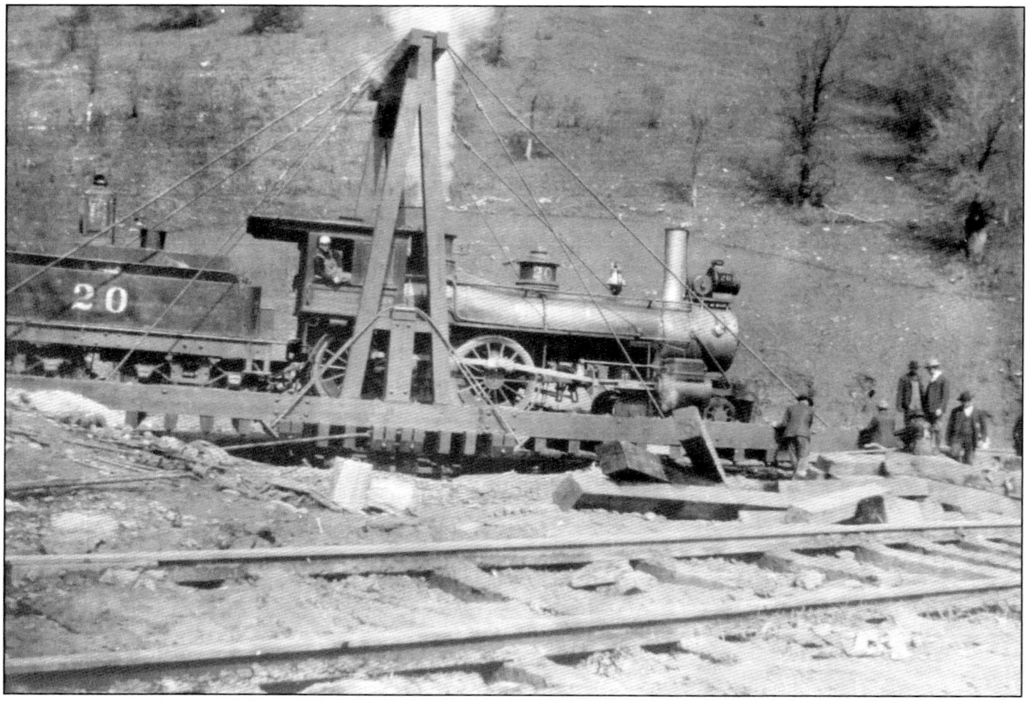

Pictured at the turntable at El Portal, the engine and tender were loaded on the table, which was then turned by hand. The 1937 flood badly damaged the turntable, so a Y system at Rancheria Flat was used to turn the engine around to allow the train to back into the station. (MHP.)

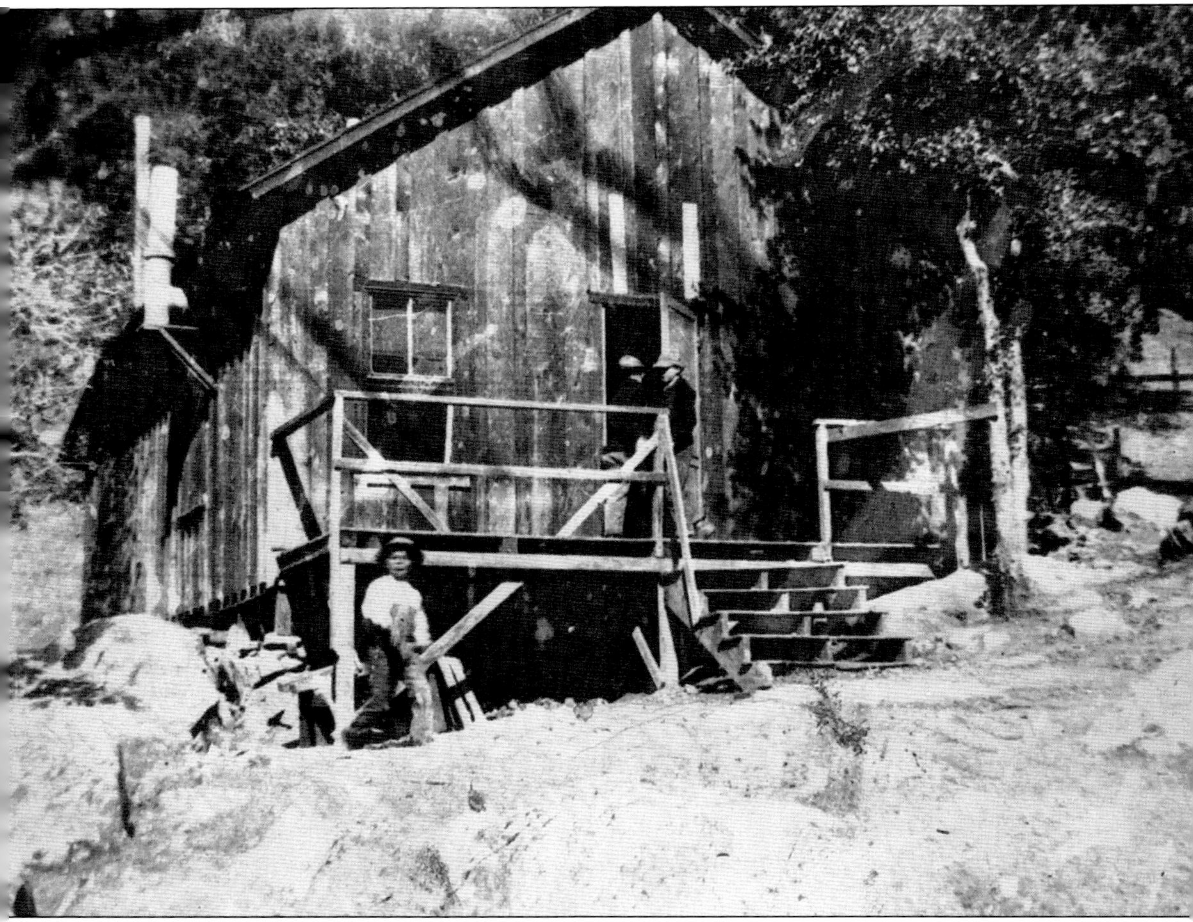

The first school in El Portal was located in this building in 1910. The pupil on the ground is Virgil "Pooch" Brown. The teacher was Daffa Morill, who taught all eight grades at the schoolhouse. (MHP.)

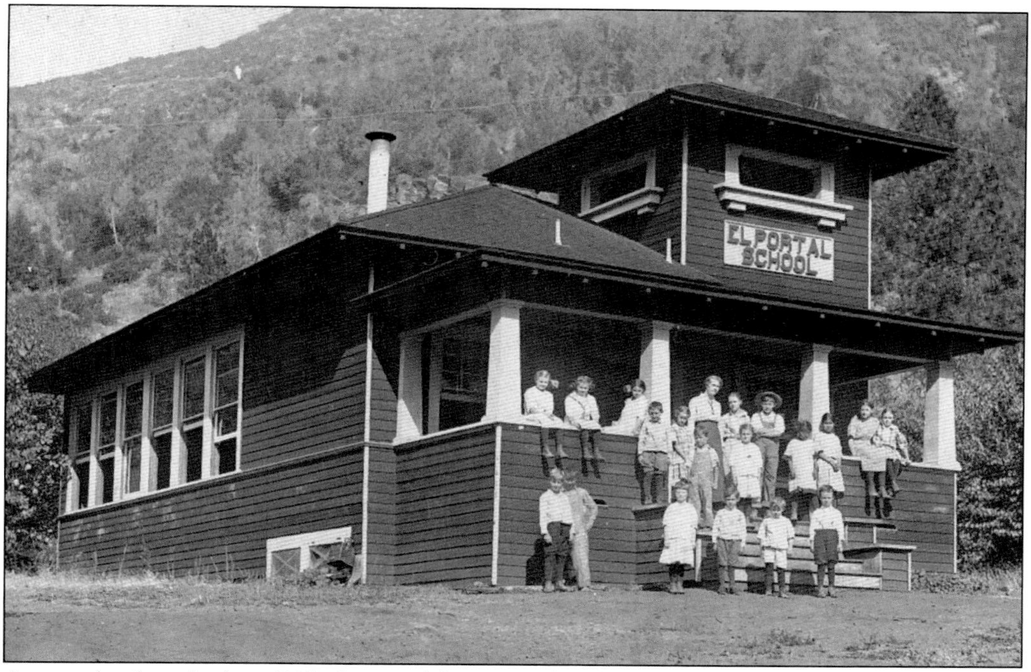

A new school was built in 1915 when work began on the El Portal incline. Families came to El Portal to work in the woods, on the incline, and with the railroad. (MHP.)

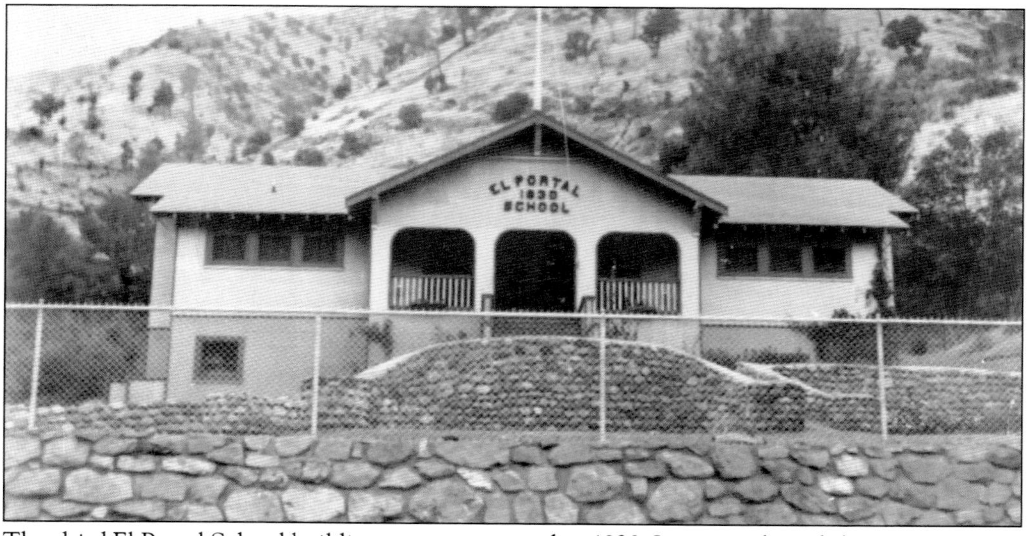

The third El Portal School building was constructed in 1930. It was used until the spring of 1963, when many families moved to El Portal from Yosemite Valley. It has since been converted into a community church. (MHP.)

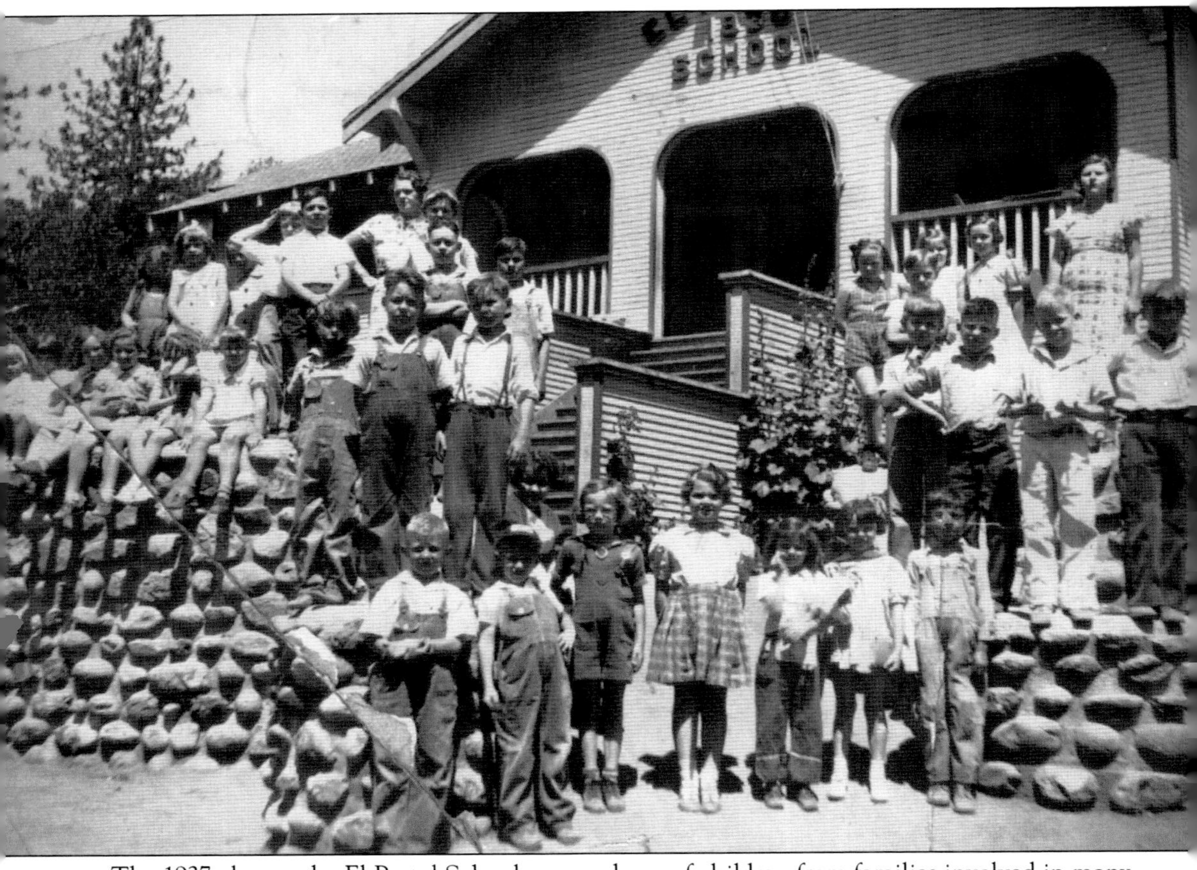

The 1937 class at the El Portal School was made up of children from families involved in many of the activities in the Merced River Canyon, which were almost always related to the Yosemite Valley Railroad. (MHP.)

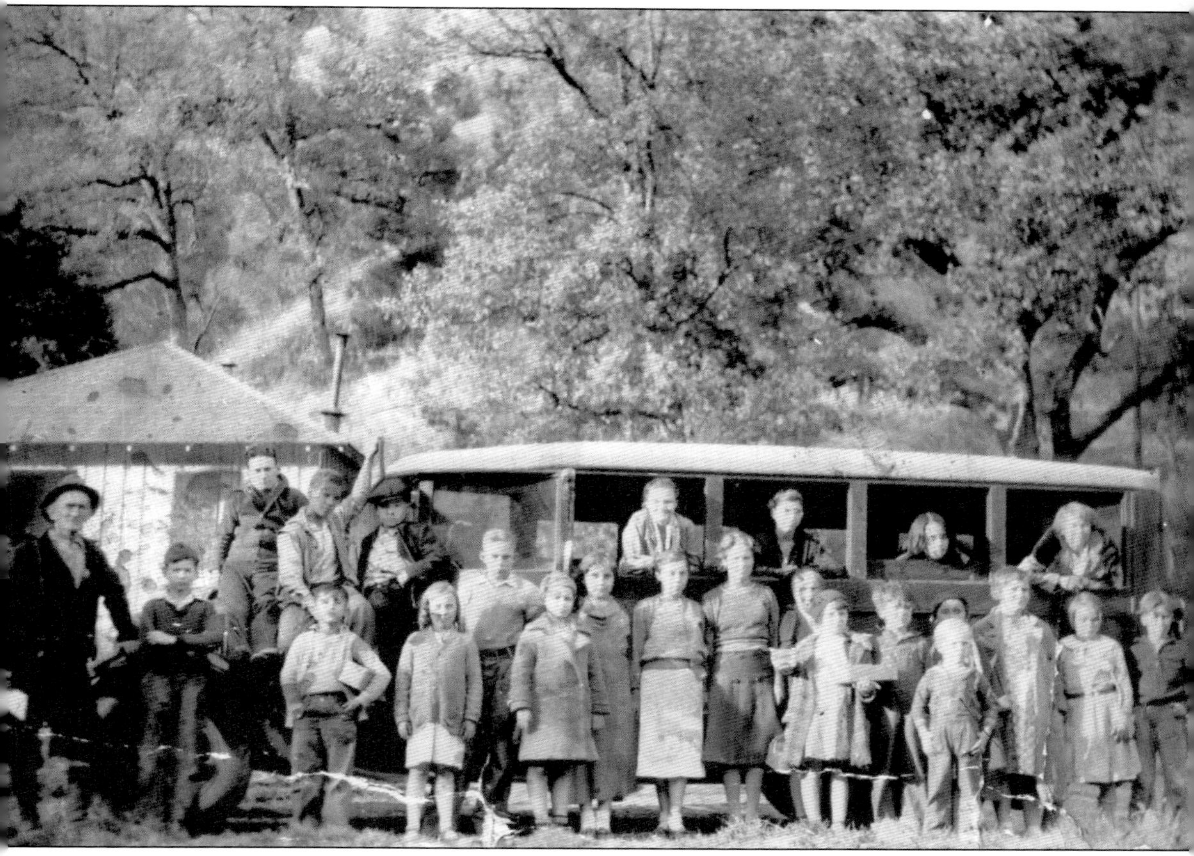

George Dukes (far left) was the school bus driver who delivered the students to the bottom of the hill, which lead to the school in 1935. (MHP.)

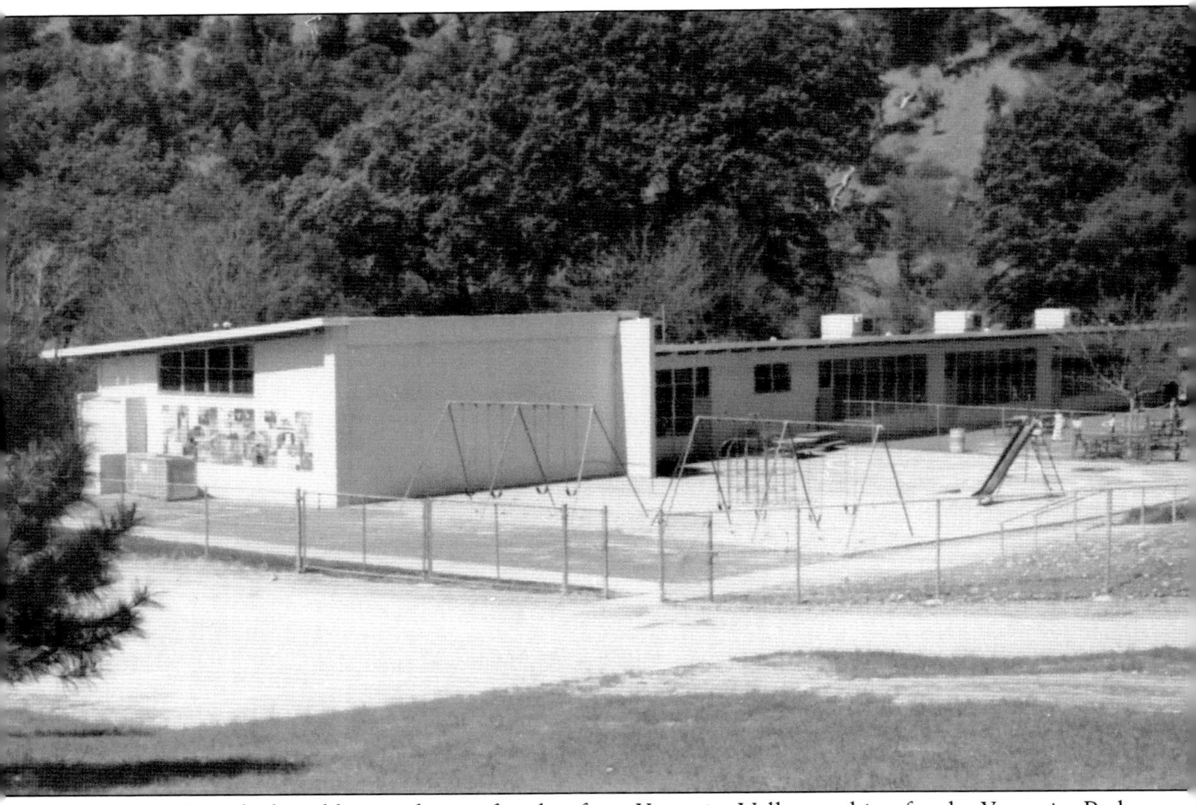

By 1963, with the addition of many families from Yosemite Valley working for the Yosemite Park and Curry Company and the National Park Service, the El Portal School grew significantly. By this time, the railroad and logging inclines had been closed. (MHP.)

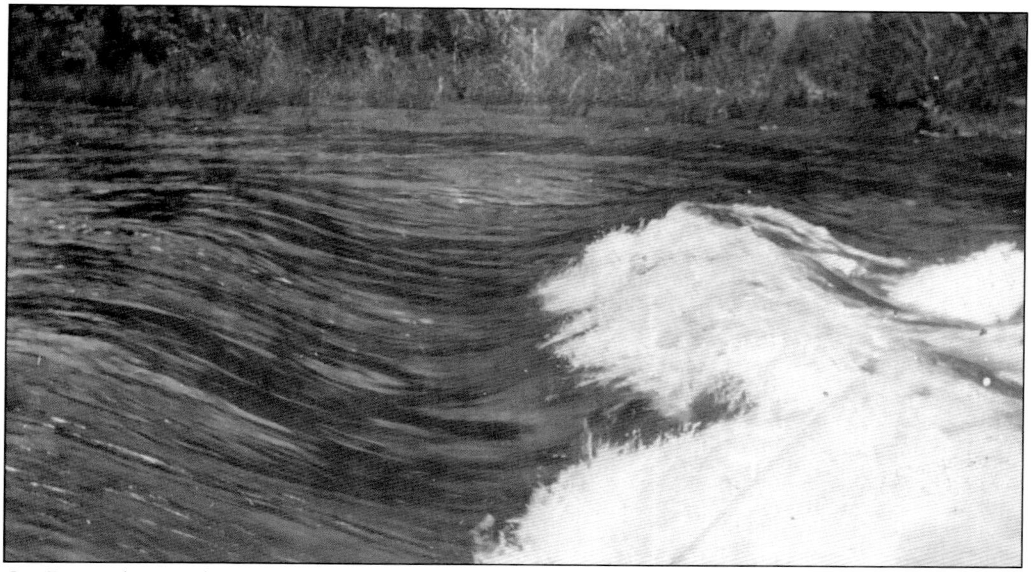

On December 11, 1937, the heavy early season snowpack was rained on, raising the snow level to 13,000 feet. This caused a torrent of water to rush into and through the Yosemite Valley. It had been 67 years since the last occurrence of this type, so residents along the river were caught unaware. (MHP.)

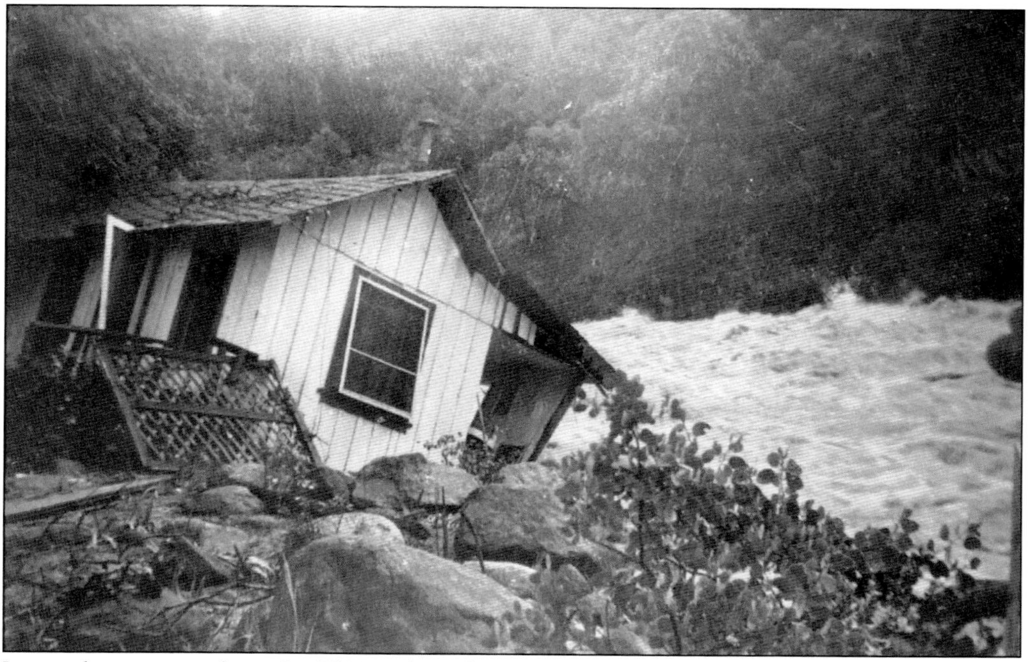

Located just across from the El Portal Market, the home of railroad engineer Al Yoakum was seriously damaged. (MHP.)

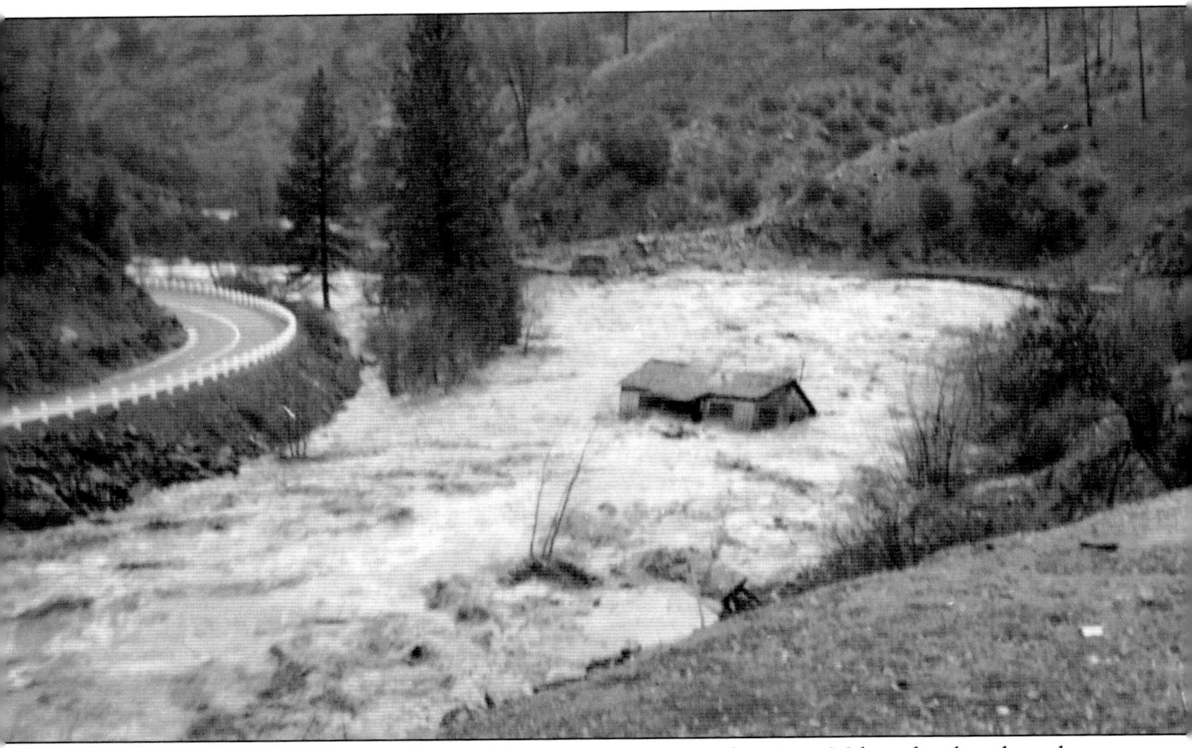

A building at the Clearing House Mine was swept into the river. Miles of railroad track were washed away, which stopped the railroad from operating for several months. (MHP.)

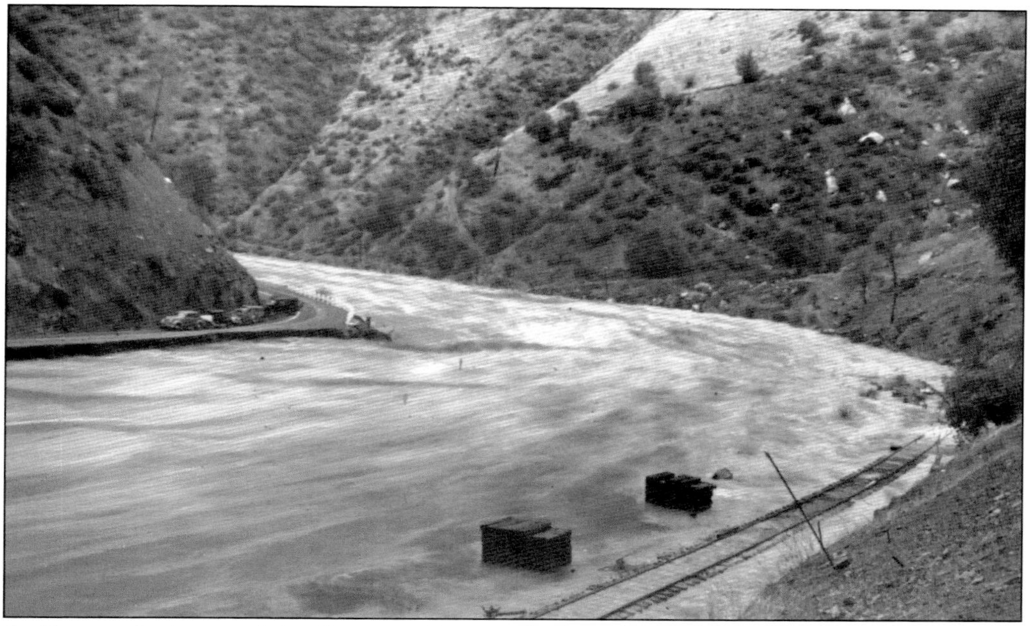

At Emory, the home of the Yosemite Cement Quarry, the tracks and loading facilities were damaged. Automobiles were still able to travel on the highway; however, the road was diminished to a single lane. (MHP.)

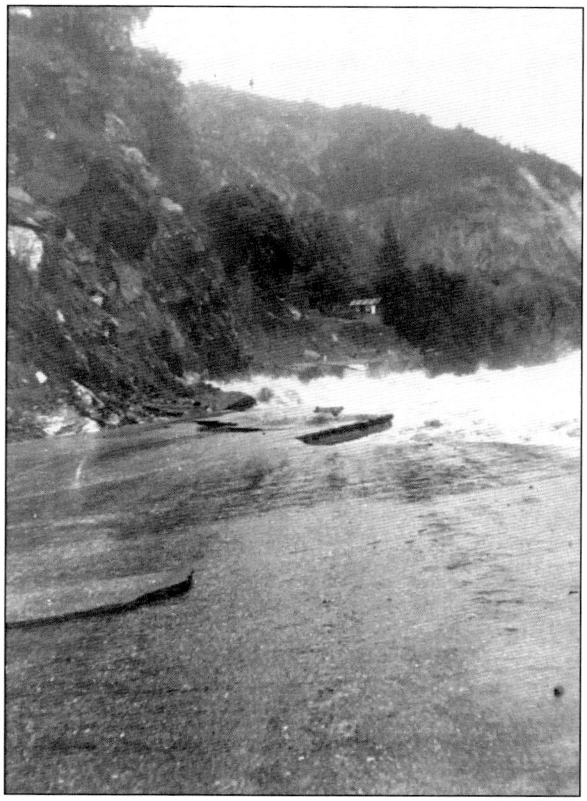

Pictured is typical damage to Highway 140 just north of El Portal. Other floods repeated this damage in 1950, 1955, and 1997. (MHP.)

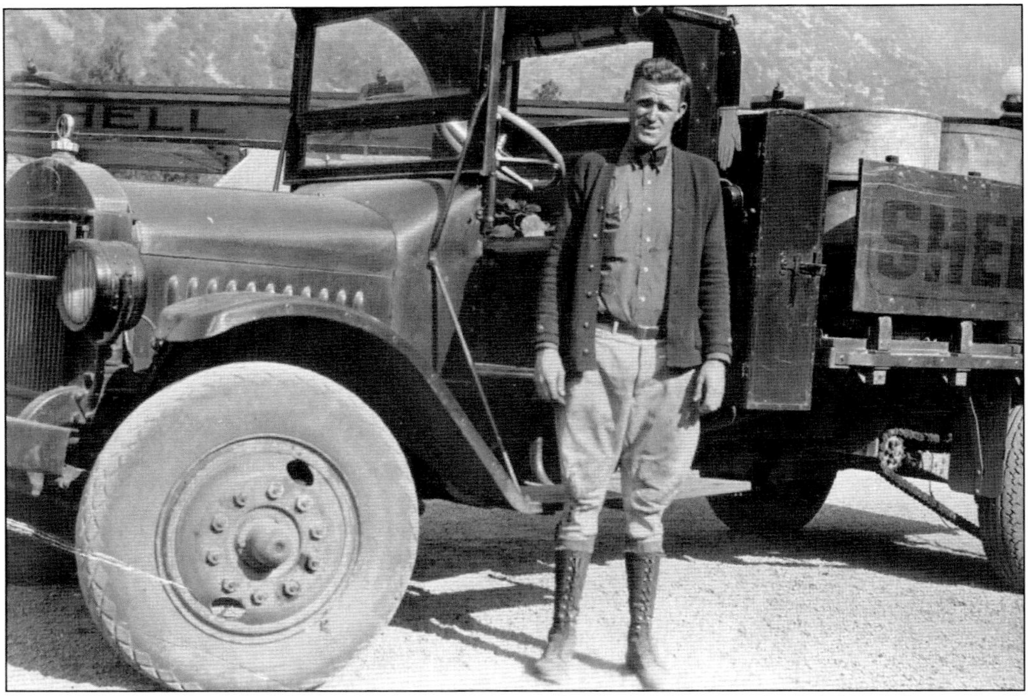

John Menzies, who would later become a Mariposa businessman, stands with his delivery truck at the Shell Station on the riverside of the highway before the 1937 flood. (MHP.)

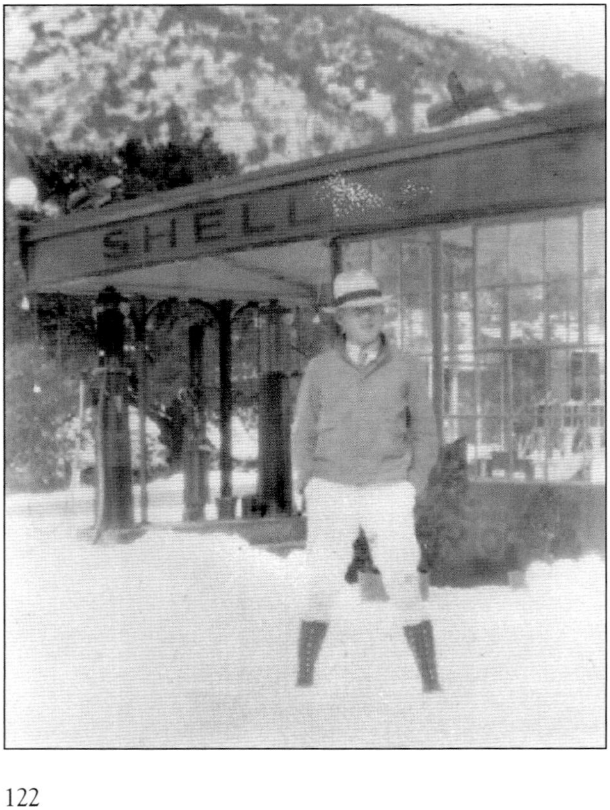

Fred Bradshaw, Menzies's partner, is shown at the station. He later became a Mariposa County supervisor. (MHP.)

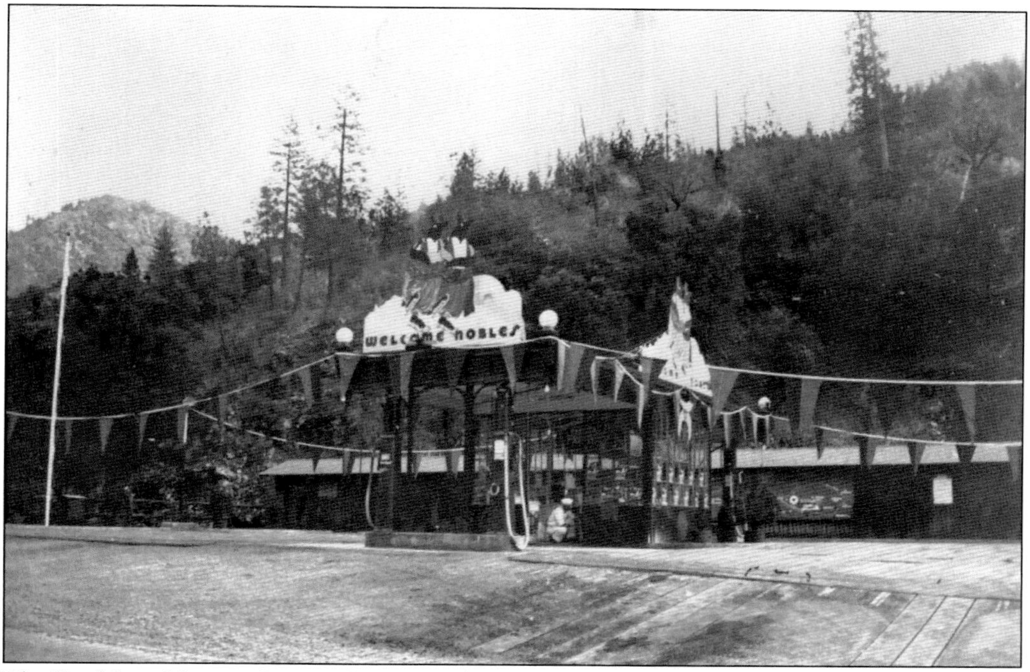

The Bradshaw-Menzies Service Station and Motel is decorated for an event. The service station and motel disappeared down the river in the flood of 1937. (MHP.)

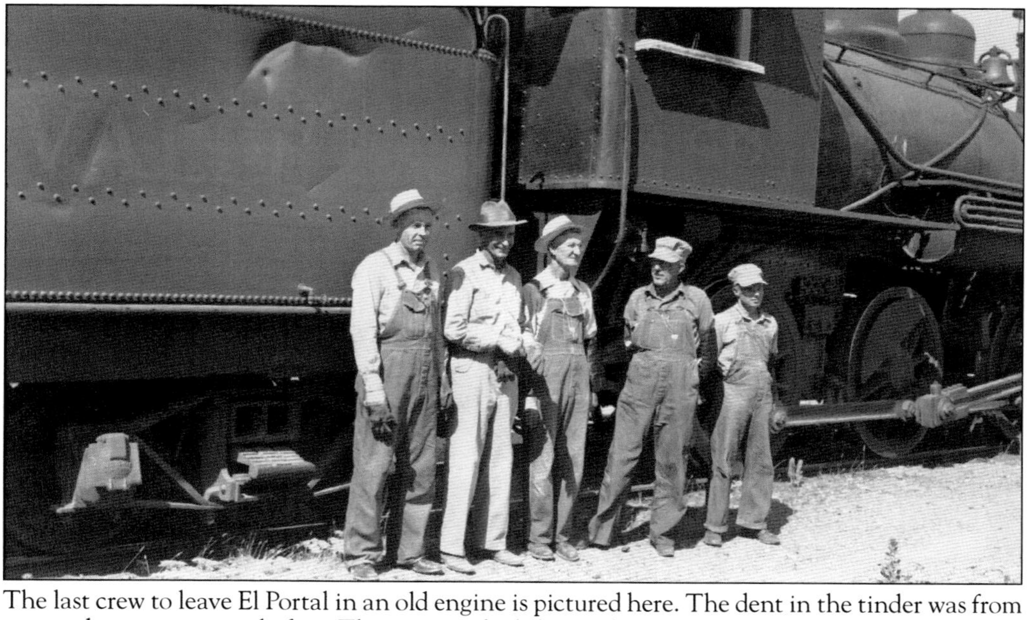

The last crew to leave El Portal in an old engine is pictured here. The dent in the tinder was from an accident many years before. The man on far left was the conductor, Bob Jirsa. (MHP.)

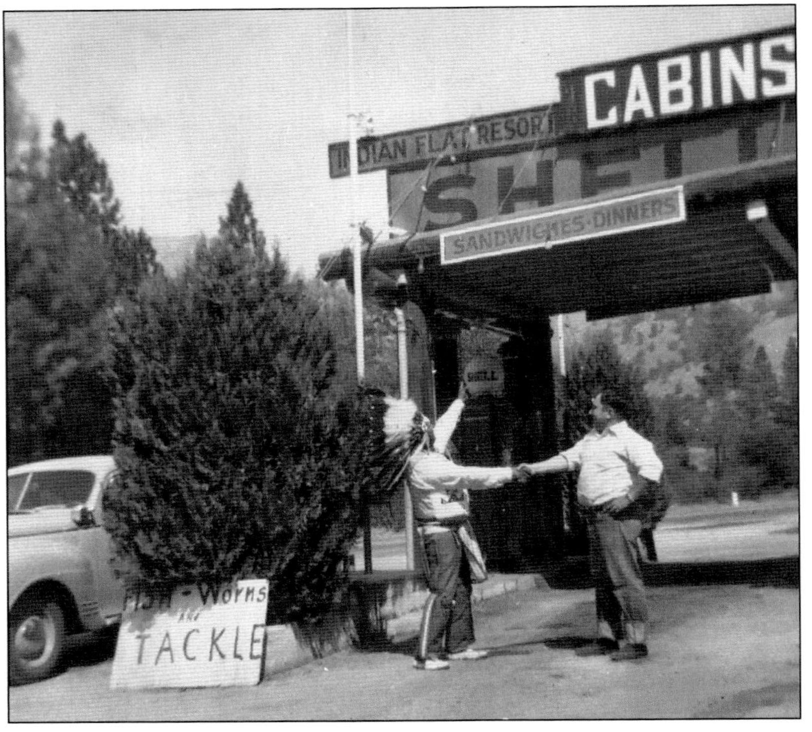

Pictured are Chief Lemee (left), born Chris Brown, and Howard Thompson, owner of the Indian Flat Resort. (MHP.)

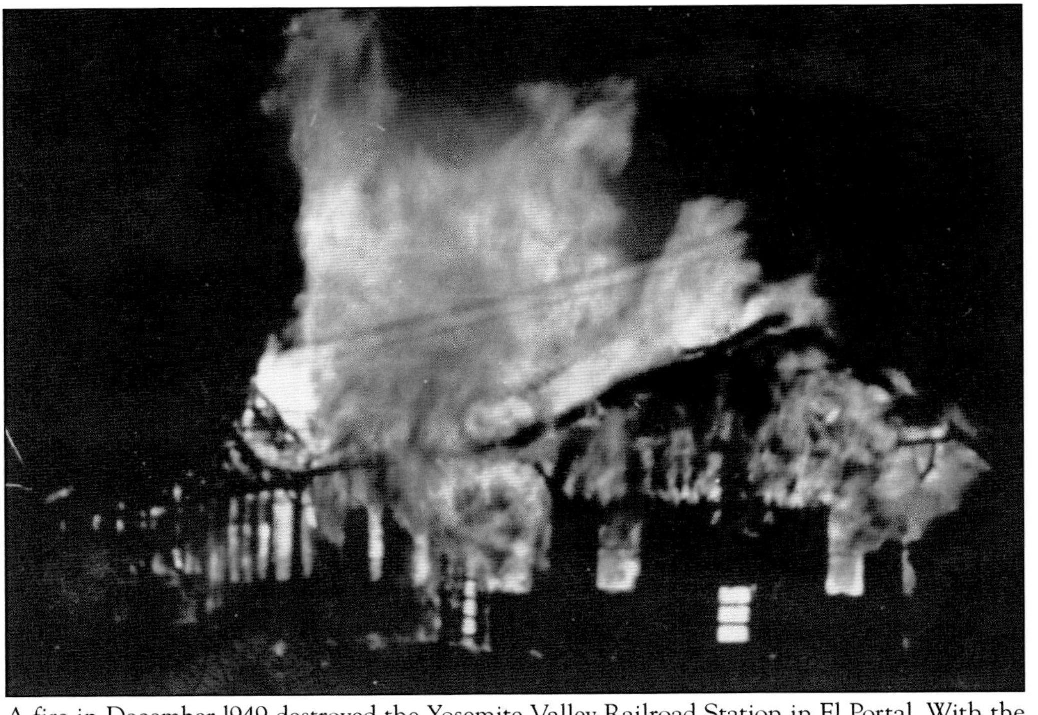

A fire in December 1949 destroyed the Yosemite Valley Railroad Station in El Portal. With the exception of a few bridges, trestles, and one caboose on display with the Shay engine at El Portal, this fire marked the end of an era for the railroad. (MHP.)

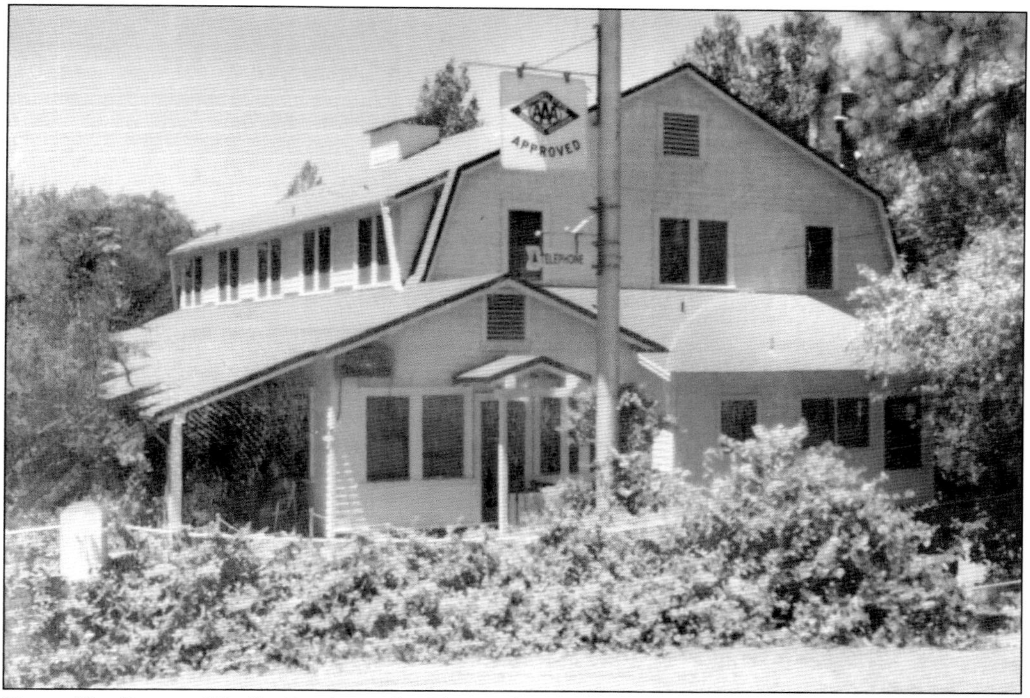

Owned by Ben and Dolly Gardner, the El Portal Hotel burned in a fire and was replaced by the El Portal Motor Inn. Dolly showed great tenacity and also built cabins and a new store. The Gardners sold the business to Bill and Adaline Brantley. (MHP.)

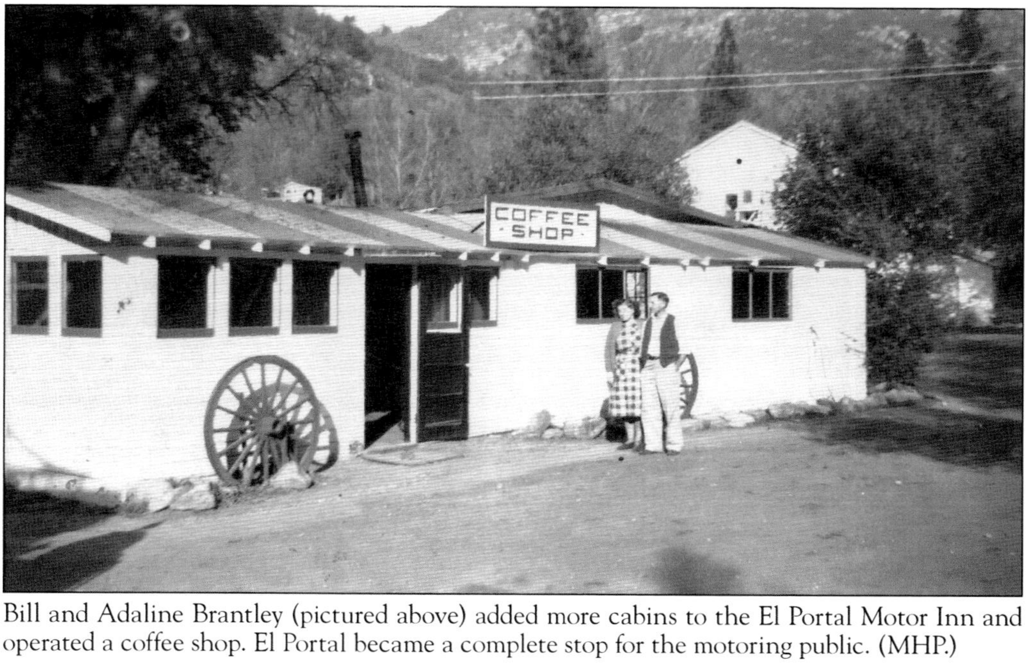

Bill and Adaline Brantley (pictured above) added more cabins to the El Portal Motor Inn and operated a coffee shop. El Portal became a complete stop for the motoring public. (MHP.)

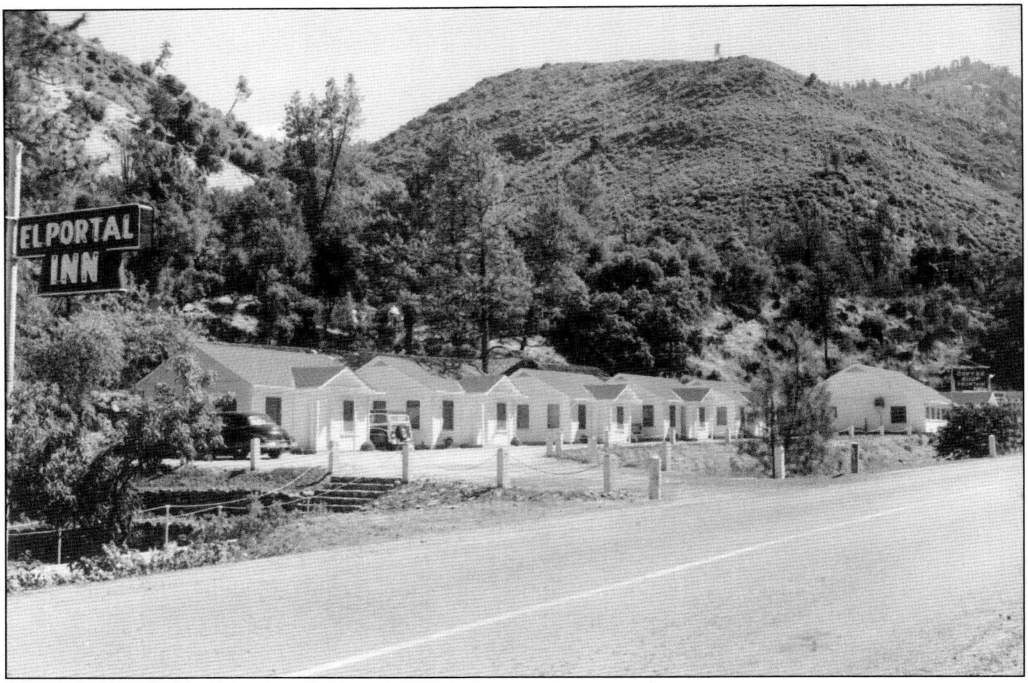

Today the El Portal Motor Inn is home to the Yosemite Institute, which is an educational organization, and the cabins are used for employee housing. (MHP.)

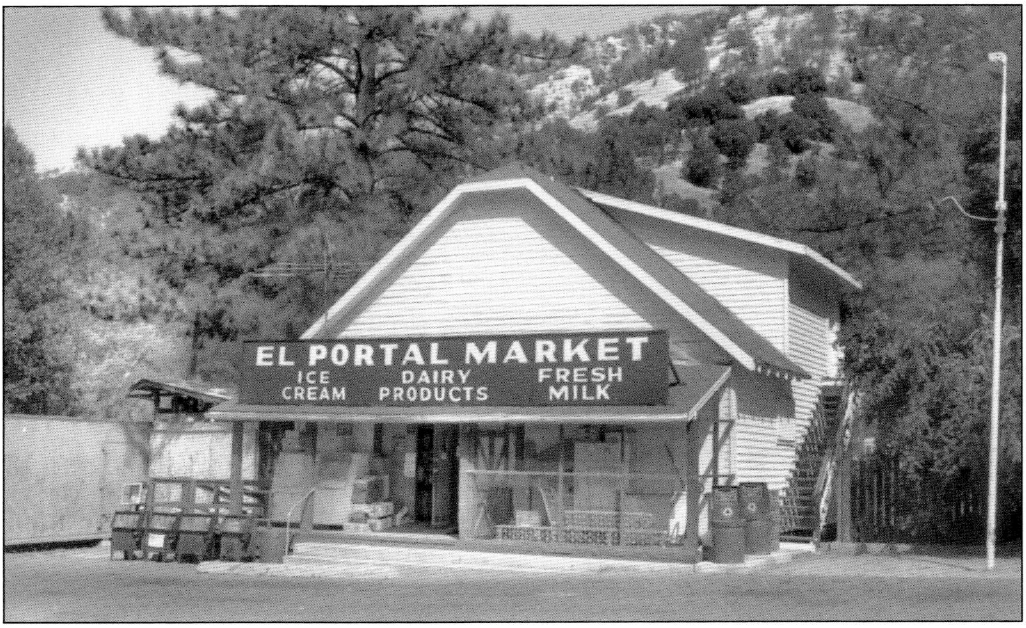

Dolly and Ben Gardner built the El Portal Market on the highway just south of the motor inn. Dolly also constructed a small building between the hotel and store for Ben to have a bar to relax in. The store burned on April 21, 2008, as it was being remodeled. (MHP.)

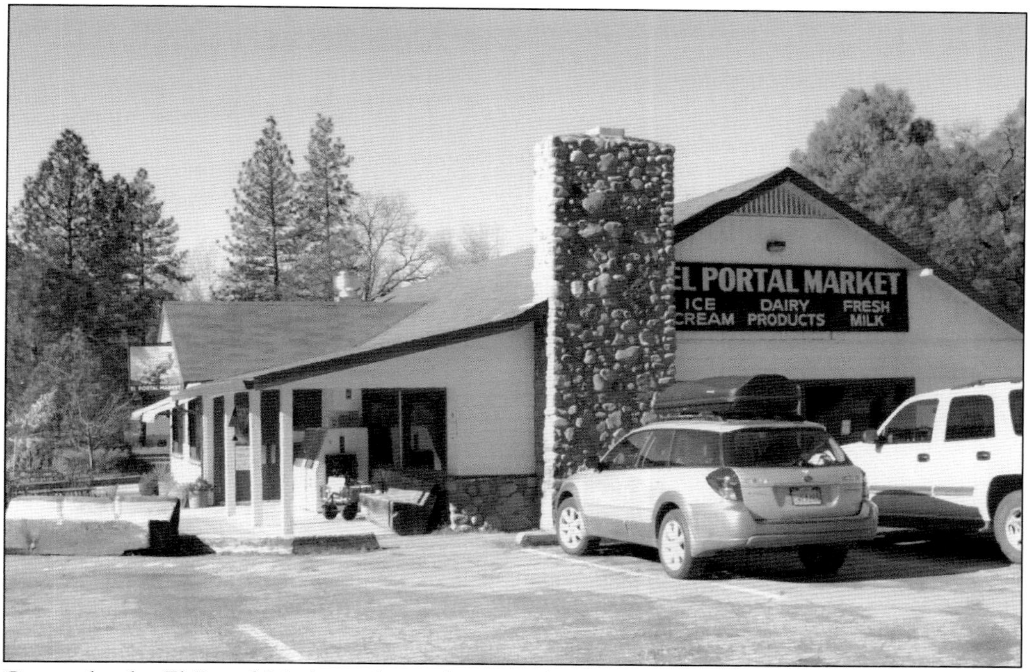

Currently, the El Portal Market is housed in a park service building near the gas station. This building was a restaurant and cocktail lounge until it became the National Park Service offices. The finest store El Portal has ever had is now under the ownership of Kristie Kari. (MHP.)

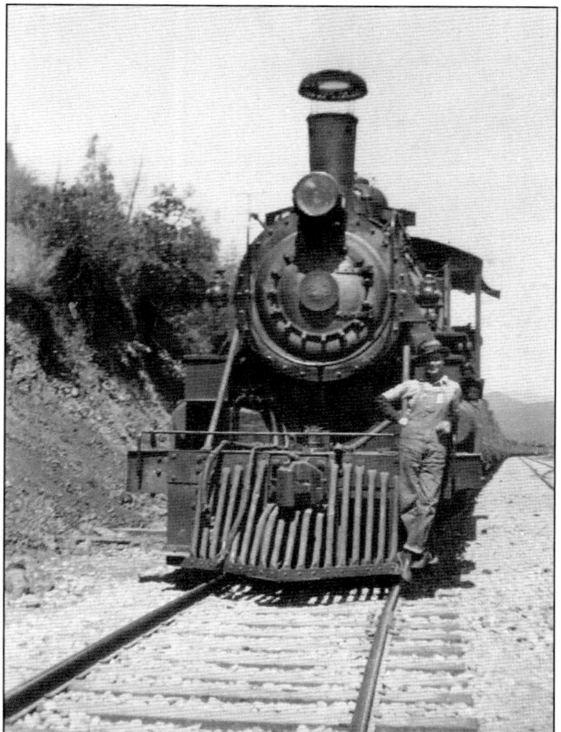

Gone, but not forgotten is the Yosemite Valley Railroad. (MHP.)